P9-CFJ-890

The
ROI
of Human Capital

The
ROI
of
Human
Capital

Measuring the Economic Value
of Employee Performance

Jac Fitz-enz

AMACOM
American Management Association
New York • Atlanta • Boston • Kansas City • San Francisco • Washington, D.C.
Brussels • Mexico City • Tokyo • Toronto

Special discounts on bulk quantities of AMACOM books are available to corporations, professional associations, and other organizations. For details, contact Special Sales Department, AMACOM, a division of American Management Association, 1601 Broadway, New York, NY 10019.
Tel.: 212-903-8316. Fax: 212-903-8083.
Web site: www.amanet.org

This publication is designed to provide accurate and authoritative information in regard to the subject matter covered. It is sold with the understanding that the publisher is not engaged in rendering legal, accounting, or other professional service. If legal advice or other expert assistance is required, the services of a competent professional person should be sought.

Library of Congress Cataloging-in-Publication Data

Fitz-enz, Jac.
    The ROI of human capital: measuring the economic value of employee performance / Jac Fitz-enz.
        p.   cm.
    Includes bibliographical references and index.
    ISBN 0-8144-0574-6
    1. Human capital.   2. Productivity accounting.   3. Labor economics.
    I. Title: Economic value of employee performance.   II. Title.
HD4904.7.F55   2000
658.14'226—dc21   00–025294

Printing number

20 19 18 17 16 15 14 13 12

To
Ellen
My teacher
My inspiration

Contents

Preface   *xi*

    The Missing Piece • Facing the Talent Shortage • The
    Structure

Acknowledgments   *xix*

Chapter 1. Human Capital: The Profit Lever of a
Knowledge Economy   1

    Effects on Organizational Management • Two Aspects
    of Human Capital • People and Information • Data-
    to-Value Cycle • Intellectual Capacity • Surveying the
    Track • The ROI Race • False Starts • Points of
    Measurement • Summary

Chapter 2. How to Measure Human Capital's
Contribution to Enterprise Goals   25

    Human Capital ROI Foundation • Human-Financial
    Interface • Putting the Human Capital in Value Added •
    Enterprise-Level Metrics: The Launch Point • The H
    in Human Capital • Human Capital Enterprise
    Scorecard • Enterprisewide Effective Practices • The
    Willy Loman Syndrome • Measuring Effective
    Enterprise Practices • Foundation Trait Metrics •
    Structural Trait Metrics • Enterprise Practices
    Measurement: Case Example • Summary

Chapter 3. How to Measure Human Capital's
Impact on Processes 61

*Positioning Business Unit Processes • Human
Capital in Processes • Anatomy of a Process • Process
Performance Matrix • Service, Quality, Productivity •
Finding Human Capital Effects • A Case in Point • A
Test Problem • Summary*

Chapter 4. How to Measure Human Resources'
Value Added 91

*Evaluating • Planning • Acquiring • Maintaining •
Developing • Retaining • Human Capital Performance
Evaluation • Change Measurement • Human Capital
Scorecard • Human Capital Accounting • A Human
Capital P&L • Human Capital Management
Consortia • Best-Practice Reports and Other Fairy
Tales • Truly Effective Practices • Summary*

Chapter 5. End-to-End Human Capital Value
Reports 129

*Pathways • Cases • An Integrated Reporting System •
Looking Ahead: Leading Indicators • Enterprise
Futures • Functional Futures • Be Prepared •
Employee Mind-Sets • Indirect Sign • Competitiveness •
Human Capital Management Futures •
Scoreboarding Overview • Summary*

Chapter 6. The Next Generation of Human Capital
Valuation: Trends, Forecasts, and Predictions 160

*Relationships and Patterns • Fallacies in Trend
Identification • Finding Meaning • Business
Applications • Data Sensors: Forecasting and
Predicting • Toward a Human Capital Financial
Index • Index Exercise • Data Sources • Summary*

Chapter 7. How to Value Improvement Initiative
Results 186

*Evolving to a New Order • Measuring the New
Human Capital • Restructuring: Back to the*

*Beginning • Outsourcing: The Latest Panacea •
Contingent Workforce Management: The New
Human Capital Challenge • Mergers and
Acquisitions: Buy versus Make • Benchmarking:
A Value-Adding Approach • Summary*

Chapter 8. How to Leverage Your Human Capital ROI 229

*The Managerial Perspective • Connecting to Results •
The Employee Perspective • A Commonsense Example •
Leverage Opportunities • Summary*

Chapter 9. Quantum Leap: A Strategy for Inventing Your Future 245

*Performance Drivers • Human Capital Signs of the
Future • The Lead Questions • Evolution of a Solution •
The Number-One Information Center • Building
Scenarios • How to Make a Quantum Leap • Reversing
the Failure Rate • Dogs Don't Fly • Reexamining Our
Nature • BEing = Vision × Culture × Strategy ×
Commitment • How to Create a New Context • Taking
the Leap • Summary*

Chapter 10. Guiding Principles 272

*The Foundation Stones of the Human Capital
Measurement Pathway*

Chapter 11. Summing Up and Looking Ahead 277

Bringing It All Together in One Place • Looking Ahead

Index 285

Preface

The Missing Piece

The classic books of management have ignored, avoided, or thrown platitudes at the question of human value in the business environment. When and if the authors did give passing attention to valuing the human contribution, their comments were either gratuitous or simplistic. Nineteenth-century capital theory claimed that wealth was leveraged from investments in tangible assets such as plant and equipment. It held that workers were entitled to compensation only for their labor, since the incremental values of the business came from investment in capital equipment. This type of thinking lit the fire under people like Karl Marx and Samuel Gompers. From the early work of Fayol[1] and Barnard,[2] which supported this thinking, to the more enlightened insights of Drucker, Peters, Handy, and others, no one has successfully taken on the challenge of detailing how to demonstrate the relative value of the human element in the profit equation. Invariably, writers attempting to do so have opted out at the last minute with weak-kneed excuses for not closing the loop with specific examples. The only exception has been some of the human resources accounting work, and that has not been accepted as a practical management tool.

The term *human capital* originated with Theodore Schultz, an economist interested in the plight of the world's underdeveloped countries. He argued correctly that traditional economic concepts did not deal with this problem. His claim was that improving the welfare of poor people did not depend on land, equipment, or energy, but rather on knowledge. He called this qualitative aspect of economics "human capital." Schultz, who won the Nobel Prize in 1979, offered this description:

> Consider all human abilities to be either innate or acquired. Every person is born with a particular set of genes, which determines his innate ability. Attributes of acquired population quality, which are valuable and can be augmented by appropriate investment, will be treated as human capital.[3]

In business terms we might describe human capital as a combination of factors such as the following:

- The traits one brings to the job: intelligence, energy, a generally positive attitude, reliability, commitment
- One's ability to learn: aptitude, imagination, creativity, and what is often called "street smarts," savvy (or how to get things done)
- One's motivation to share information and knowledge: team spirit and goal orientation

The great irony is that the only economic component that can add value in and by itself is the one that is the most difficult to evaluate. This is the human component—clearly the most vexatious of assets to manage. The almost infinite variability and unpredictability of human beings make them enormously more complex to evaluate than one of the electro-mechanical components that comes with predetermined operating specifications. Nevertheless, people are the only element with the inherent power to generate value. All other variables—cash and its cousin credit, materials, plant and equipment, and energy—offer nothing but inert potentials. By their nature, they add nothing, and they cannot add anything until some human being, be it the lowest-level laborer, the most ingenious professional, or the loftiest executive, leverages that potential by putting it into play. The good news is that measuring the value added of human capital is possible. In fact, it has been going on in a dozen countries since the early 1990s. Why this is known by only a relatively few managers will be addressed later.

Viewed from either an economic or a philosophic perspective, the thing that matters most is not how productive people are in organizations. That is a by-product of something more fundamental. The most important issue is how fulfilled people are in their work. No amount of compensation can restore the soul of a person who has spent his or her life in mindless toil. In fact, even a modicum of economic comfort cannot overcome the bitterness of that experience. Curiously, fulfilling work is truly its own reward for the individual and the enterprise. In the final analysis, there is clear and abundant evidence that an organization that makes work as fulfilling as possible will develop and retain the most productive workers and enjoy the most loyal customers.

One of the key drivers of fulfillment is knowledge. Knowing how well we have done leads directly to job satisfaction. The only thing that is more satisfying than seeing data that show our accomplishments is having our supervisor see the results of our labor and compliment us on a job well done.

Facing the Talent Shortage

For the foreseeable future, organizations in most developed countries will be faced with a talent shortfall. In the United States, the demographics are such that it will be impossible to sustain strong economic growth due to the paucity of talent. Since 1965, the end of the baby boom era, the birth rate has declined by about one-third. This has resulted in a workforce population that is decreasing. Concurrently, the national economy as measured by the gross domestic product has nearly doubled over the same period. Obviously, the economy and the working population are on diverging growth curves. Although the current robust economy will surely slow to some degree, the availability of indigenous talent is not going to reverse its course overnight. From 1996 to 2006, the percentage of workers ages 25 to 34 will shrink 9 percent, and those 35 to 44 will slip 3 percent.

Such data are available to anyone who chooses to look for them. Drucker accuses organizations of focusing data collection on the inside of the enterprise.[4] These data treat only costs. Yet results are outside, and management has largely ignored demographic and customer trend data. He claims that the most important factor for planning and for strategy is whether the share of income that customers spend on an industry's products is increasing or decreasing. On the human side, it was pointed out in an article in 1990 that the most significant problem organizations would face in the last half of the decade would be a shortage of talent.[5] The economic and population data were available to management and were ignored. If we want the economy to continue its upward pace, something has to be done to compensate for the declining number of qualified workers at all levels.

There are several ways to accomplish that—some potentially more effective than others. The first reaction is to bring in millions of immigrants to fill jobs. This is not going to happen. Congress is under pressure to control immigration by various self-interest groups such as labor unions. Immigrants will help, but they will be a very small part of the solution. Even if the gates were opened, the data show that between 1980 and 1990, 41 percent of the new immigrants age 25 and older did not have a college equivalency education, compared with 23 percent of native-born Americans of the same age group.[6] This is not going to fill a knowledge economy's talent shortage in the near term.

Outsourcing work to other countries is an increasingly popular method of coping with the shortage. Manufacturing has been doing this successfully for the past thirty years. However, managing professional workers engaged in qualitative, judgmental designs thousands of miles across oceans and continents is a more complex matter and not so trouble-free.

Another simplistic answer stems from outmoded beliefs about people. Some managers believe in their hearts that rank-and-file workers are not a whole lot smarter than Skinner's pigeons who learned to peck levers to obtain food pellets. Those managers believe that providing tangible incentives, the human equivalent of food pellets, is the answer. However, it doesn't matter how tasty the incentives might be; a pigeon who doesn't know which lever to peck is not going to get a pellet. This is a way of saying that if we don't have people with the inherent talent, training, or work experience, along with the right tools and information to do the job, we are not going to get the results we need. All we will have is frustrated pigeons. To maintain a competitive position in the marketplace of the twenty-first century, management will have to find methods for increasing the power of the human information lever. The availability of valid and reliable performance data is at the heart of the issue.

The most cost-effective, long-term solution to the talent shortfall lies in helping each person become more productive. This charges management with the task of figuring out how to invest in human productive potential. During the industrial age, the primary production tools moved material. In the post-industrial age, the production tools move information, which in turn tells us how and when to move the appropriate materials and services. Electronic technology is just beginning to be employed to generate useful data and move them quickly. The loop of productivity begins to close when human beings learn what data are needed, where, when, in what form, and by whom. The loop is completed and productivity enhanced when people learn what the data mean. Training in data analysis and interpretation turns data into information and eventually intelligence. That is the only feasible path to solving the talent shortage. Schultz was right, decades ago.

The Structure

This book shows how data, especially data on human capital activity, are aggregated to become information and eventually intelligence. It describes the variables, the combinations, the contexts, and the applications. It provides explicit examples of the connections among the corporate, business unit, and human resources levels.

Chapter 1 takes the first steps toward a methodology for measuring the return on investment (ROI) of human capital. It lays out the issue of integrating intellectual and human capital. I focus on this because to measure the ROI of human capital, we have to understand how it interacts with other aspects of intellectual capital. The chapter traces the linkages among the four elements of intellectual capital and value added. Then it outlines how the elements have to work together to optimize enterprise effectiveness.

Chapter 2 launches the process of finding the ROI of human capital from an unusual starting point. It begins by reminding us that instead of starting with process improvement, we must move up the corporate ladder. Everything must flow from the goals of the enterprise. This provides the context for process and employee management. My concentration is on quantitative metrics. Perceptual measures are also addressed and incorporated into a scorecard model. Examples are provided for designing objective and perceptual human capital metrics at the enterprise level. The amounts or degrees of change shown through successive metrics are a function of the five basic indicators of change: cost, time, volume, errors, and human reactions.

Chapter 3 is the bridge between the enterprise and the human capital management levels. This is the process arena, the center of functional performance. I describe how to find value in processes, as well as how to tease out the human aspect. Metrics for functional unit service, quality, and productivity are displayed alongside the five indices of change and linked upward to the enterprise and downward to the human capital. Examples are given that show the interactive effects of change on several performance indices.

Chapter 4 brings us to the drivers of all enterprise success: people. It explains that there are five basic activities in managing human capital: planning, acquiring, maintaining, developing, and retaining the human asset. A matrix is constructed of the five human capital management activities and the five indices of change. From this, virtually all service, quality, or productivity changes can be identified, measured, and evaluated. A scorecard format is offered as a comprehensive example for monitoring human capital.

Chapter 5 integrates the three levels—enterprise, process or function, and people—together in one end-to-end system of human capital valuation reporting. It shows the linkages among them, the drivers, and the effects of one level on the others. An extensive look at the future begins with a set of leading indicators. This is followed with futures scorecards for each level. The chapter concludes with an overview of the integrated reporting model.

Chapter 6 moves to the next level: trending and predicting. In a marketplace that moves as rapidly as this one, success is not a function of hindsight. We have to improve our ability to see what might be over the horizon. The chapter discusses the sources and uses of demographic data and builds on the leading indicators and futures concepts of Chapter 5. It introduces the human capital financial index as another way of monitoring changes in human capital revenue, cost, and profit.

Chapter 7 dissects five of the most common human resources and human capital initiatives and demonstrates how to find economic value in the workings of each. It covers restructuring of the human resources department, outsourcing, contingent workforce management, mergers and acquisitions, and benchmarking.

Chapter 8 reports on two of the longest-term, largest-scale studies of human capital management. One is a study by the Gallup organization, which focuses on management practices that have been shown to bring out the best in employees. The other, conducted by the Saratoga Institute, deals with the employee perspective and what it takes to retain and motivate key talent. After examining these two research projects, I provide a commonsense example of successful management and point out a high degree of correlation among the three.

Chapter 9 shows you how to take your organization on a quantum leap over the competition. By standing in the future and managing it from today, you learn how to change the context of the organization to make it highly effective five years out. This approach creates the desired new organization by designing systems today that position us in the future.

Chapter 10 is a compilation of guiding principles. These are the underlying lessons of the preceding chapters. They are the key points that need to be remembered above all the specific activities.

Chapter 11 sums up the basic measurement system. It provides a coda to the book by looking at how electronic technology is changing the human and financial dynamics of the workplace. The conclusion is that knowledge management is the key to unlocking the incomprehensible potential of the twenty-first century.

References

1. Henri Fayol (1841–1925), *Administration Industrielle et Générale* (General and Industrial Management), trans. Constance Storrs, with a foreword by L. Urwick (London: Pitman, 1949).
2. Chester Irving Barnard (1886–1961), *The Functions of the Executive* (Cambridge, Mass.: Harvard University Press, 1938, 1962).
3. Theodore W. Schultz, *Investing in People: The Economics of Population Quality* (Berkeley, Calif.: University of California, 1981), p. 21.
4. Peter Drucker, "The Next Information Revolution," *Forbes ASAP*, August 24, 1998, pp. 47–58.
5. Jac Fitz-enz, "Getting and Keeping Good Employees," *Personnel Journal*, August 1990, pp. 25–28.
6. *Workforce 2020*, Hudson Institute, 1999.

Acknowledgments

The models and methods described are the result of the collective insights and efforts of many people over a long time. At the beginning, in the 1970s, Barbara Davison and Bob Coon tested the earliest methods with me in the human resources department of a Silicon Valley computer company. Over the years, Barbara and later Bob worked with me again at the Saratoga Institute, when we went public with our first crude survey of human resources metrics in 1985. The staff at the institute, through their daily work of supporting clients with valid, reliable data on human capital, added immeasurably to the content of this book. The work of Eric Stanger, David Flores, and Charlotte Cox was especially valuable. Clients too numerous to mention have tested our ideas over the past fifteen years.

Throughout the struggles of the 1980s and 1990s, my incomparable wife, Ellen Kieffer, listened to my babbling, challenged my hyperbole, and gave me the strength to continue during the dark days. To her especially and to the others, I wish to express my deepest appreciation and gratitude for their faith in my wild idea that we could find the economic value that people contribute to organizations.

Finally, I thank the thousands of indifferent and contentious people whose apathy and sometimes hostility spurred me to prove that it could be done.

A special word of thanks to my acquisitions editor, Adrienne Hickey. She never let me produce anything less than the best I had to offer.

1

Human Capital

The Profit Lever of a Knowledge Economy

"Only the investment of capital assets can increase the productivity of labor."

—*Nineteenth-century economic theory*

In the closing years of the twentieth century, management has come to accept that people, not cash, buildings, or equipment, are the critical differentiators of a business enterprise. As we move into the new millennium and find ourselves in a knowledge economy, it is undeniable that people are the profit lever. All the assets of an organization, other than people, are inert. They are passive resources that require human application to generate value. The key to sustaining a profitable company or a healthy economy is the productivity of the workforce, our human capital. In the American economy, where over half of the gross national product is allocated to the information sector, it is obvious that knowledgeable people are the driving force.

The stock market has recognized the leverage of human knowledge by awarding a market value for service and technology companies that exceeds their book value by many times. Leverage is the use of certain fixed assets to enhance the return on investments or sales. Typical examples are com-

mon stock leverage and borrowed capital. Companies acquire
funds through stock offerings or borrowing. The objective is
to use these funds to generate greater returns than the cost
incurred. Most managers and financial analysts have finally
acknowledged that human capital has great leverage potential.

In April 1999, investment bank Goldman Sachs launched
an initial public offering (IPO) that drew a market value of
$36 billion on its opening, a value four times that of its hard
assets. If we subtracted the book value from the $36 billion
and divided that by the number of employees at the time of
the IPO, we would see a dramatic example of the market's
appreciation for human capital leverage.

Effects on Organizational Management

Organizations are undergoing wrenching change not only due
to globalization but also because of the force that makes truly
global companies competitive—information exchange. Senge
puts a framework on this capability:

> For the first time in history, humankind has the ca-
> pacity to create far more information than anyone
> can absorb, to foster far greater interdependency
> than anyone can manage, and to accelerate change
> far faster than anyone's ability to keep pace.[1]

Information has always been of great value. America's
first recorded millionaire was Elias Derby of Salem, Massa-
chusetts. Salem was our first major port and the place where
fortunes were made and lost in commanding sailing ships. But
the clever Derby never had to brave the dangers of the deep.
He remained safe and dry on shore while accumulating his
fortune. While ships were coming from and going to many
destinations around the known world, Derby stayed in Salem
gathering data from shipmasters, sailors, and port documents. He learned what types of cargoes were trading between which ports and the prices being paid. With this

information, Derby was able to invest in cargo that promised the greatest security and profit margins.

Drucker claims that the greatest challenge for organizations today and for the next decade at least is to respond to the shift from an industrial to a knowledge economy. He reminds us that the purpose and function of every organization is the integration of specialized knowledge into a common task.[2] This shift toward knowledge as the differentiator affects all aspects of organizational management, including operating efficiency, marketing, organizational structure, and human capital investment. Each of these directly or indirectly hinges on an understanding of the ability of people to cope with unforeseen, massive, and usually hurried change. Bontis shows us that human capital, as the employer of information technology, is the critical antecedent in effectively managing the organizational knowledge that yields higher business results.[3] At the end of the day, it is blindingly obvious that without hard data on human capital activity and productivity, there is virtually no chance of competing effectively.

The irony underlying the need for data on human capital is that the capability that information technology puts at the disposal of organizations can be a barrier to understanding events and responding effectively. The vast majority of data resident on organizational databases is not gathered and organized in a manner that helps executives manage their

> Since employee costs can exceed 40 percent of corporate expense, measuring the ROI in human capital is essential.

human capital problems or exploit their opportunities. Since employee costs today can exceed 40 percent of corporate expense, measuring the ROI in human capital is essential.[4] Management needs a system of metrics that describe and predict the cost and productivity curves of its workforce. Beyond that, and more important, are qualitative measures. Quantitative measures tend toward cost, capacity, and time. Qualitative measures focus on value and human reactions. The quantitative tells us what happened, whereas the qualitative gives us some idea of why it happened. Together, they offer insights into results and drivers, or causes. For example, if we see costs or delivery times increasing, we might find that quality problems are at the source. Product defects cause work to be recycled, thus slowing down delivery time. In turn, this causes customers to be dissatisfied and perhaps to look for other suppliers. Lost customers drive marketing costs up, which increases product cost, and so on.

Rummler and Brache draw on their experience in process improvement to state, "we believe that measurement is *the* pivotal performance management and improvement tool and as such deserves special treatment."[5] They go on to point out that without measurement we cannot:

- Communicate specific performance expectations.
- Know what is going on inside the organization.
- Identify performance gaps that should be analyzed and eliminated.
- Provide feedback comparing performance to a standard or a benchmark.
- Recognize performance that should be rewarded.
- Support decisions regarding resource allocation, projections, and schedules.

In short, if we don't know how to measure our primary value-producing asset, we can't manage it.

Two Aspects of Human Capital

When we speak of measuring the value of people, we have to acknowledge the two aspects of that issue: the economic and the spiritual. We can accept the intrinsic spiritual value of people and focus on the economic side. In essence, all measures of value contribution are really measures of human value as economic units and as spiritual beings. Only people generate value through the application of their intrinsic humanity, motivation, learned skills, and tool manipulation.

In addition, we must deal with the myth that only standard financial information is accurate. Because we have practiced double-entry bookkeeping for 500 years, we have come to believe that the numbers on financial statements are truths. This is not the case. They are facts, but seldom truths. There is only one number on a balance sheet that is verifiable as a truth. That is the first asset: cash. All other numbers are a combination of hopes, agreements, and expectations. In effect, we have constructed a system that changes whenever the Financial Accounting Standards Board (FASB) decides to change it. We admit willingly that the system works to some extent in telling us what happened last period—so far as the agreed-upon practices show it. But the data are only as accurate as the inputs, which every businessperson knows are manipulated.

How well accounting has ignored human capital can be seen in practically any book on business ratios. A typical example is *The Vest-Pocket Guide to Business Ratios.*[6] In over 300 pages, the only time that employee-related metrics show up is as costs, never as leverage. The guide closes with a list of thirteen ratios that are published by the likes of Dun & Bradstreet, Standard & Poors, Moody's, Value Line, and Robert Morris Associates. Not a single one involves human capital, even as a cost element.

Standard accounting fails to solve today's mandate at two levels. First, accounting looks inside the organization. Its primary role is to conserve the assets of the enterprise. Second, it is focused on the past. If we want an internal, backward look, accounting does the job. Conversely, today we need to focus on the issues that will create wealth, the actions that will extract value from the marketplace. And we need to focus on the future. We cannot be successful by backing into the future with our eyes locked on the past. The advent of new forms of accounting—namely, economic value added and the balanced scorecard approach—is a promising step in the right direction. So let us accept accounting for what it is, but not worship it to the exclusion of other useful data.

Next, we must confront those who say that invested capital greatly determines the productivity of people. In an absolute sense, that is correct. If you give me a gazillion-dollar supercomputer, I can solve large mathematical equations faster than I can using my laptop. But the question is, can I do it as fast as a mathematics professor using the same equipment? No way! This is the human leverage.

A related argument says that brand equity has much to do with the success of a given salesperson. It's true that if I am selling Coca Cola versus Joe's Cola, I will probably sell more Coke than Joe's with less effort. But if you are a better salesperson than I am, you will sell more Coke than I will. So, it is fair to claim that factors other than human knowledge, skill, and effort affect the outcome of a given situation. (I address this momentarily as part of the discussion of the intellectual capacity of an enterprise.) Nevertheless, it is also true that human knowledge, skill, and effort make the marginal difference in just about every situation.

People and Information

The knowledge, skills, and attitudes of the workforce separate the winning companies from the also-rans. It is a complex combination of factors. Still, people per se are not the only force behind the inherent power of human capital. If the key to wealth creation were only a head count, then the dullest, lowest-level person would be as valuable as the brightest, highest-level person. In actuality, it is the information that the person possesses and his or her ability and willingness to share it that establish value potential. Data and people are inexorably linked as never before. Either one without the other is suboptimized. Rather than bigger buildings or more equipment, employees need timely, relevant, and, most important, organized data. (Later cases will illustrate that equipment without operating instructions or data without the knowledge of what they mean are useless.) Management's imperative is to put useful data at the fingertips of its human capital on a timely basis and to train them how to use such data. The ability and experience of a person allow him or her to:

- Convert data into meaningful information.
- Turn information into intelligence related to a business issue.
- Share that intelligence with others.

The motivation to share data is the unrecognized barrier to information systems and value extraction. Once more, having data per se is no more useful than having any other resource unless we know how, why, and when to share it. Experience has proved repeatedly that without the knowledge of what to distribute and the motivation to do it unselfishly, information is just another expensive, underutilized asset. The inevitable conclusion must be that long-term profitability is dependent on the creation of an information-sharing culture. It is the prequisite to any attempt to manage intellectual capital.

Dunnigan and Masterson studied the methods of twelve great generals from Alexander the Great to Norman Schwarz-kopf.[7] In almost every case, they found two characteristics that helped these men win decisive battles. First, they paid great attention to details. They gathered and analyzed as much relevant data as they could. They studied not only the size and disposition of the enemy but also the terrain, logistical challenges, and weapons technology. Second, they concentrated on communications. By relaying accurate, relevant information more rapidly than the enemy, they could move their forces faster, giving themselves a great tactical advantage.

Gengis Khan presaged the American Pony Express by 650 years. He established stations at intervals of twenty-five to fifty miles. Travelers possessing a "tablet of authority" could get fresh horses and supplies at these stations. When a messenger carrying an important letter neared a station, he blew a horn, and a fresh horse and saddle would be waiting. This way, a rider could cover over 200 miles a day. For really important messages, fresh riders were ready. This doubled the daily miles traversed. This method allowed Temujin (his real name) to control and move troops over an enormous area. In those days, it took a ruler weeks to assemble an army. He depended on travelers and spies to let him know if an enemy was preparing to mount a campaign. Temujin's communications system gave him the ability to strike before the enemy was ready. Today, 700 years after the great Khan, the imperative is still to manage information so that people can act swiftly and decisively. Sun Tzu put it succinctly: "What enables the wise sovereign and the good general to strike and conquer, and achieve things beyond the reach of ordinary men, is fore-knowledge."[8]

Data-to-Value Cycle

At the heart of the data-to-value cycle is people. It is a cycle rather than a continuum, because data from one phase can cycle back to influence the previous phase or phases. To understand how to assess the value of human capital, we have to look at it in application. To reiterate, human knowledge or skill is of no organizational value until it is applied to a business situation. Value adding always starts with the enterprise's goals. Operationally, those goals flow down through the business units to the starting point of human capital management—the activities of the human resources department. At this point, the process of connecting human capital data to demonstrate value begins.

> Human knowledge or skill is of no organizational value until it is applied to a business situation. Value adding always starts with the enterprise's goals.

Value can be traced from the inception of data collection through processes to economic results. The cycle starts with the processes having to do with the planning, acquisition, maintenance, development, and retention of human capital. The values are the economic effects resulting from investment in human capital. Human capital is organized in the human resources department and transferred into operating units. There it is invested, along with other resources. As improvements are realized, value ensues. Value comes through reduction in expenses as well as through revenue generation, which ultimately lead to profitability and other enterprise goals. The cycle is seen in Figure 1-1.

Schematically, it works like this: Phase one of the cycle is the point of obtaining, supporting, and retaining human capital. Internal efficiencies within the human resources department lead to expense reduction. Improvements in cycle times, incentive compensation plans, or development programs also

Figure 1-1. Data-to-value cycle.

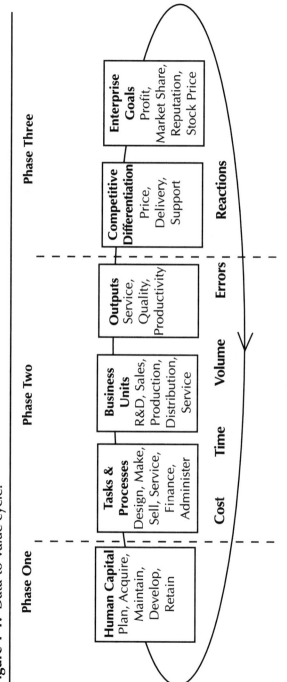

can affect revenue generation. In phase two, human capital is applied to tasks and processes within the various business units. The outputs are differentiating improvements in customer service, product or service quality, and/or productivity as measured in unit cost terms. It is then a matter of determining whether the gains are attributable in part to human actions. Phase three focuses on the competitive advantages those improvements generated, which lead to economic goals. When this is viewed as a continuous recycling process, we can find many points at which to assess the impact of internal improvements on a corporation's profitability.

Intellectual Capacity

Intellectual capacity is the ability of a company to extract value from the organization's intellectual capital. Intellectual capital is composed of two types of organizational capital: intellectual property and a complex intertwining of process and culture, plus relational capital and human capital. Figure 1-2 shows the intellectual capital setup. People are the catalyst that activates the intangible, inert forms of intellectual capital and the equally passive forms of tangible capital—material and equipment—to improve operational effectiveness. To optimize and measure the ROI in human capital, we have to understand how it interacts with other forms of capital, both intangible and tangible.

Organizational capital includes intellectual property and process data. Executives often look at organizational capital from an internal ownership perspective. This is a protectionist view, which is not totally bad but is certainly limiting in terms of exploiting its potential. They want to know how to secure the intelligence contained within their documents and processes, as well as within the minds of their employees. It is relatively easy to slap a brand, trademark, copyright, or patent number on a piece of intellectual property. It is a bit more bewildering to find a method for putting one's brand on the human brain. A judicial battleground is forming, with lawsuits flying in all directions as we try to establish a body of legal precedents for intellectual assets.

Figure 1-2. Intellectual capital.

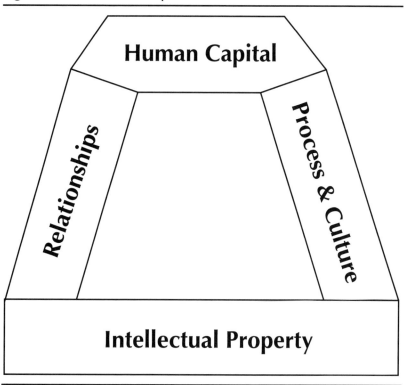

The second organizational capital artifact is process management. Documenting how to do something makes it an asset. For example, superior inventory management helped Wal-Mart take the number-one position in retailing away from perennial leader Sears. Fred Smith, founder of Federal Express, created an industry by changing the process of small package delivery. Distribution systems, manufacturing methods, and administrative efficiencies represent potential value. Codifying and applying them is an attempt to build intellectual capacity.

One process capital issue that has been largely overlooked has to do with an organization's culture. This is arguably at least as important as process management. Some would say that culture is a human capital issue, but it is not. Culture

is the defining aspect of every organization. It is its *signature.*
Deal and Kennedy launched the corporate culture concept in
1982.[9] They described how it covers the expectations, rituals,
taboos, and underlying rewards and punishments of the corporate society. Trompenaars and Hampden-Turner extended
the concept to global issues of corporate value systems and
diversity around the world.[10] This has caught on to the point
where a currently popular cultural goal is to become an "employer of choice." *Fortune* magazine has jumped on this bandwagon with an annual issue devoted to "The 100 Best
Companies to Work For." Beyond competitive remuneration,
some companies are struggling to build environments
wherein people want to work. Other executives roll their eyes
and claim that they have no time for changing the culture.
This is like saying, "My people are dying of malaria, but I
don't have time to drain the swamp that breeds the anopheles
mosquitoes." Executives with this type of short-term, simplistic attitude invariably produce short-lived, weak organizations.

This brings us to the folks who are trying to corral another
kind of capital or intelligence that is focused outside the organization. It is relational information. Relations include interactions not only with customers but also with suppliers,
partners, competitors, media, community, government—
indeed, all stakeholders or observers of the organization.
Compelling arguments can be made regarding the economic
value of knowledge about, and good relations with, any external force that impinges on the organizational corpus. I suspect
that books will soon be written rediscovering relational capital. McKenna introduced the idea in 1986 when he argued
that traditional product-focused marketing was an anachronism.[11] He claimed that building relationships was one of the
three underpinnings of marketing:

1. Understand the market.
2. Move with it.
3. Form relationships.

Whereas information may have a fleeting moment on the
stage of consciousness, relationships have a permanence that

can be very powerful. People might not remember what someone said yesterday, but they will remember what others did.
Somewhere along the way, McKenna's third element got lost
because it was not a traditional marketing activity. However,
as one who spent several years in sales and then founded a
company, I can state unequivocally that personal relationships are absolutely a competitive advantage. We will look at
relational capital as it connects with human capital ROI.

Finally, we encounter the fourth position, which is dedicated to expanding the skills and knowledge of employees for
the sake of the person as well as the company. There are two
concerns here. The first is with trying to build "learning organizations"—another recent term for which there are a number of fuzzy definitions. In short, according to Senge, who
popularized the term, a learning organization is "a place
where people are continually discovering how they create
their reality."[12]

This construct is undergoing a great deal of experimenta-
tion in its own right. A learning organization is not a simple
idea. Senior executives, first-line supervisors, employees,
trainers, accountants, and lawyers all take different views.
The definitive model, notwithstanding Senge's work, has yet
to be proved. To compound matters, another incomplete concept, human capital, is being added to the mix. The combination of two uncertainties raises the odds against success on
either one of them to a very high level. In my opinion, this
interdependency has not yet been recognized.

The second and corollary human concern is the right of
the individual to trade on the knowledge that he or she possesses. Humanists and lawyers argue over the rights of persons within whose brain cage and experience base lies the
germ of human capital. This is no less important a topic. Several well-publicized cases of appropriation of knowledge
through recruitment have already arisen. Most are being settled out of court. Eventually, one or more will work itself all
the way through the legal system, and a body of human capital
law will begin to emerge.

Consultants and some academicians have joined the race
to intellectual capital for what they see as an opportunity to
sell their newfound erudition. Every major consulting firm

has formed a human capital practice. The media are supporting this with clichés. Spouting platitudes like "people are the
most important product," they encourage the building of new
management vehicles, thereby inserting more ignorance into
the race. By touting every new employee service fad for which
there is scant evidence of effectiveness, they generate confu-
sion and frustration. Figure 1-3 displays many of the management panaceas that have hit the market in the past fifty years.
The top is left open, because tomorrow someone will come up
with the latest solution to all of management's problems.

Typically, people choose just one of the lanes on the intellectual capital track (organizational, relational, or human).
But they drive off in every direction, each toward what he or
she believes is the finish line. The irony is that they are partly
correct, but only partly, and therein lies the rub. So long as
they never need to meet, there will be no problem. However,
even in this embryonic stage, intellectual capital looks less like
a racetrack and more like a maze. Having said that, there is
still undoubtedly value in this frenzy, for it is by the trials and
errors, the running in wrong directions and the collisions
along the track, that we will one day understand what intellectual capacity involves. The race will be more painful and less
successful until we accept that we must survey the track and
understand the vehicles. I fear that in the near future we are
in for fewer Indianapolis 500s and more Demolition Derbies.

Surveying the Track

To build intellectual capacity and maximize the ROI in human
capital, we should consider all aspects of intellectual capital
simultaneously. In addition, the decisions that come out of
this search must always be focused on achieving competitive
advantage through improvements in service, quality, or productivity. Figure 1-4 is an example of the intellectual capacity
pathway.

We need to turn the four lanes into one. When we grasp
how to integrate property, process and culture, external relations, and human capital into our management thinking, we

Figure 1-3. Fifty years of management panaceas.

2000	? ? ? ? ?
	Intellectual Capital- Learning Organization
1990	Rightsizing - Balanced Scorecard - EVA
	TQM - Reengineering - 7 Habits - Delayering
	Downsizing - Customer Service - Benchmarking
1980	Kaizen - Empowerment - Continuous Improvement
	Corporate Culture - Change Management - MBWA
	Intrapreneuring - Relationship Marketing - Excellence
1970	Quality Circles - Diversification - One Minute Managing
	Work Simplification -**Needs Hierarchy**- Statistical Process Control
	Organization Renewal - Value Chain - Portfolio Management
1960	Managerial Grid - Matrix - Hygienes and Motivators - Theory Z
	Theory X & Y - Plan - Organize - Direct - Control - Human Relations
1950	Management by Objectives - Management Science - Decision Tree

EVA = Economic Value Added: net operating profit after tax — cost of capital.
TQM = Total Quality Management: systemwide application of quality philosophy.
MBWA = Management By Walking Around.

Figure 1-4. Intellectual capacity pathway.

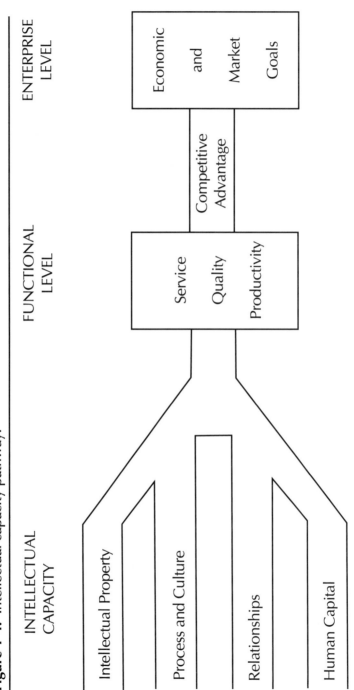

INTELLECTUAL
CAPACITY

FUNCTIONAL
LEVEL

ENTERPRISE
LEVEL

Intellectual Property

Process and Culture

Relationships

Human Capital

Service

Quality

Productivity

Competitive
Advantage

Economic

and

Market

Goals

will be moving in the right direction. Strategy and tactics must fuse the four perspectives into a broad-based synergistic solution that can be economically valued. That integration represents the final step on the path to intellectual capacity.

The ROI Race

The strategic business plan is like a race plan. The plan's goals are to reach the finish line first. Data systems are the vehicle. Information is the fuel. But the vehicle is not a self-propelled, perpetual-motion machine. It needs a driver, the human being. Measurement is the dashboard gauges. They tell us how fast we are going, the condition of the car, and how far we have gone. Only the driver knows if we are headed in the right direction. When management is the sole driver, the only one who has access to the travel plan and the odometer, we can go a long way in the wrong direction before we realize it. By having someone checking the map against the road signs while others watch the speed, fuel gauge, and temperature and pressure lights, we increase the probability that we will arrive at our destination on time, as well as enjoy the trip.

To have a successful trip to profitability, we need to know more than how to read traditional dashboard gauges. If you look inside a race car, you see a dashboard that is quite different from the one in your car. It is very utilitarian and contains detailed information beyond what we are used to seeing. So it is in business. We have to design a human capital dashboard that gives us new data and then teach everyone how to read the gauges efficiently and accurately. Everyone includes management. Human capital data analysis has only lately come into the management education and training system. Although businesspeople have been exposed to courses on financial analysis, they have focused primarily on standard accounting instruments such as income statements and balance sheets. Human capital ROI analysis uses the same principles, but some data points are not found on corporate financial documents. Furthermore, it teaches us how one gauge affects another. If the temperature gauge shows an overheated condition, we need to know if it is due to lack of water in the radiator or a broken fan belt. Recognizing that it is hot but continuing to push the accelerator to the floor is a good way to cause the pistons to overheat and seize the engine.

The starting point is to know specifically what our goal is, as well as what our competitors are doing. This information evolves into distance, direction, and time requirements. Next, we must specify the type of information that different people will need to manage the race. Finally, we have to learn how people, data systems, and information interact to impact profitability. It comes down to where, what, who, when, and how:

1. Where do we want to be?
2. What data do we need to capture and manage to get us to the finish line?
3. Who should generate what data?
4. When do we need it?
5. How do we accomplish this most efficiently and effectively?

It is also useful to know how fast and in what direction the competition is moving. Currently, we call that benchmarking.

False Starts

The most common reaction to the information challenge is to invest in technology. This is necessary, but by itself, it seldom yields a solution that we want. Technology is a passive asset. Computers and programs don't add value until knowledgeable human beings put their trained hands on the keyboard and begin to draw out the potential within the software programs. Informal surveys have shown that few organizations invest in the training necessary to exploit

> Computers and programs don't add value until knowledgeable human beings put their trained hands on the keyboard and draw out the potential within the software programs.

the capability of the technology. One example from within my family is typical of this shortsighted practice.

My son Peter worked at a major department store for several years as a retail clerk. At one point, a new cash register program was installed throughout the store. When the clerks asked for training, they were literally "tossed" a manual and told to read it. It is an undeniable fact that (1) software manuals are not written in a language most of us learned in school, and (2) no one reads the bloody things anyway. The result in Peter's store was that for several weeks the clerks struggled with the cash registers until they muscled their way through the program by trial and error. The problem for the store was that during this self-teaching period, after several false starts with a purchase price input, the frustrated clerk would give the product to the customer at whatever price came up. Naturally, this price was always less than the tag price, or the customer would not have accepted it. The clerk's explanation to the delighted customer was that this was a special sale or a closeout price. According to Peter, this sometimes represented a discount of 50 to 75 percent. The many thousands of dollars lost far exceeded the cost of basic training. (Note: Of course, Peter never did this.)

So, we see that technology plus training should make workers at all levels more productive. This is the first step. But there are two parallel steps that must accompany it. One is the issue of data production. All processes generate data as a by-product. Most data are not sorted, collected, and shared. Organizations lean on the signposts and never see them. Some executives realize that they have a vast pool of useful data within their organization, but they seldom make the investment or issue the mandate to turn it into productivity-enhancing intelligence. I have had countless discussions with executives who acknowledged this shortcoming yet never did anything about it. I believe the reason is that they have been trained in financial data analysis, but not in the utility of human performance or information data. They know they can't run the enterprise without financial information, but they don't appreciate the value or necessity of applying human capital data. Rather than admit their ignorance, they squeeze financial data ever tighter. The one light at the end of the proverbial tunnel is the gradual adoption of the balanced scorecard.[13] Here, data beyond financials make up 75 percent of the information.

The first, last, and most important piece is information culture. Investing in information technology and training is necessary. But again, technology and data are passive. Even information possessed by workers is suboptimized unless it is shared. Putting up an intranet knowledge exchange does not automatically cause useful information to be shared. Millions have been spent on technology and training to create internal knowledge exchanges. In very few cases have they met expectations. Andersen Consulting invested a great deal of money in its "KX" (knowledge exchange). But it wasn't until the staff learned how useful shared data could be that they began to input their knowledge and experience. Now, consultants around the world enter project experiences and post queries. In many cases, they receive prompt replies that help them serve their customers more efficiently and effectively.

In the final analysis, it comes down to creating an information-sharing culture. Only then is it worthwhile to invest in information technology, train people in its use, and implement policies aimed at gathering useful by-product data. The fundamental question remains, What information do we need?

Points of Measurement

There are three levels at which the leverage of human capital investment can be measured. The principal focus must always start at the enterprise level. Here we are looking at the relationship between human capital and certain enterprise goals. These goals include strategic financial, customer, and human issues. The second level of measurement is the business unit. At this stage, we are watching for changes in intermediate-level service, quality, and productivity outcomes. Measurement is fundamentally about assessing degrees or amounts of change. All business objectives can be reduced to service, quality, or productivity categories. All changes can be measured through some combination of cost, time, volume, errors or defects, and human reactions. The third, but in a sense the primary, stage is human capital management per se. Now we can see the effects of the human resources department's work on planning, hiring, compensating, developing, and retaining the enterprise's human capital. When we break down the subject of human capital measurement like this, the mystery should disappear.

However, this is where the barrier seems to be for many people. They can't seem to get past a mythology that claims that the economic value or effectiveness of people in business cannot be calculated. I grant that it is not easy to measure the economic effectiveness of people in service work or professional-level activities. The problem has been that measurement initiatives often applied manufacturing methods. Except for clerical jobs, measures of efficiency or productivity are not appropriate in a nonmanufacturing situation. The input to white-collar work is data. The applicable skill is judgment. The output is information and, if we're lucky, intelligence. There is no single metric for professional-level staff work. As I will demonstrate later, there are five basic paths to measuring the value of this type of output. The greatest value is found in staffs' effects on line function objectives and ultimately the corporate goals. The bottom line is that although it is not easy to evaluate staff work in quantitative terms, it can be and is being done.

> Although it is not easy to evaluate staff work in quantitative terms, it can be and is being done.

I have spent twenty years explaining and demonstrating this by showing the linking methodology and publishing company, industry, national, and international benchmark data, but some people still won't let go of the myth and deal with the reality. Either I am a lousy communicator or I'm talking to a bunch of zombies. Fortunately for all of us, the zombies are being left behind in greater numbers every day as people with open minds, new values, and different perspectives come into business, especially into staff functions. The following chapters show how to measure the ROI in human capital and process management, which leads to competitive advantage and economic value at the enterprise level.

Summary

Management's responsibility today is to combine people with information on a timely basis for several purposes. First, information on employee-based activities is necessary to partner with financial data. Second, financial data tell us what happened. Human capital data tell us why it happened that way. Third, if we are going to manage for the future rather than the past, we need leading as well as lagging indicators. They cannot be found in traditional profit and loss statements.

Information is the key to performance management and improvement. Without it, we have only opinions with no supporting facts and no directional signals. Information does not move by itself. There has to be an information-sharing culture that promotes and rewards data distribution. Improvements in one area need to be published centrally, where people can access the information and save themselves from reinventing effective practices.

The three types of data—organizational, relational, and human—must be integrated. Organizational data tell us what we have. Relational data tell us what outsiders—customers, competitors, and other stakeholders—need or want from the enterprise. Human data show us how the only active assets, people, are doing in their quest to drive the organization toward its goals. When we begin to understand how the three relate to one another, support and drive one another, we have started down the track to intellectual capacity. The costs to the enterprise of not doing this are often hidden but potentially devastating. At the very least, the failure to manage all types of data separates the winners from the also-rans.

Not only is it possible to measure the effect of human performance; it is necessary for maintaining a viable position in the market. Since white-collar, information-focused judgment is fundamentally dissimilar from blue-collar, product-focused labor, a different measurement methodology is required. A spectrum of metrics can be developed that, in total, show the value added of professional-level work. The value is not found in the initial output per se, but rather in the effect it has on enhancing the outputs of its operating-unit customers. As staff groups utilize human capital more effectively, they increase their contribution to the goals of the enterprise.

References

1. Peter M. Senge, *The Fifth Discipline* (New York: Doubleday, 1990), p. 69.
2. Peter Drucker, *Managing in a Time of Great Change* (New York: Dutton, 1995), p. 76.
3. Nick Bontis, "Managing Organizational Knowledge by Diagnosing Intellectual Capital," *International Journal of Technology Management*, 118, 5/6/7/8 (1999), pp. 433–462.
4. *Human Resource Financial Report* (Santa Clara, Calif.: Saratoga Institute, 1999).
5. Geary A. Rummler and Alan P. Brache, *Improving Performance: How to Manage the White Space on the Organization Chart* (San Francisco: Jossey-Bass, 1990), p. 141.
6. Michael R. Tyran, *The Vest-Pocket Guide to Business Ratios* (New York: Prentice-Hall, 1992).
7. James Dunnigan and Daniel Masterson, *The Way of the Warrior* (New York: St. Martin's Griffin, 1997).
8. Sun Tzu, *The Art of War*, ed. James Clavell (New York: Dell: 1983), p. 77.
9. Terrence E. Deal and Allan A. Kennedy, *Corporate Cultures* (Reading, Mass.: Addison-Wesley, 1982).
10. Fons Trompenaars, *Riding the Waves of Culture* (Chicago: Irwin, 1994); Charles Hampden-Turner and Fons Trompenaars, *The Seven Cultures of Capitalism* (New York: Doubleday, 1993).

11. Regis McKenna, *The Regis Touch* (Reading, Mass.: Addison-Wesley, 1986).
12. Senge, *The Fifth Discipline*, p. 13.
13. Robert S. Kaplan and David P. Norton, *The Balanced Scorecard* (Cambridge, Mass.: Harvard Business Press, 1996).

2

How to Measure Human Capital's Contribution to Enterprise Goals

"Attaining one's objectives is not a cause for celebration; it is a cause for new thinking."

—*Peter Drucker*

It is axiomatic that all resources should be directed to serving the enterprise's purpose. This purpose can be, should be, and most often is expressed through a combination of economic and human goals. It often starts with a statement of corporate management's vision, values, and mission. Then it moves to the financial goals of seeking an exceptional rate of return on shareholder investments. Finally, there is obeisance to serving the interests of employees and the communities in which the corporation operates. However, this last goal is sometimes more a platitude than a sincere expression of values.

In the mid-1990s, the Saratoga Institute undertook a retroactive study of the five-year financial and human performance of 1,000 companies. The objective was to uncover the human resources programs and employee-related financial practices that separated top performers from all others. Exceptional performance was defined as top quartile financial standing within a company's industry plus top quartile performance on human metrics of staffing, compensation, benefits, turnover, and training in Saratoga's annual *Human*

Resource Financial Report. The data were drawn from this on-going study of employee and financial metrics, which the institute had launched in 1985. Of the original 1,000-plus companies in the pool, 110 qualified on both employee and financial performance. The findings regarding effective practices were surprising. Rather than identifying a series of human resources–based programs that led to top perform-ance, the results showed that the most effective firms shared a common set of eight beliefs, traits, and operating stratagems that were not so common among the other 900.[1] The prime hallmark was an effort to consistently balance financial and human values. That study is detailed later in this chapter.

I believe strongly, based on my personal contact with many of these firms, that their balanced focus and reporting system are driving forces in their financial performance. An-other way of saying this is that the focus on the interaction between human capital and financial outcomes is a leading rather than a coincidental reason for their long-term financial success. This does not mean that management is constantly trying to reduce human capital costs per se. Rather, managers see the leverage potential in people and work to unleash it. They see this effort as an investment, not as a cost. This opens up the left side of the income statement—revenue—the side that has much more room to add value. This is an important insight. In fact, the belief in people as a financial lever is ex-tremely rare.

I struggle for words of sufficient power to cause you to stop and contemplate this. No matter what the public rela-tions department puts out about people being important, on a daily basis in the executive aerie, people are considered to be an expense. This leads to cost cutting through layoffs. How-ever, after several rounds of cost cutting, the expense side quickly reaches a point of diminishing return. But the revenue side always has room to grow, and beyond the sales function, executives don't have the slightest inkling of how to tie human effort directly to financial results.

From the revelations in its research project, the Saratoga Institute launched a program to establish a set of macro human and financial metrics that would go beyond standard accounting ratios. These metrics have been tested, published, and refined through the institute's annual report.

Human Capital ROI Foundation

Over a period of about five years, we field-tested various human-financial ratios that could eventually be used to provide a link between people and financial results. The simplest measure is revenue per employee. This was the first metric that appeared in the first report, the 1985 *Human Resource Effectiveness Report*. At the conclusion of the research into exceptionally effective companies, we began to search for more sophisticated and discriminating metrics.

We tried combining revenue, operating expense, profit, pay, and benefits with employee head count and full-time equivalents. We split pay by level from nonexempt through supervisor/manager and up to the executive level. Each combination yielded a different aspect of the relationship of people, their costs, and the economic results of the enterprise. In the course of the testing, we gathered insights into the forces that drove financial performance. It became clear that there were relationships between and among the many employee and operating variables. We could see that movement in pay programs, turnover rates, staffing strategies, and training investments influenced productivity, customer service, and product quality. Although we could not statistically demonstrate causality, there were obviously some connections that were more than coincidental. From that work over the past five years, we can now suggest structures that bring people and profitability closer together.

Human-Financial Interface

For many years, the general practice of matching human and financial variables at the corporate level has been confined to a single gross measure derived from the income statements of corporations. This metric is revenue per employee. It is simplistic, in that it does not separate the effects of human effort from the leverage of other assets. For instance, we cannot see in revenue per employee the effects of automation, better inventory control, improved quality, training, effective marketing programs, monopolistic conditions, or anything else. All it yields is a general trend. Adherence to this single metric has driven the myth that the impact of human effort cannot be measured at the enterprise level. The fact is that there are a number of metrics that can be applied to the relationship of human capital to corporate financials.

When we look at any metric, we are looking at a result, not a cause. So it is with corporate-level human capital metrics. It is the same as looking at gross sales or operating expense. These metrics are simply the end point of a large number of activities that occurred within the organization, many of which were affected by outside forces. For example, the gross sales metric does not tell us what activities within the sales and marketing function were the primary drivers of the result. It could have been due to a cadre of great salespeople, a brilliant advertising campaign, having the best product, price discounting, or myriad other factors. It also could have occurred despite having a marginal sales force, based on great customer loyalty, a competitive advantage in delivery capability, or a series of competitor mistakes. In order to find causes, we have to break the corporate-level metric down and look at it from various angles over time. This segmented, longitudinal view will eventually tell us what drove the end result, be it good or bad. So, as we view several combinations of revenue, costs, and employees, keep in mind that the causes will be found later in the organization's processes, along with the way in which we acquire and deploy human capital.

A continuous series of events and reactions drives organizations. Many improvement programs, such as reengineering projects, start at a business unit process level with presumed but untested assumptions of some distant, vague value. This is a common, fundamentally flawed approach. Value can be added only if the goals of the enterprise are foremost. Everything starts there. Figure 2-1 outlines the basic interactions

Figure 2-1. Human capital value circle.

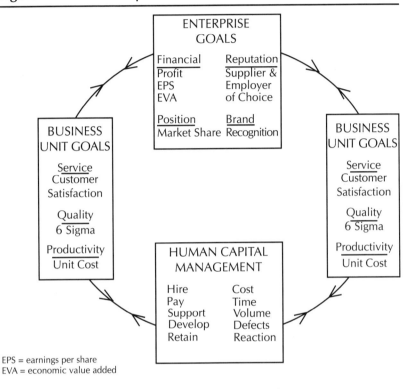

and interdependencies among corporate goals, business unit objectives, and human capital management. From the enterprisewide financial, market, and human goals, the business units derive their service, quality, and productivity objectives. The objectives are achieved or not achieved through the actions of people, the human capital. Hence, the flow is both clockwise and counterclockwise as intermediate and final results drive still more efforts to improve at each level. In essence, everything in an organization oscillates across processes between corporate goals and human capital management. We need tactical-level metrics to measure improvements within the human resources–based functions and to monitor the human capital effects on business unit objectives. We need strategic-level metrics to show the effects of human capital on corporate goals.

Putting the Human Capital in Value Added

When choosing one measure over others for a performance reporting system, keep in mind that what we select is a reflection of what we value. What we select will be the issues on which our people will focus their attention and energies. In addition, if we are going through some type of organizational change (and who isn't?), we can use metrics to focus the direction of the change. If the move is aimed at improving customer responsiveness and service, then we should measure that. Likewise, if it is targeting cost reduction or product quality, we can use those types of metrics to drive the change in that direction. Best of all, when we choose enterprise-level metrics, we are telling everyone that their change and improvement programs must service these metrics.

Hamel and Prahalad claim that change programs often fail due to a lack of proper measures. They state: "Competitor and customer benchmarks may be the most underused motivators in management's administrative tool kit."[2] They describe one multinational that watched its market share decline for years. Employees received messages in various forms urging them to do better and berating them for substandard performance. The missing element was competitive data. They did not know the exact nature and magnitude of the competitive shortfall. Without specific data, there was no focused sense of urgency around improvement. The fault lay on the doorstep of top management, which at first did not have a method for systematically collecting market data. Later, when the data did arrive, they were explained away. The impasse was resolved only after the chairman was dismissed and a new top management team was put in place. As they gathered pertinent data and acted, things began to change for the better. However, the denial and lost time cost thousands of employees their jobs.

Enterprise-Level Metrics: The Launch Point

Macro-level data is the launching site of an ROI assessment system. The most common takeoff point is corporate sales or revenue.

Human Capital Revenue Factor (HCRF)

A first step in looking at the human capital aspect of financials is to revise the traditional revenue per employee metric. Sales per employee is the standard measure used by the federal government and most business media. This equation is not only simplistic; it is out of date. In the days when management first began to look at sales or revenue per employee, the corporate landscape was considerably simpler than it is now. In other than seasonal businesses, most employees were hired to work full-time. But in today's market, organizations employ human talent in several ways. In addition to the traditional full-time employee, many people work part-time. This changes the corporate denominator from employee to full-time equivalent (FTE). As a simple example, if ten people work half-time, the FTE is five people, although the number of "employees" is ten. The number ten represents what is commonly referred to as head count.

> Sales per employee is the standard measure of revenue per employee. This equation is not only simplistic; it is out of date.

To further complicate matters, a growing percentage of the American workforce is what has come to be called "contingent." These are often referred to as "rented" employees. According to government statistics, in 1998, contingent workers represented about 14 percent of the American workforce population. These people are not truly employees, since they are not usually on the payroll. Nevertheless, their labor has to be accounted for in order to have a valid representation of the labor invested to produce a given amount of revenue.

At the end of the day, we have converted revenue per employee into what the Saratoga Institute reports as revenue factor, which is revenue per FTE (including full-time, part-time, and contingent labor hours). FTE is a surrogate for total labor hours invested. It is a basic measure of human productivity, in that it tells us how much time was spent to generate a given amount of revenue. Although this is a better starting point than revenue per employee, it is still too simple. We need more sophisticated metrics to understand the relationship of human capital to financial outcomes.

Human Economic Value Added (HEVA)

Recently, the work of the Stern Stewart organization has popularized the term *economic value added*.[3] EVA, as it is called, is defined as *net operating profit after tax minus the cost of capital*. The objective of this measure is to determine whether the actions of management have added true economic value rather than simply generated the typical financial statements, which can mask actual outcomes. EVA is very useful, in that it shows how much true profit is left not only after paying all expenses, including taxes, but also after subtracting the cost of invested capital. As Stern Stewart has pointed out, this can be a revealing measure of managerial performance.

EVA can be given a human capital perspective by dividing it by the FTE denominator described earlier:

$$\text{HEVA} = \frac{\text{Net operating profit after tax } - \text{ Cost of capital}}{\text{FTEs}}$$

By converting EVA into HEVA, we can see how much EVA can be ascribed to the average amount of labor contracted for. I say *labor*, because the term *employee* is an anachronism in this case.

The following formulas are variations on a set of financial and human capital variables. For the sake of example, I have produced a set of figures for a hypothetical company, SamCo, to illustrate the formulas. Figure 2-2 lays out the vital statistics of SamCo that are needed for this exercise.

Figure 2-2. SamCo financial data.

Revenue	$100,000,000
Expense	80,000,000
Payroll and benefits	24,000,000
Contingents cost	3,750,000
Absence cost	200,000
Turnover cost	3,600,000
Employees (FTEs)	500
Contingents (FTEs)	100

Human Capital Cost Factor (HCCF)

Just as the income statement displays both revenue and expenses, we can show human capital expenses to go along with various revenue and value calculations. The principal costs of human capital are four: pay and benefit costs for employees, pay costs for contingents, the cost of absenteeism, and the cost of turnover.

Each of the four cost variables needs some explanation. Keep in mind that contingent labor normally includes neither benefits expense nor the cost of absence or turnover. In some contracting situations, the agency pays benefits for its contract personnel, and this cost is passed on in the hourly labor rate charged to the contracting company. In the case of absence or turnover, contingent labor that does not report to work is most often replaced promptly by the contracting agency. Although there may be a couple of hours lost until the replacement arrives, overall, the costs are too negligible and variable to track. All measurement programs from business to politics to the social sciences have some error. Macro measures such as ours have a small inherent standard error. Nevertheless, they have been proved over twenty years to be at least as accurate as the other line items in corporate financial statements. When we use the same formula over an extended period, the effects of a minuscule error are fractional.

Pay, as we use it, is simply the number that appears on an employee's W-2 form at the end of the year. It is all current cash compensation. Pay does not include long-term incentives until they are paid out. In the case of options that are exercised, we would include the cost to the company of the stock option.

Benefit costs are the monies paid by the company to provide employee benefits. Portions paid by the employee are not included, since they are not an expense to the company. We use the U.S. Chamber of Commerce list of benefits as the standard.

Absenteeism is an expense to the company, in that the work ascribed to a given job is not getting done by the person paid to do it when he or she is absent. One can argue that someone else does the work when a person is absent. However, that cannot be proved, and the variations in how an organization copes with absenteeism are so great that we must take a consistent stand in order to have a reliable measure. A small cost of absenteeism is factored into our metric by taking out one-half the value generated per hour by all jobs. It works like this:

Revenue per FTE per hour is X (hypothetically $100)
Absenteeism is 2 percent
Subtract 1 percent or $1 per FTE hour

Although the cost is minuscule, we include it to keep the issue of managing absenteeism in view.

Turnover is obviously costly. An argument has raged for many years about the true cost of turnover. Despite several credible studies, some executives like to argue over how to cost turnover. An individual organization can choose to measure turnover costs any way it likes. But to have a reporting system that transcends the idiosyncrasies of the individual, we have developed and tested a standard formula for calculating turnover.[4] It includes the cost of termination, replacement, vacancy, and learning curve productivity loss. These four variables generally cost a company the equivalent of at least six months of a nonexempt person's pay and benefits and a minimum of one year's worth for a professional or manager.

The combination of pay, benefits, contingents, absence, and turnover yields a total cost of human capital for the organization. Obviously there are equipment and facility costs implied with the employment of labor, but these are not truly human capital costs. It is the responsibility of management to control these direct and indirect costs of human capital, just as it controls the cost of other resources. The HCCF is a convenient, tested metric for monitoring the base costs of an organization's human capital over time.

Applying the scenario and figures for SamCo, we find the following human capital cost:

$$\text{HCCF} = \text{Pay} + \text{Benefits} + \text{Contingent labor} + \text{Absence} + \text{Turnover}$$
$$\text{HCCF} = \$24,000,000 + \$3,750,000 + \$200,000 + \$3,600,000$$
$$\text{HCCF} = \$31,550,000$$

It is clear that labor cost is not $24 million, but $31,550,000, or 31.4 percent more than appears on the employee pay and benefits line in the financials. If we extend this a bit further, we calculate that true average FTE cost is not $24 million for 500 FTEs, or $48,000, but $31,550,000 for 600 FTEs, or $52,583 each. Both numbers include overtime, shift pay, and all forms of pay for time not worked. Now we have a more comprehensive and descriptive cost metric.

Human Capital Value Added (HCVA)

The issue of human capital productivity was seen in a simplistic form as revenue per employee. Then we saw a more accurate form in revenue per FTE (HCRF). Next, we introduced cost with HCCF. Now, if we want to move to profitability per FTE, we have the following formula:

$$\text{HCVA} = \frac{\text{Revenue} - (\text{Expenses} - \text{Pay and Benefits})}{\text{FTEs}}$$

In this case, we are looking at the profitability of the average employee. By subtracting all corporate expenses, except for pay and benefits, we obtain an adjusted profit figure. In effect, we have taken out nonhuman expenses. Then, when we divide the adjusted profit figure by FTEs, we produce an average profit per FTE. Note that this can be set up to include or exclude the cost of contingents, absence, and turnover. We'll look at it both ways using SamCo's figures—first, with only pay and benefits:

$$\text{HCVA} = \frac{\$100,000,000 - (\$80,000,000 - \$24,000,000)}{500}$$

$$\text{HCVA} = \frac{\$44,000,000}{500}$$

$$\text{HCVA} = \$88,000$$

If we include the cost of contingents, absence, and turnover, we would have an adjusted profit figure of $51,550,000 ($100,000,000 − [$80,000,000 − $31,550,000] = $100,000,000 − $48,450,000) divided by 600 FTEs, or $85,917 per FTE. The 600 FTEs include employees and contingents.

You can see that with a minimum of effort you can have several views of the effects of people on financials. To contend that there is no valid and consistent way to do this is simply to admit one's ignorance.

> With a minimum of effort, you can have several views of the effects of people on financials. To contend that there is no valid and consistent way to do this is simply to admit one's ignorance.

Human Capital Return on Investment (HCROI)

Another relationship of human capital investments to profitability can be made visible through a ratio that follows from the formula for HCVA. HCROI looks at the ROI in terms of profit for monies spent on employee pay and benefits.

$$\text{HCROI} = \frac{\text{Revenue} - (\text{Expenses} - \text{Pay and Benefits})}{\text{Pay and Benefits}}$$

Again, by subtracting expenses except for pay and benefits, we have an adjusted profit figure. In effect, we have taken out only nonhuman expenses. Then, when we divide the adjusted profit figure by human capital costs (pay and benefits), we find the amount of profit derived for every dollar invested in human capital compensation (not counting training and the like)—in effect, the leverage on pay and benefits. This can be expressed as a ratio.

Applying the SamCo figures, we have the following with no contingent, absence, or turnover costs added in:

$$\text{HCROI} = \frac{\$100,000,000 - (\$80,000,000 - \$24,000,000)}{\$24,000,000}$$

$$\text{HCROI} = \frac{\$44,000,000}{\$24,000,000}$$

$$\text{HCROI} = \$1.83$$

In this case, the HCROI ratio is $1: $1.83. If we want a complete and true return on our direct and indirect human capital expenditures, we have to use the $31,550,000 figure as shown before, rather than $24 million. The HCROI ratio in that case is $1: $1.63. In effect, less of the total expense was for nonhuman costs because we transferred the contingent, absence, and turnover costs to where they belong—cost of human capital. For every dollar spent on human costs with no change in total expense, we got a smaller human capital profit ratio. Now that you see the logic, you can design additional metrics that include training and other employee-related costs to suit your special needs.

With the examples so far, we can see that the cost of human capital can be much more than is normally realized. However, the important point is that no matter what the costs are or in which direction they are moving, it is clear that the relationship of human capital to productivity and profitability has been definitely established.

Human Capital Market Value (HCMV)

"Tobin's Q" is a ratio that measures the relationship between a company's market value and its replacement value. It is a metric that is sometimes cited by the naïve as a measure of human capital value. Economists or stock analysts may find it interesting, but as a management indicator, it is not very useful. In one sense, it is the market's view of the value of intangible assets. This can include not only human capital but also other forms of intellectual capital such as process capability, brand recognition, or marketing acumen. It is an interesting number, but it is subject to wild stock market fluctuations having nothing to do with the capability of the organization's human capital or the utilization of tangible assets. Thus, if it is going to be used at all, it should be tracked over a long period to smooth out external market machinations. For the intellectually curious, one variation on it would be to subtract book value from market value and divide that by FTEs. This gives us a market value premium per FTE. The formula would look like this:

$$\text{HCMV} = \frac{\text{Market value} - \text{Book value}}{\text{FTEs}}$$

An example of the effect of market action on HCMV comes out of the earlier Goldman Sachs case (see Chapter 1). The company offered stock in its IPO at \$15.72 per share. At the opening, the stock jumped, and at the end of the first day, it closed at over \$50. On any given date since then, the share price could be anywhere. Does the fluctuation represent an increase in intellectual capital at Goldman Sachs since the opening? Tobin's Q would argue that it does. I leave it to you. Does Goldman Sachs's intellectual capital fluctuate on a daily basis, or are we really looking at the needs of investors (read gamblers)?

The *H* in Human Capital

We've discussed a set of financial-based human capital metrics. Now we have to balance it with a set of human-based human capital metrics. Most monitoring of employee metrics is basically a body count. How many employees do we have? How many are male and how many are female? What is the racial and ethnic mix? How many affected class personnel are in managerial positions? All that is fine, and it needs to be monitored for equal employment opportunity purposes, if nothing else. However, no one has yet shown that a given mix of people correlates with high performance. Before the diversity gods get me, I want you to know that I wholeheartedly believe that all people, regardless of any demographic label, need to be cherished, supported, and helped to grow. And I believe that a diverse workforce is better than a homogeneous one. My interest here is to look for metrics that will tell us something about the effectiveness of certain human-financial ratios in our operating systems.

Workforce Demographics

It is useful to know things like how many exempt versus nonexempt people you have and what percentage of the work is being done with regular versus contingent personnel or is being outsourced.

Exempt Percent

The exempt percent is the number of exempt FTEs as a percentage of total FTEs. The proportion of your workforce that is exempt versus nonexempt tells you something about the nature of your organization. If your employees are predominantly nonexempt, you are probably in the processing business—building products, processing paper transactions, or running some type of call center. If your employees are predominantly exempt, you are probably more of a nonbank financial service or a technology or marketing business.

There are well-known examples of marketing companies. Nike enjoys a major share of the sneaker market and a significant piece of the sports apparel market. Yet it does not manufacture its products. It is principally a marketing company. In late 1998, Levi Strauss announced that it was closing almost all its manufacturing plants. It planned to have its products made by other people while it shifted its attention to marketing and to opening retail outlets. As that transition progresses, the mix of employees will change to suit the new business model. Fidelity Investments has a mix of exempts and nonexempts. It offers both a variety of financial services, such as mutual fund management, and transaction processing through its benefits and payroll businesses. Predominantly professionals populate the investment advisory functions, whereas the transaction processing services have a higher percentage of nonexempts. Automobile manufacturers are heavily weighted toward production workers, who are mostly nonexempt. If one of them decided to sell its manufacturing facilities and focus on design and marketing, its mix would flip, just as Levi's will.

In conclusion, knowing your mix is useful because you can see it begin to get outside of acceptable levels. This is what happened to many American businesses up through the early 1980s. The proportion of exempt to nonexempt staff in manufacturing firms got out of balance and created a breakeven point that made some companies noncompetitive. This led to the downsizing tsunami. If we had been watching the mix all along, we probably would not have experienced that pain.

Contingent Percentage

The contingent percentage is the number of contingent FTEs as a percentage of total FTEs. The growth of the contingent workforce has reached a point where it bears monitoring. We cannot keep adding contingents to the workforce without some type of plan. If we do not pay attention, one day we may find that contingent workers who have no company loyalty hold many of our core competencies. They can go at a moment's notice and leave us incapable of competing. It would be like the story of the camel who was allowed to put his nose into the tent during a sandstorm. After the nose came the head, and no one resisted. Then came the shoulders, trunk, and finally the hindquarters. At that point, the original inhabitant found himself out in the storm. When we don't pay attention to the key signals of our business, we will sooner or later find ourselves in the middle of a storm.

> One day we may find that contingent workers who have no loyalty to us hold many of our core competencies. They can go at a moment's notice and leave us incapable of competing.

A little side note about contingents: We tend to think that contingents are cheaper than regular employees. This can be true, but it is not axiomatic. Often in technical and professional ranks, contingents cost more on an hourly basis. Some companies that don't keep track may eventually realize that their contingents have been around for more than a year. In those cases, it might have made more economic sense to hire a regular worker. Contingents have a way of blending in and disappearing in large organizations. I know of cases in which both regular employees and contract workers were paid for more than a year after they had left. Some firms, most notably Microsoft, found to their embarrassment that the courts considered their long-term contingents eligible for benefits, just like the regular employees. There is no magic here. It is just called management.

Workforce Movement

Obviously, the workforce is not static. People come and go every day. Some are replacing terminated personnel, and some are taking newly created positions. It's not a bad idea to know how many are doing each, because movement is expensive.

Accession Rate

The accession rate is the number of replacement hires and hires for new positions as a percentage of the workforce.

How many people did your company hire last year? The cost to hire a nonexempt person can run between $900 and $1,100, as reported in Saratoga's annual *Human Resource Financial Report*. The cost of exempts averages $8,000 to $9,000, with the top 25 percent of companies averaging $12,000 to over $20,000. None of these costs include training the new hire or the effects on productivity or customer service.

Separation Rate

The separation rate is the number of voluntary and involuntary separations as a percentage of total head count. Turnover is a costly and disruptive event. Whether you fire someone or the person quits, it causes a break in routine. Surviving employees have to pick up the slack until a replacement is hired or divide the work among themselves if this is a downsizing. The cost of turnover is detailed in Chapter 4. At this point, we'll say only that retention of talent is a serious responsibility. We should use terms like human capital "loss" or "depletion." They more accurately describe what is actually happening. By any term, it is something that top management should be monitoring.

Most of the quits can be prevented. Not everyone who goes was a bad employee, nor do they all leave for higher pay. We all know that this is true, yet we seldom address turnover until it reaches epidemic levels. If the separation rate starts to climb, you had better jump on it and find out why.

Cost Management

Although it is good to know about percentages and movement, it is even better to know about cost. The cost of an average employee's pay, according to the 1999 Saratoga report, was right at $44,000. Add to this another 25 to 30 percent for benefits, and you are approaching the $60,000 level.

Total Labor Cost Revenue Percentage

This figure is all labor costs as a percentage of total revenue. TLC does not stand for tender loving care in this case. It covers the cost of pay and benefits for regular employees plus the cost of all contingent labor, including contract professionals. The best way to look at it is to see how much of each sales dollar is being absorbed by labor cost. In 1999, Saratoga's data showed that the median for 891 companies in 25 industries was 26 percent, with a range of 11 percent to 46 percent by industry.

This metric tells you that you are investing an average of twenty-six cents in compensation to capture a dollar in sales. Downsizing programs were launched to bring the percentage down. For every penny you reduce it, you add that penny to earnings, since expense reductions go directly to the bottom line. But rather than laying people off, you could consider how to leverage them into greater revenue. After all, this is an equation with two sides. When management truly believes that people create profit, it balances cost control with investments in skill building. Deming told us that performance is affected more by managerial barriers than by employee effort. Research has shown for decades that executives who use the balanced approach to people management consistently outperform the reactive, feast-and-famine managers.

Investment Management

This is the other side of the cost management approach. We know from the human capital value added and the human capital ROI formulas earlier that people do make money for companies. It only makes sense, then, to invest in them and to monitor that investment.

Employee Development Investment

This is the cost of all education, training, and development programs as a percentage of payroll. But there is a problem here. No one has figured out what constitutes employee development. Yes, tuition refund programs clearly qualify. Formal training classes inside and public seminars also count. But what about coaching and counseling? What about the conference that was really a three-day vacation in Las Vegas to reward performance? Add to this uncertainty the ambiguous way in which training is accounted for, and you realize that we don't really know what we are spending on training. I've talked to about 200 training directors, and not one is willing to stake his or her career on a cost figure. The American Society for Training and Development has been working on this since the mid-1990s and it does not have a satisfactory, standard, and practical method yet.

Nevertheless, let's not let ignorance stand in our way. There is a workable solution, even though its factual basis is suspect. Set your own standards for what constitutes a developmental expenditure. You can do it any way you like, because there is no generally accepted standard. Then, collect data according to your model and monitor those data every quarter. Pretty soon you will see movement, and you can begin to judge the value of that investment. Ask yourself, did we see productivity, customer service, product quality, or sales increase as the training investment increased?

Motorola made a major commitment to training around 1980. For years, it allegedly spent somewhere between 3 and 5 percent of payroll on training. It set up a model corporate university, which still cranks out a multitude of developmental programs. For this it is to be admired. But in the late 1990s, when business turned sour and Motorola began to lose market share, it decided that it could no longer be cavalier about such a large investment. Now the company is trying to determine how effective its programs are. Faith in people is a wonderful thing, but you have to manage, Bubba.

Faith in people is a wonderful thing, but you have to manage, Bubba.

These are just a few of the things that can be tracked and managed at the enterprise level. Knowing how much is being produced and sold, what it costs, and whether you are getting a decent ROI is essential for corporate management. Ignoring human capital costs, or using only gross pay and benefit costs as your benchmark, is somewhere between simplistic and inexcusable. Of course, we all want and need to manage cost to stay competitive. But the real opportunity is in managing contribution to revenue and profits. We can cut costs only so far. But there is always room for more revenue generation. Human capital management takes us down that side of the path as well.

Human Capital Enterprise Scorecard

In 1996, the work of Kaplan and Norton culminated in their book *The Balanced Scorecard.*[5] It followed a series of articles by the pair that described their experiments with this method of management monitoring and reporting. Since then, the balanced scorecard has become a very popular management tool. Its premise is that standard accounting is too insular and focused exclusively on financial performance. They suggest that issues such as learning and growth, customers, and business process should be added to financial data. From their basic model, variations have appeared across the landscape. It is a refreshing and much needed break from total reliance on standard accounting.

To make some order out of all the indicators we've discussed so far, I suggest that an enterprisewide human capital scorecard be developed. There would be two topical sections to start: financial and human. After some experience, others could be added, such as a learning or growth section or one on costs and ROI in workforce development. Figure 2-3 lists the recommended starters drawn from the metrics detailed earlier.

Norton makes a key point about what differentiates the scorecard from other business performance measurement frameworks in the marketplace:

> The primary differentiator is that the balanced scorecard is based on organizational strategy. Many people will build a list of measures which are nonfinancial and think that they have a balanced scorecard, but in our view the scorecard has to tell the story of your strategy. The biggest mistake organizations make is that they think that the scorecard is

Figure 2-3. Sample corporate human capital scorecard.

Financial	Human
Human Capital Revenue *Revenue divided by FTEs* Human Capital Cost *Cost of pay, benefits, absence,* *turnover, and contingents* Human Capital ROI *Revenue minus (expense minus* *total labor cost), divided by total* *labor cost* Human Capital Value Added *Revenue minus (expense minus* *total labor cost), divided by FTEs* Human Economic Value Added *Net operating profit after tax* *minus cost of capital, divided by* *FTEs* Human Capital Market Value *Market value minus book value,* *divided by FTEs*	Exempt Percentage *Number of exempt FTEs as a per-* *centage of total FTEs* Contingent Percentage *Number of contingent FTEs as a* *percentage of total FTEs* Accession Rate *Replacement hires and hires for* *new positions as a percentage of* *the workforce* Separation (Loss) Rate *Voluntary and involuntary separa-* *tions as a percentage of head* *count* Total Labor Cost Revenue Per- centage *All labor costs as a percentage of* *total revenue* Employee Development Investment *Cost of all training and develop-* *ment as a percentage of payroll*

Notes: FTEs include contingent workers unless noted otherwise.
Total labor cost includes pay and benefits plus contingent worker cost.

just about measures. Quite often they will get some lower level staff group in the organization to develop the measures, but the scorecard has to be owned by the executive team as only they are responsible for the fundamental corporate strategy.[6]

So far, my focus has been on objective data. I did that deliberately. Executives live on numbers, although they sometimes act on feelings. We need the quantitative side as a consistent reference set. Still, there is value in the subjective. Qualitative measures of employee satisfaction, commitment, and corporate culture balance the hard numbers. Whereas you can monitor volume and costs every month, you cannot take the pulse of the workforce that often. Semiannual or annual surveys of employee groups are common. If you need more frequent signs, you can sample the workforce. Cut it by level, function, job group, or geography. This way, you can obtain partial signals every quarter.

You can also compare movement in the qualitative indices against movement in the quantitative metrics. I'm not suggesting that you will find causation. If you see parallel movements, it might be coincidental. But at the very least, you will have something to check out. There just might be some correlations buried in the data that you can test. The more of this you do, the more experience you gain, and your sixth sense will sharpen. Eventually, you will sense things that you didn't see or feel before. You'll look at data and know that something has changed, even though the data do not look that different. This is your reward for diligence. With this heightened sensitivity, you will be able to suggest preemptive strokes that cut off a nuisance before it becomes a problem or to take advantage of an opportunity that others have not seen. People will think that you are wise, and you are.

Enterprisewide Effective Practices

Most alleged best-practice reports detail a particular process or project. The report usually describes how someone responded to a problem and found a solution that worked in that situation. This singular success is often extrapolated to an acclaimed universal solution. In fact, a follow-up inquiry usually finds that the process and the results were embellished somewhat. Furthermore, it is common to find that the process is no longer being used or is being confined to just one location. One consulting company goes so far as to request self-nomination. It invites people to send in their stories of effective practices. These are written up, published, and sold with very little verification against any type of quantitative standard. The object lesson is that one person's single, idiosyncratic success does not make for an organizational best practice applicable to other situations or organizations.

The Willy Loman Syndrome

My experience in nearly twenty years of collecting data worldwide is that the best performers usually don't self-nominate.
They are too busy widening the gap between themselves and
the pack, and they seldom feel the need to blow their own
horns. In Arthur Miller's classic play *Death of a Salesman*, the
main character is talking to his best friend. You need to know
that Willy's sons have not done much since high school to dis-
tinguish themselves, but Willy puffs up their every little ac-
complishment. His friend mentions somewhat offhandedly
that his lawyer son recently presented a case before the U.S.
Supreme Court. Willy is dumbfounded and asks why the man
didn't tell him sooner. His friend's reply is that, when you do
it, you don't have to talk about it.

The good news is that at the Saratoga Institute, we were
able to cut through this sea of stories to discover what appear
to be organizational truisms. In the early 1990s, Saratoga
began a series of annual studies of effective practices among
the 500-plus companies that participated in its annual survey
of financial aspects of staffing, compensation, benefits, training, and turnover. Over a period of four years, the institute
monitored the outcomes of what grew to be over 1,000
companies. In a fifth-year retrospective, we sought to find
something generic about the work of the top performing companies. The culmination of this work was briefly cited at the
beginning of this chapter. At this point, I want to describe
what we found to be the eight practices common to the top
performers and, most important, how to measure the effectiveness of such practices. These practices are discussed in
depth in my book *The 8 Practices of Exceptional Companies*.

Measuring Effective Enterprise Practices

The eight practices and their companion measurements can
be linked through both objective and subjective assessment
techniques. Hard data are available in many cases, and employee testimony taken in formal surveys produces scores that

can be monitored over time. For enterprise-level measurement, we must ask ourselves what the end value of the practice is for the organization rather than for just one function. For example, if one department improves something within its operation, what positive effect will that have on other functions involved in the same process continuum? Ultimately, how will the total outcome add value to the enterprise in terms of creating a competitive advantage that can be converted into financial, market, or human value? A hard test is, Will the market reward the enterprise for this measurable change? When the honest answer is, "Yes, and here's how," you have a winner.

The eight practices and their various assessment methods are outlined in the following sections. They are divided into two groups. The first three are what I call the foundation traits. The next five are the structural traits. The foundation traits are the bedrock on which long-term, exceptional performance is laid. The structural traits can be stylized to suit the times.

Foundation Trait Metrics

Balanced Values

This is a constant, conscious focus on adding value in every activity. The key question at each investment decision point is, What is the value of this? The corollary question is, What is the human *and* financial value in each case? The human capital enterprise scorecard shown in Figure 2-3 is the measurement model for the foundation traits. It gives us several examples of both financial and human metrics that apply at the enterprise level. All the following examples should roll up to and affect enterprise-level metrics.

The measure of how well balanced values are being practiced is, Where does the question of balance come up in discussions of important issues? As an example of monitoring the frequency and importance of a fundamental issue, I cite the practice of Bob Galvan, retired chairman of Motorola. His support of the quality program was such that it was the first item on the agenda at all top management meetings. Financial and operating topics came later. If the balanced value question is always number one in the discussion sequence, you've got a de facto metric that is the guiding hand of the enterprise.

Commitment

Enlightened executives strive to build an institution of enduring success and value through commitment to a long-term core strategy. There is an openness to change as a means of continual renewal. However, the change is in structure and processes, not in strategic commitment to all stakeholders. Measurement depends on putting the commitment into visible behaviors and results. For example, if management dedicates itself to building the best-quality product possible, it is an easy matter to test that against the competition's product characteristics. Is our price-performance ratio better than all others, or has the company begun to produce middling-quality products? If the commitment to the workforce is to position compensation 5 percent above the mean for all positions and to provide benefits that support certain outside personal needs such as family programs, those commitments are verifiable. They are budgeted, so we know the expense. We can look for ROI through ongoing employee surveys and exit interviews. Eventually, these programs should show at least an indirect connection between the commitment to support them and the enterprise-level metrics of turnover and productivity. Fewer quits positively drive greater financial returns.

Culture

The more I study organizational profitability, the more I am convinced of the power of culture. One of the recent reinforcing studies was published as a sidebar in *Fortune*, which reported on the 100 most admired companies in the world. It found that corporate culture was a key factor differentiating the top performers from average companies. According to Bruce Pfau of the Hay Group, who led the study, "the single best predictor of overall excellence was a company's ability to attract, motivate and retain talent. CEOs said that corporate culture was their most important lever in enhancing this key capability."[7]

In a follow-up, in-depth study, the contrast between cultural priorities in the top companies in the *Fortune* survey versus average performers studied by Hay was remarkable:

Top Performer Priorities	Average Performer Priorities
1. Teamwork	1. Minimizing risk
2. Customer focus	2. Respecting the chain of command
3. Fair treatment of employees	3. Supporting the boss
4. Initiative and innovation	4. Making budget

The top performers consciously manage their corporate culture and attempt to link it with systems into a congruent, mutually reinforcing package. This is the same thing we found in our study of 110 top performers reported in *The 8 Practices of Exceptional Companies*, cited earlier.

If a participative culture is desired, systems must be flexible and authority devolved to the lowest level possible. Assessment of the success of that desire can be found through employee surveys focused on organizational climate, resource availability, and system operations.

For measurement purposes, there are many commercial survey instruments on the market. The previous value, commitment, can be assessed in the same survey. The questions can be asked in several ways. It comes down to, How easy is it to work here? Is there consistency? Do most people understand the culture and work within it? Does management follow through on its commitments to employees and customers? In summary, scores on key concepts such as consistency, commitment, support, values, loyalty, and other terms used in vision and culture statements can be generated and reviewed. This set of measures will be unique to each organization. Yet potential for external benchmarking does exist. We have organized groups of companies, within and across borders, into consortia that agree to use a common system. Results can be shared periodically, and everyone learns.

Those three issues—values, commitment, and culture— form the foundation of every organization. Among the top performers, there is an honest attempt to be consistent. When it is successful, employees, customers, and competitors recognize the inherent strength of the enterprise. This recognition is often rewarded in mar-

> Values, commitment, and culture form the foundation of every organization.

ket valuations. We've seen market analysts consistently give the benefit of any doubt to companies such as General Electric under Jack Welch, Motorola under Bob Galvin, and Wal-Mart under Sam Walton.

Structural Trait Metrics

The remaining five traits form the structure that rests on the foundation of values, commitment, and culture. The next three—partnering, collaboration, and innovation and risk— share common assessment methods. They are all open to process measurement. In each case, there are specific projects that can be isolated for analysis and subjected to qualitative and quantitative measures and reporting systems. The final two practices—communication and competitive passion— pervade the total organization at all levels. These provide the vehicle and the energy to support the total enterprise.

Partnering

Top performers are champions of joining with outsiders to enhance performance. They aggressively support partnering and joint venturing. They regularly look outside the enterprise for organizations with which they can leverage resources. Customers, vendors, schools, community agencies, and even competitors are engaged in programs of common interest.

Assessing the ROI of a partnership requires an explicit

statement of the goals of the venture. Every venture is different, so no single standard metric can be applied. Instead, ask these types of questions; the answers will yield quantitative data.

- Was there a new product or service that was to be generated? If so, what was the price-performance profile of the result?
- Was there simply information to be shared? If so, exactly what was wanted, why, and what is the financial, market, or human value of that information?
- Was it an attempt to improve human capital ROI by generating job applicants, reducing health care costs, or leveraging training investment?

As always, the lesson of measurement is: Be explicit. If we make our goal visible in terms of a specific thing or a noticeable behavior, we can always find a way to measure it. At the end of the day, how did it contribute to the enterprise metrics?

Collaboration

Collaboration involves the cooperation and involvement of several sections *within a function*. The top performers research, design, launch, and follow up new programs in a collective manner. The value of this practice is cohesiveness, efficiency, and better solutions built on multiple viewpoints. Measurement of a collaborative effort is nearly identical to that in a partnering case.

- What was the purpose?
- Is there a visible, measurable, desired result?
- Will it help us hire and keep better talent?
- Will it cut costs or improve organizational productivity, quality, or service?
- How will it roll up to a competitive advantage at the enterprise level?
- What data support that assumption?

Measures of improvement start with a purpose question and end with a competitive advantage answer.

Innovation and Risk

Innovation is recognized as a necessity in a highly competitive marketplace. There is a willingness to shake up the organization, shutting down out-of-date methods and structures and restarting in different forms. Innovation's companion is risk. Where there is innovation, you find risk. Risk must be accepted but managed.

The measurement of innovation is relatively easy, because it is a specific project that can be outlined from beginning to end. That level of specificity makes it easy to describe the intended values at the functional and enterprise levels. After the fact, it is usually a simple task to find the ROI at either or both levels. A case example is provided later to show how this works.

Communication

Communication is the most pervasive human activity. Organizational communication is the lifeblood of the enterprise. The absence of information lights the fire under the rumor boiler. It takes people away from the job in a search for the meaning behind their observations. The top performers exhibit an extraordinary commitment to communicating with all stakeholders. Constant, extensive use of all available media, sharing all vital information with employees and other stakeholders, builds extraordinary levels of employee loyalty and productivity.

> Communication is the most pervasive human activity. Organizational communication is the lifeblood of the enterprise.

Assessment of communication programs and processes typically focuses on the media in use rather than the information conveyed. Before deciding to put out a communiqué, management needs to understand its audience's information needs. It is similar to market research, except that in this case, the customers are employees. Start by surveying a random sample of employees to learn what types of information they need and want and from whom they want to get it. With that as a base, a communications system can be built. Its value to the employees can be assessed through a later survey. Ask people to indicate how important each key topic is to them and how well the company did in communicating different types of information. There are a relatively small number of basic topics for employee communication. They include the following, roughly in this order of interest to the average employee:

1. Job performance: How am I doing?
2. Career opportunity: How far, how fast can I go?
3. Personnel programs: What changes are coming in pay and benefits programs?
4. Organizational change: What's happening, what's coming?
5. Organizational financial state: How healthy is the company?
6. Company policies: What's new in general administrative systems?
7. Competitor activity: What and how well is the competition doing?
8. General company and employee news: department news, anniversaries, and so forth.

The follow-up question is, From whom do they want to get each type of information? Satisfaction scores point to problems and opportunities. Low scores suggest that absenteeism and turnover will probably rise and productivity will drop. High scores across the board are indicators of a turned-on workforce, and the degree of "turn on" can be measured in service, quality, and productivity.

Competitive Passion

Leaders constantly search for improvement. They maintain systems and processes to continually seek out and incorporate ideas from all sources. If we want a "passionate" organization, we need passionate people. One way to get them is to incorporate questions relating to energy levels, aspirations, values, and financial and personal needs, among others, in hiring interviews. Once we have them, we can measure passion or zeal for continual improvement. Verifiable indices can be found by asking, How do we know whether we are meeting all important goals and objectives at the operating and enterprise level? Referring to the balanced scorecard mode, how do we stand on our financial, customer, process, and innovation and growth goals?

Enterprise Practices Measurement: Case Example

Let's take an example of a project that is focused on getting a new product to market in order to achieve a competitive advantage and regain market share—an enterprise-level measure. We have, as a starting point, the financial and human values shown earlier in Figure 2-3. Assume that these set us off on this quest. A simplified format of assessment, measurement, and evaluation could go like this:

Q: What corporate-level financial measure told us that we needed a new product?

A: Loss of market share.

Q: How will that harm employees if it isn't fixed?

A: Potential freezing of wages, followed by layoffs if it drops another two points.

Q: Can we continue to meet our long-term commitment to shareholders, customers, and employees to have the top-quality products and be number one in this industry niche if we don't come up with the new product quickly?

A: Probably not, all other things being equal.

Q: Do we have any inherent problems with our culture and systems that will jeopardize getting the new product out within the window of opportunity?

A: We've gotten a little complacent lately. We haven't kept up our employee communication program, and we haven't run an employee survey for two years. I don't know what's on their minds or what's bothering them, but you can feel the lethargy.

Q: Sounds to me like the problem is in this room. We're not managing our human capital. What do we have to do to get people excited again?

A: Take a quick sampling of the employees' "passion" level. Find out how our neglect has affected them. Then, design a program of employee communiqués that talk honestly about the pros and cons of our situation.

Q: Is this product a high-risk move, and do we need to partner with someone outside to manage our risk and accelerate development?

A: We've never worked in composites before. We could completely blow it. We ought to talk to Professor Jones at State University who has published some interesting papers on this technology; bring in new vendors who will have to supply modified materials just-in-time to keep inventory costs down; and involve the outside engineering firm to speed up design of a new high-speed, high-quality production system.

Q: Who inside needs to play a role besides the production team?

A: Market research needs to get fresh customer data very quickly. Human resources will have to plan right away to hire the new skills we'll need to move from metal to composite forming. Accounting has to set up an activity-based costing system once we know our specs so we can monitor costs during test and ramp-up. Legal should check patent registrations in this area. Advertising must be involved early on so they will understand the new product's advantages and can have an ad campaign ready.

Q: What are our production targets and corporate goals?

A: We have to deliver by the third quarter, or we'll miss the window of opportunity.

Q: Where are the data to support that?

A: We know from the market research we commissioned that at least one competitor is coming on market by year-end with a new product of this type. Our product has to have a unit cost of no more than $1,100. And if we can make that, to meet

*expected demand, we have to be shipping in quantity by the start
of the fourth quarter. When we do all this, we should pick up at
least two points in market share next year, which is worth $150
million per point annually.*

Q: Okay, let me review our production-level targets:

Cost: not to exceed $1,100 per unit
Time: launch by July 1
Volume: full production by October 1
Defect rate: 99 percent defect-free products by middle of
    third quarter to meet our commitment to customers as
    the top-quality producer
Customer satisfaction: 95 percent in the third quarter,
    and 100 percent by the fourth quarter

At the corporate level, if we do this, the company gains back
two points in market share, picks up $300 million in revenue
next year at our standard profit margin, and avoids a layoff. It
should also restore some of our reputation with our customers. Right?

A: Right!

The key to assessing enterprise value added is to demand a
projection of expected value *at the beginning.*

Summary

Measurement of the effectiveness of human capital has been
conspicuous by its absence in corporate financial reports.
Only with the advent of the balanced scorecard has there been
any attention paid to this most important of resources. The
single typical measure, revenue per employee, is simplistic
and out of date. Since human capital costs currently can absorb upward of 40 percent of revenue, they certainly warrant
better attention. Couple that fact with management's belated
realization that people can be viewed as an investment rather
than as a cost, and it is absolutely imperative that more so-

phisticated metrics be devised to monitor human performance at the enterprise level.

This chapter has demonstrated with formulas and examples that human capital can be linked to economic value added, corporate productivity, cost structure, and profitability. Metrics have been placed into a scheme that includes quantitative and qualitative indicators of performance at the enterprise level. A human capital enterprise scorecard template shows how to view a set of financial and human metrics. Collectively, it displays for top executives a target against which functional unit performance can be judged. This performance measurement and reporting system has life breathed into it through eight enterprise-level practices that are common to top performing companies: balanced values, long-term commitment, culture and system linkage, partnering, collaboration, innovation and risk management, communications, and competitive passion.

In the end, it should be evident, even to skeptics, that human capital's effect on corporate performance can be traced, analyzed, and evaluated. This base, along with the metrics for business units and human capital management (covered in the next two chapters), gives executives a method for managing their human capital in objective terms rather than relying on clichés, hunches, and unverifiable opinions.

References

1. Jac Fitz-enz, *The 8 Practices of Exceptional Companies* (New York: AMACOM, 1997).
2. Gary Hamel and C. K. Prahalad, *Competing for the Future* (Cambridge, Mass.: Harvard Business School Press, 1994), pp. 141–42.
3. G. Bennett Stern III, *The Quest for Value* (New York: Harperbusiness, 1991).
4. *Human Resource Financial Report* (Santa Clara, Calif.: Saratoga Institute, 1985–1999).
5. Robert S. Kaplan and David P. Norton, *The Balanced*

Scorecard (Cambridge, Mass.: Harvard Business Press, 1996).
6. David Norton, "Keeping the Score," *Fast Track* (spring 1998), pp. 14–15.
7. "1998 Survey: The World's Most Admired Companies," *Fortune,* October 26, 1998.

3

How to Measure Human Capital's Impact on Processes

"To say that what can't be easily measured really doesn't exist is suicide."

—Robert McNamara

Everything that happens in an organization is the result of a process. A process is a series of steps designed to produce an effect. All processes share a common pattern. They consume resources, and they generate a product or a service. This is as true for a social service program as it is for lead mining. The reason we want to study business processes is that an organization is only as effective as its processes. It is referred to as the ability to execute.

American business devoted a great deal of effort during the last two decades of the twentieth century toward improving process efficiency. To its credit, significant gains have been achieved in some areas. Productivity of manufacturing processes has increased to the point where we have been able to recapture market share and improve margins in international markets. Unfortunately, the same is not true in the staff side of the house. Since the 1920s, administrative costs as a percentage of sales have increased from 8 to 20 percent. *Fortune* described this in pithy terms: "on the staff side of the house— which processes information—they have gotten worse, unable even to achieve economies of scale, let alone truly take out costs."[1]

Keen makes a compelling argument for processes as assets of the enterprise.[2] He points out that traditionally, accounting has treated business processes as expenses. This ignores the fact that a process is more accurately an asset if it generates value. If we talk to managers about their most important resources, they seldom list balance-sheet assets. Instead, they mention items such as people, technology and the information it generates, corporate culture, brand recognition, management capability, and distribution systems, all intangible, off-balance-sheet assets. The key issue within Keen's hypothesis is to differentiate processes on the basis of their ability to generate a return on invested capital. Processes that return more money than they cost are assets, and those that cost more than they return are liabilities. Reengineering an administrative process that is inherently a liability does not magically transform it into a valuable asset. At best, reengineering can only reduce the expense of running the process.

Others agree with Keen that a process should add value and not merely move something around. To the extent that processes are liabilities, they ought to be outsourced. Those processes that have the potential to add value should always show a direct link from the process outcome to an organizational goal. Rummler and Brache state it unequivocally:

> Each customer process and each administrative process exists to make a contribution to one or more Organization Goals. Therefore, each process should be measured against Process Goals that reflect the contribution that the process is expected to make to one or more Organization Goals.[3]

Every discussion I have had over the past decade with practitioners of process management started with the same belief statements. Typical examples are:

> "A process must always be linked to strategic, external, customer satisfaction, or retention goals."

"A process must be part of something bigger [the enterprise's objectives]."
"A process should support achievement of the business's
   objectives."

Process values are not static. They change over time as
the corresponding competitive issue becomes more or less important. However, if we decide that a given process does not
affect our competitive position, then it is probably a liability,
by definition. Yet tomorrow, something in the marketplace
could change it into a potential asset to be improved. For example, if prompt delivery is not a competitive advantage, then
there is no value to be gained from reengineering the order
entry–to–shipment process. This would be the case in a mo-
nopoly. If we have such a strong market position that there is
no competition, then speed is not an issue. When we had one
telephone company, if AT&T could not deliver service or a new
phone quickly, we had no choice but to wait. Now, there are
many manufacturers as well as long-distance and cell phone
companies, so everyone has to be competitive on speed as well
as on quality and service. Process value is the foundation of
the discussion in this chapter. Our concentration is on the effect of human capital on the value added of processes.

Positioning Business Unit Processes

Processes are the link between human capital management
and the enterprise's strategic goals. Human capital, often
called people, is an asset. Through
processes, which are activities,
assets are put to work. The investment of human and other forms of
capital in the process propels it on
a course of contributing, or not, to
the imperatives of the enterprise. If
the imperative is to reduce operating expense, processes can be
streamlined, automated, elimi-

> Processes are the link
> between human capital
> management and the
> enterprise's strategic
> goals. Human capital,
> often called people, is an
> asset. Through processes,
> assets are put to work.

nated, or outsourced in support of the imperative. The decision and cost-reducing action give us a way to measure one of the three basic objectives of an organization: productivity. If customer satisfaction or that current cutesy phrase— *delight*—is the goal, customer-oriented processes can be improved and measured in terms of another objective: service. Lastly, if it is imperative that we reduce the number of errors or defects in product manufacturing or administrative processes, they can be overhauled in pursuit of the third objective: quality. In every case, my agenda in this book is to look at how the role or deployment of human capital in the process affects outcomes in a measurable way. The outcomes will be defined within productivity, service, or quality terms.

As Keen pointed out, a process is either an asset, because it leverages the assets within it, or a liability, because it costs more than the value it produces. To gain leverage and ensure that our in-house processes are truly assets, we have to engage both types of capital investments: human and structural. The first investment can be improved by doing a better job of acquiring, maintaining, developing, and retaining the human capital. Simply put, we need to generate better strategies and tactics around hiring, compensating, training, and caring for our human talent. The second investment can be improved by shaping, organizing, and positioning the various elements within our structural capital base. This means more effective acquisition and deployment of materials, equipment and technology, information, and systems.

One of the more pleasing discoveries one makes when improving a process is that it yields gains in more than one objective. When we improve quality, we naturally reduce production or service costs as a by-product and usually make customers happier in the end. Naturally, this leads to customer retention. Happier customers also buy more and refer other potential customers. This improves a company's market reputation. In turn, that saves the marketing expense required to obtain new customers, which in turn improves profit margins, and so on. If we were to add up the dollar value of each of those outcomes, we could test it against the cost of running and improving the process. This tells us whether a process is a value-generating asset or a liability with little verifiable, tangible value. Figure 3-1 is a sample of three such cases. After we have the dollar values on the right side, we can compare them to the cost of running the process. We might find that it is more cost-effective to outsource the process.

Another example of the multiple-value phenomenon comes from Allstate's work on nonfinancial measures, as described by Epstein and Birchard.[4] In an effort to improve its insurance claim processes, Allstate found that shorter contact time leads to higher customer satisfaction, higher customer satisfaction leads to higher renewal rates, higher renewal rates lead to higher premium revenues, and higher premiums lead to higher operating income and share prices. In a parallel chain, shorter contact time leads to lower legal fees, lower claims payments, lower loss ratios, and higher operating income and share prices. The basic idea is to always trace possible linkages between the process improvement and the enterprise goals. If there is a driving connection, then there is potential, measurable value added. The only question left is, How do we find the human capital effect?

Human Capital in Processes

Human, material, equipment, facilities, and energy capital are invested in a process. At the end, we want to know with some degree of certainty how much the human asset affected the outcome. At one level, this is obvious, since all other forms of capital are passive. It is only the action of the employee that causes an outcome. Practically speaking, what we are trying to ascertain is how much more value the employee leveraged from other capital investments such as computerization. A basic question is, If we invested in the automation of a process, how well did the worker leverage that investment? An economist might make the argument that the marginal improvements of automation have nothing to do with how the human leveraged that piece of equipment. However, if we get down off the economics horse for a moment and put our hands on the process, it becomes clear that the person contrib-

Figure 3-1. Process value analysis.

Process →	Change →	Impact →	Values
Time to respond to calls for customer service and to repair product was too long	Shortened response time and time to repair through new phone system and training for service technicians	Customer complaints dropped, and survey showed customer retention increasing	Reduced marketing expense to gain new customers: average cost to obtain a new customer = $XXX saved Satisfied customer continues to spend: average sales per customer = $XXX Customer referrals: each customer typically refers X new customers, who spend an average of $XXX Uncalculated: improvement in market reputation, leading indirectly to new customers
Time to fill key professional and technical positions was increasing	Shortened time to fill positions through new recruiting program without denigrating quality of new hires	Key jobs filled an average of 14 days faster; new product release and production schedules met; customer service phones covered	Each day a job is filled, the estimated average value (revenue−pay) = $XXX Better customer service values
Accounts receivable invoice errors were intolerably high	Computer invoice screen redesigned and accountants trained	98% of invoices mailed within 48 hours of receipt and error rate decreased to 1%; less rework	Receivables aging dropped 10 days; cash flow increase = $XXX; less rework saves $XXX; fewer calls from customers' accountants enhances reputation, perhaps attracting applicants for accounting positions and reducing cost per hire

uted the knowledge and skill to fulfill the promise of the machine's specifications. Some people like to ignore that and claim that the human element was not critical. But when the promise of the structural capital investment is not fulfilled, they quickly turn to the operator as the source of the problem. So, one more time, the machine is potential. The person is the catalyst.

Assume for the sake of example that if the work output doubles, we will believe that the combination of automation and human capital created it. Can we prove what percentage of the change resulted from human effort? Pragmatically speaking, we cannot separate the person from the machine in a business setting. It would be like trying to separate the computer from the software in terms of relative value. Proof is the stuff of the laboratory. Degree or amount of improvement from invested capital is the concern of the business executive.

Can a person add value beyond the capability of the machine or the work process? Of course! There are thousands of stories of how the human element turned around a deficient situation without the addition of new equipment. Nobel laureate Richard Feynman, who worked as a physicist at Los Alamos on the Manhattan Project that built the A-bomb, recounts one of the best ones.[5] The short version of his story goes like this:

> I was asked to stop working on the stuff I was doing and take over the IBM group. Although they had done only three problems in nine months, I had a very good group. The real trouble was that no one had ever told these fellows anything. The army had selected them from all over the country for a thing called Special Engineer Detachment. They sent them up to Los Alamos. They put them in barracks. And they would tell them *nothing*.
> Then they came to work, and what they had to do was work on IBM machines—punching holes, numbers that they didn't understand. The thing was going very slowly. I said that the first thing there has

to be is that these technical guys know what we're doing. Oppenheimer went and talked to the security and got special permission so I could give a nice lecture about what we were doing, and they were all excited. "We're fighting a war! We see what it is!" They knew now what the numbers meant [they were pressure and energy readings]. They knew what they were doing.

Complete transformation! They began to invent ways of doing it better. They improved the scheme. They didn't need supervising in the night; they didn't need anything. They understood everything: they invented several of the programs that we used. [They physically rearranged the machines and got better output from them through a new process flow.]

So my boys really came through, and all that had to be done was to tell them what it was. As a result, although it took them nine months to do three problems before, we did nine problems in three months, which is nearly ten times as fast.

That is an illustration of the central point of the process question. Human value is found through the leverage it applies to structural capital. What we measure is the marginal improvement that occurs when a person picks up a tool and makes something happen. It can be rightfully claimed that in the truest sense, all leverage is a function of human effort. A machine is not a machine in the hands of everyone. For some, it is an incomprehensible combination of metal, plastic, wood, or rubber. To others, it is a tool in the true sense of the word—a productivity lever. People make the difference through how effectively they employ other forms of capital. In effect, the result is the value added of human capital.

> What we measure is the marginal improvement that occurs when a person picks up a tool and makes something happen.

Anatomy of a Process

Figure 3-2 shows the position of the person, the human capital, within a process. Everything starts with the desired outcome of the process, which is allegedly linked to the goals of the enterprise. But here we run into the first of several problems with process management, or, I should say, mismanagement. Quite often, particularly in the administrative processes found in marketing, advertising, accounting, information services, human resources, and other support groups, process management is nearly nonexistent. I intend to show that there is value in managing those processes and that we can see the value added by human capital.

Thirty years ago, Mager and Pipe led the whole human performance management analysis process by asking the fundamental question, "If their life depended on it, could they do it?"[6] This put people squarely in the middle of the value-adding game.

These questions set up the requirements of the process:

- Is there a clear, specific, quantitative outcome?
- Do the people involved know what it is?
- Are the expectations easily attainable, or are they a stretch?
- Do the people understand the importance of the outcome?
- Are the people committed to its attainment?

These questions may sound naïve, but more often than not, I've encountered vague, incomplete, or no answers. The following discussion draws on my studies with Rummler and Brache on process improvement.

The first external element impinging on the process is the interferers. These are forces or factors that get in people's way as they try to perform the tasks within the process. They are:

- Inputs from the preceding unit or person that don't arrive on time or are unworkable

Figure 3-2. Anatomy of a process.

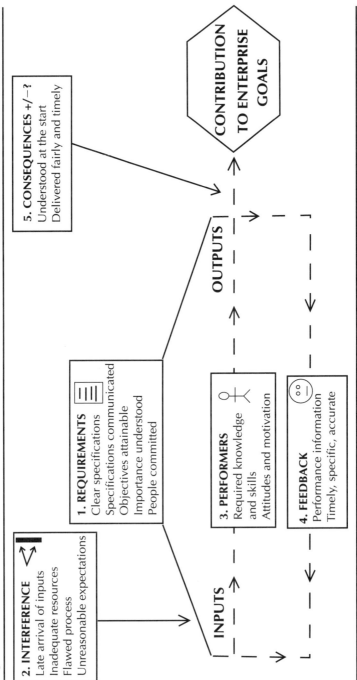

- Resources that are inadequate to perform the tasks
- A flawed process, making performance difficult
- Unreasonable expectations of output speed

The central element, the person, is next. This is the one element that makes all the difference. It can make up for weak points elsewhere or break the process. Key questions are:

- Do the people have the knowledge and skill to perform up to expectations?
- Are they psychologically capable—emotionally and motivationally?

The other inside element in the process is feedback. The questions are:

- Do the people receive information of their own making or from others as to how effectively they are performing during or at the end of the process?
- Is the information relevant, accurate, timely, understandable, and specific enough to prompt an appropriate response?

After the fact, there are consequences surrounding the results. These include, basically, rewards or punishments. The relevant points are:

- Do the people understand the consequences?
- Are the rewards or punishments delivered in a fair and timely manner?

What stands out in this schema? It is the performer! Most of the factors in the five boxes of Figure 3-2 deal with the personality, skills, and behavior of the people carrying out the work. Take these factors out, and what we have left is a static shell of a procedure. Now, let's take a look at how we locate and measure the effects of human capital in a business unit process.

Process Performance Matrix

Every function should have an ongoing set of operational metrics. Production, sales, and service units normally do. But when we move to staff groups, we often find a lack of metrics that tell us how efficient or effective the unit is. There is a solution to this deficiency. Just as there is an accounting system to tell us what is happening on the P&L, there is a basic methodology for process management. It is called the performance matrix.

> Just as there is an accounting system to tell us what is happening on the P&L, there is a basic methodology for process management: the performance matrix.

Figure 3-3 illustrates the performance matrix. You'll see it again in Chapter 4. It is the fundamental template to lay over any function or process. Down the left-hand column, you see cost, time, quantity, errors, and reaction. These are the five ways to evaluate things in organizations and in life.

1. How much does it cost?
2. How long does it take?
3. How much was accomplished?
4. How many errors or defects occurred in the process?
5. How did someone react to it?

This is as applicable to shopping for groceries, taking your child to the movies, having your car serviced, or working in an organization. It even applies to making love. You figure it out. Granted, each of the five measures is not equally important in a given situation. In some cases, you may use only one or two of the measures. Nevertheless, these are the five possibilities.

The matrix gives us the three basic criteria for judging intermediate value added: service, quality, and productivity. These are the three essential elements of business. Researchers call them dependent variables. We call them change objectives. They are the steps along the way to competitive advantage and, eventually, profitability—one of the enter-

Figure 3-3. Performance matrix.

	SERVICE	QUALITY	PRODUCTIVITY
COST		Warranty Cost	Unit Cost
TIME	Mean Time to Respond Mean Time to Repair	Delivery Time	Time to Market
QUANTITY	Number Served		Number of Orders Filled
ERRORS		Scrap Rate; Programming Bugs	
REACTION	Customer Satisfaction		

prise's goals. Although we treat them individually, they are interdependent. It is hard to imagine good service based on overly expensive products of low quality. Likewise, improvements in quality reduce the unit cost of the product or service because it doesn't have to be recycled. Everything that everyone does at all times can be dropped into one of these three columns.

Service, Quality, Productivity

Service

Taking care to satisfy the needs of people is service. Usually we think of customers as the prime target of service. Although that is true, we also have to serve employees, people in the community, government agents, strategic partners, and, of course, stockholders. In effect, all relations with other human beings are measurable in service satisfaction terms. In Figure 3-3, satisfaction is found in the reaction cell, at the bottom of the service column. Other ways to measure service include the cost of the service event, the time to deliver it, the amount delivered, and the rate of errors made in its delivery. When a customer service person takes a call at a service center or makes a call at the customer's site, each of those measures can be applied. Despite the fact that the customer defines the level of satisfaction, and even though each customer is different, we can measure service on the five dimensions in the matrix.

Quality

The customer also defines quality. But again, there are concrete measures of both product and service quality. The customer usually judges quality in terms of a combination of factors. The cost of the product and its utility and durability are the criteria that underlie a subjective judgment of quality. The quality movement of the 1980s focused on cycle time to produce the product and the error or defect rate. Motorola became famous in the quality field for its 6 Sigma program. This was a measure of defect rate that was six standard deviations above the mean. In concrete terms, it meant that there were no more than three errors per million items processed. This applied to manufacturing, shipping, and any other high-volume operation. The company believed not only that it had to aspire to this level to compete in international markets but also that customers were raising their level of expected quality to this range.

Productivity

The most concrete of all measures is productivity. The most common metric is unit cost. Manufacturers strive to reduce the average cost of producing each product in their lines. Whether it is paper cups or locomotives, the basic measure has always been unit cost. As international competition increased in the 1960s, American business started to worry about production costs and delivery times. The volume-oriented phrases "do more with less" and "lean and mean" became mottoes behind the great downsizing of the 1980s. Error rate reduction was a way to reduce unit costs and meet delivery schedules. Finally, reaction to the product became a key way of looking at production success. But behind that was the reaction of the people doing the work. Stress levels increased and employee complaints became more prevalent with the speed-up of manufacturing processes. There was a famous case in the 1980s of an automobile assembly-line rebellion. The assembly-line workers revolted against the continual increase in line speed demanded by management. This attracted other management's attention, and the drive for productivity improvement took on a more humanistic tone.

■ ■ ■ ■ ■ ■

I've filled in some of the cells in Figure 3-3 with a few of the typical process and outcome metrics. The degree or amount of change in the sample outcomes that could result from any improvement effort is measured by some combination of the cost, time, quantity, error, and human reaction indicators. In all, there are fifteen possibilities to find positive change. The caution is to remember that a positive change does not necessarily mean that it contributed to corporate goals. This has to be recognized at the beginning of the process. The question is, If we improve this process, what difference will it make to the customer and therefore to enterprise value? Assuming that we have figured this out ahead of time and we are right, at the end of the day, we should be able to give specific examples of the improved metric and how that contributed value—as well as find the human capital contribution.

Cortada and Woods provide a guideline for deciding what to put into a business unit's performance measurement system: "The preference in the development of measures should be for those that aid improved understanding of customer preferences, employee motivations, or investor expectations, rather than those that offer only precision, convenience, or low cost."[7]

Finding Human Capital Effects

We've looked at processes per se, where they fit in the enterprise–to–human capital continuum, and the issues that need be addressed regarding people's ability to perform within the process. Now we come to the point that stymies most people: It is how to find the effects of a human intervention in a process. Specifically, we want to tease out the human contribution within the general effects. This can be accomplished with a four-step analytic process called process value analysis. The steps are situation analysis, intervention, impact, and value. The critical step is the first one. If we thoroughly understand the situation in which we intend to intervene, it is not that difficult to find the value added at the end. Most failures emanate from this point. If we aren't diligent in laying out the situation, we have little chance of answering specific value-added questions at the end.

Step One: Situation Analysis

1. *What is the business problem: service, quality, or productivity (SQP)?* There seems to be a natural tendency in business to throw a solution at a problem, which is often no more than a symptom. Consultants, trainers, and even managers all have their pet panaceas. They are solutions in search of a problem. The proper first question is not What shall we do? It is What is the business problem? I say "business problem" because I want to improve service, quality, or productivity. If someone is upset because of the way employees are acting, I suggest they gulp down some Maalox or Prozac and chill out. So tell me, how does what is bothering you affect SQP? Which of the three basic business goals is suffering? Often it is more than one. But whatever it is, you have to locate it before you can try to fix it.

> The proper first question is not What shall we do? It is What is the business problem?

2. *What is the current performance level in terms of SQP indices?* Once you have defined the arena, give me the evidence in hard and soft data. Are there cost, time, quantity, error, or human reaction problems? It is helpful to have as much historic data as possible so that you can see how long this deterioration of performance has been going on and how far it has slipped. At the very least, you need it described in one or more of the five indices.

3. *How is the current performance affecting competitive advantage?* Again, if you just believe that you ought to be doing better, don't bother me. Come back when you can see how your company is being disadvantaged in the marketplace. For example, if this problem continues, will it eventually affect your ability to compete? Will the competition be able to offer a better-quality product at a cheaper price? Will they be able to deliver faster than you can? Will they be servicing customers better? Why aren't you able to match the competition's SQP? If it is something like this, you have my attention. An-

swers to these types of question take us to an element we can fix one way or another.

4. *What are the critical work processes in this situation?* First, is it a manufacturing, service, or administrative process? Are you making a product, providing a service to a customer, or both? Who and what are involved: first-level employees, technicians and professionals, supervisors, materials, equipment? What about the process itself; can you outline its steps for me?

From these four questions we should be able to understand all the important elements that define a situation. As we proceed, we will look for causes. When we have intervened and monitored ensuing changes, we will have a good idea of the source of and reason for change. This will tell us how and where an investment in human capital will contribute to the process improvement. It is this degree of preparation that unlocks the mystery of human value. Perhaps for the first time we will really understand the process and its effect on enterprise goals.

Step Two: Intervention

1. *What is the source of the problem?* You have made a list of all the elements in the process. As we review these and begin to discuss how they interact, it will become clear what is causing the breakdown or holding you back from making improvements. The source of the problem will be found within or among the following elements: people, equipment, material, the process, or if it is a manufacturing situation, sometimes the product itself, which is designed in such a way that it is difficult to produce in quantity and quality consistently.

2. *What is the best solution?* At this point, it always becomes obvious what at least one of the interventions should be. With practice, people learn to ferret out all the possible problem sources and assign priorities to their solution. Sometimes we don't know whether an issue is really part of the problem or just a possibility. In those cases, we have to send

someone with technical skills into that area to study the process in action. This could be anyone from a materials engineer to a psychologist. Before acting, we might want to go outside the organization and benchmark the process elsewhere. We might decide that training, counseling, reengineering, or providing incentives is part of the solution.

3. *Agree on a solution, plan the action, and do it.* It is hard to believe that people will go through a lengthy analysis and never act, but every consultant has faced this problem. Clients sometimes get cold feet when they discover the source of the problem and the people involved. This is when they claim that discretion is the better part of valor and slip quietly back into the shadows. As Scott Adams reported in *Dilbert,* "I was part of a 'Quality' initiative where the only tangible change was to our notepads."[8]

Step Three: Impact

1. *Did performance change? If yes, was the change in a positive or a negative direction?* We have defined the problem, found the cause, and acted. After an appropriate time lapse to let the solution take effect, we want to know what happened. If nothing changed, the reason is usually so obvious that no analysis is necessary. Frankly, I have seldom gone through the intervention stage and seen no change whatsoever. When that does happen, it is because someone did not do what he or she was supposed to do. Assuming there was change, what was it?

2. *What and how much change occurred?* Here we go back to the basic indicators: cost, time, quantity, error, and human reaction. Perhaps you see now how this framework makes value analysis rather easy. The key again is thorough analysis in step one. From that, we know the situation so well that any later deviation is easy to spot, along with its cause, direction, and amount. At the end of the day, we can see whether we are saving money or time, increasing throughput with the same or less input, reducing errors, and making someone happier.

3. *What caused the change? Was it the action we took or*

extraneous factors? This is the moment of truth. This is where we answer the question that many people believe cannot be answered. I'm sure that at this point you see that it is not a sleight-of-hand trick. We have analyzed and observed this process for some time. We know it inside and out. We've monitored its rhythms. We've watched it operate within the larger organization and seen inputs from other areas. We've witnessed unforeseen forces impacting it and watched it either absorb and rebound from the blow or be laid low by it. We know this baby. Now we are able to say with a good degree of certainty that the change amounted to *this much* in *these areas* (percentages or dollars). It was driven principally by *these actions* (training, reengineering, automation, counseling, and the like) and was or was not affected by *extraneous forces*.

Step Four: Value

1. *What are the* internal *effects on service, quality, or productivity levels?* Using the five change indicators, we can show how, where, when, and how much service, quality, and productivity changed in the business unit in question. We may also be able to trace changes and improvements outside the unit to other stakeholders of the process. Did we cause any problems on the input side? Did we deliver an improvement that helped on the output side? In all cases, we can quantify much of the change. Some effects will be perceptual, in that employees may report reduced levels of stress or fatigue or attitude improvements as a result of the change. In these cases, we don't need to put a dollar value on the scale responses to a survey. Keep in mind that we are not doing a doctoral dissertation. We are just trying to figure out where the improvement is coming from and whether it was worth the investment.

2. *What are the* external *effects on competitive advantage?* If we were correct at the start (see step one, question three), we knew where we were being hurt in the marketplace. We knew that if we didn't fix the problem or exploit an opportunity, eventually we would probably see lower sales and mar-

gins, declining customer relations, or other negative effects. Now, we can turn around and add the changes back in as gains in competitive advantage. As we said at the beginning, if the problem that started this action was affecting the organization's key goals, it qualified as an area of concentration. If we were right then, we can see the value gained for the enterprise now. And we will have convincing qualitative and quantitative data regarding the ROI in human and structural capital.

Figure 3-4 is a form that can be used to do the process value analysis.

A Case in Point

We had a client in the agricultural products business on the West Coast. It grew and sold seeds, plants, and cut flowers. The business was expanding rapidly, so the company was hiring salespeople without having much time to train them. At one point, it found that sales growth was stagnating. When management talked to the sales force, it was told that the problem was partly due to the number of new salespeople and partly due to the sales force's not having current information on inventory and shipments in progress. The story went like this:

We make a call on a customer who supplies flowers for the football games in this area. These are the big mums that they tie to sticks with ribbons of the school's colors and sell at the stadium. The customer says, "My regular supplier had a flooded field and can't supply the mums. I need 10,000 mums by Wednesday because it takes a couple days to make them up. Can you supply them, and what will they cost?"

We look at our inventory book to see what we have in stock. The only problem is that it is out of date within a couple days after it is printed because we are all selling against it. So we tell the customer that we will have to call in to find out what we have in stock or on the way. By the time we get an inventory control clerk on the

Figure 3-4. Process value analysis.

Situation Analysis

1. What is the business problem: service, quality, or productivity (SQP)?

   _____

2. What is the current performance level: SQP indices?

   _____   _____

   _____   _____

3. How is current performance affecting competitive advantage?

   _____

   _____

4. What are the critical work processes in this situation?

   _____

   _____

Intervention

1. What is the source of the problem?
   _____Equipment   _____Material   _____People   _____Process
   Describe: _____

   _____

2. If people or process, what is the best solution?
   __Benchmark __Reengineer __Provide incentives __Counsel __Train
   Describe: _____

   _____

3. Agree on a solution, plan, and act.
   Describe: _____

   _____

Impact

1. Did performance change?   _____Positively   _____Negatively

2. How much change occurred?
   Cost: _____
   Time: _____
   Quantity: _____
   Error: _____
   Human reaction: _____

3. What caused the change?
   Your action: _____
   Extraneous factors: _____

Value

1. What are the *internal* effects on service, quality, or productivity?
   _____
   _____
   _____

2. What are the *external* effects on competitive advantage?
   Sales: _____
   Margins: _____
   Customers: _____
   Time to market: _____
   Other: _____
   _____
   _____

phone, it might be hours or the next day. Finally, we get back and tell the customer, for example, "We have 6,000 in stock and another 15,000 that will arrive on Thursday morning. I can have 6,000 in your hands on Wednesday and the remaining 4,000 by noon on Thursday. How's that?"

The customer says, "Thanks, but I had a call from another supplier this morning and I gave him the order because I couldn't take the chance that you couldn't deliver in time. Sorry."

The sales manager felt that a little training probably would have helped in this situation, in that the salesperson should have asked the client for a commitment to wait an hour or so for an answer regarding availability. Based on these two issues—skills and information—the sales manager decided to do two things. First, all the sales force, new and old, was put into refresher sales training. Second, all the salespeople were given laptops with modems. Inventory data were loaded on the laptops. When the salespeople hit customers' sites, if there was a question about inventory, they could instantly hook into a phone and dial up the warehouse to find out the up-to-the-minute availability of stock. The result was an increase in sales within the first month and a continuing positive trend for the rest of the quarter. At that point, the sales manager and the training manager went to the CEO to describe their actions and report the outcome. When the CEO heard how well the double-barreled approach was going, he *did not* ask, "What percentage of the increase came from fresh inventory data versus improved sales skills?" Instead, he shook their hands and said, "Do some more."

The point is simply that senior managers don't really need or want sophisticated "proof." In fact, most of them are suspicious of statistical methods. They are experienced people who are neither gullible nor stupid. They tell me that if the evidence is not compelling on its face, no amount of statistical maneuvering will make it believable.

A Test Problem

Figure 3-5 is a list of basic process and function metrics for eight functions. If you look closely, you will see metrics for cost, time, quantity, error rates, and human reactions (customer satisfaction). Here is the problem:

1. Take one of the time measures, such as mean time to respond and repair, percentage of filings on time, average time to process a requisition, or work order completion time. Although these come from different functions, they have one thing in common: They are processes that involve employees, equipment, supplies, a procedure, and supervisory management.

2. What are the consequences of these processes falling out of a tolerable range of performance?

Process Deficiency	Possible Consequence
Mean time to respond and repair	Dissatisfied, potentially lost, customers
Percentage of filings on time	Penalties levied by government
Average time to process a requisition	Production slowdown and late delivery
Work order completion time	Inconvenience to employees

Figure 3-5. Process and function metrics.

MARKETING	CUSTOMER SERVICE
Marketing costs as percentage of sales	Service costs as percentage of sales
Advertising costs as percentage of sales	Mean time to respond and repair
Distribution costs as percentage of sales	Service unit cost
Sales administration costs as percentage of sales	Customer satisfaction level

INFORMATION SERVICES (IS)	FINANCIAL
IS costs as percentage of sales	Accounting costs as percentage of sales
Percentage of jobs completed on time and within budget	Aging of receivables
Overtime costs	Accuracy of cost accounting
Backlog hours	Percentage of filings on time
Value of regular reports (use paired comparison)	Percentage of on-time closings

FACILITIES	SAFETY & SECURITY
Work order response time	Safety & security costs as percentage of sales
Work order completion time	Accident rates
Level of employee complaints	Lost days level
Maintenance costs as percentage of sales	Worker compensation costs
Recycling percentages	Security incident rates

PURCHASING	ADMINISTRATIVE SERVICES
Purchasing costs as percentage of sales	General & administrative costs as percentage of sales
Average cost to process a requisition	Outsourcing cost/benefit
Average time to process a requisition	Average project response time
Inventory costs	Internal customer satisfaction level
Percentage of purchases defective or rejected	Percentage of projects completed on time and within budget

3. Choose one problem to work through the process value analysis. Assume logical causes and effects. I'll demonstrate using the first possible consequence: A dissatisfied customer may leave us and cause a loss of sales.

4. In going through the process value analysis, you can speculate on what could cause a delay in mean time to respond and repair. It could be a communications problem, in that the customer's request was not given to the service department promptly. It could be that the process of assigning service people is cumbersome or illogical, causing them to drive back and forth across the service area, incurring travel expense and slowing response time. It could be that the service people are not properly trained. It could be a breakdown of equipment.

5. For each of these causes there is a logical remedy. If it is the service people's skill deficiency, we can train them and see if the problem goes away. If that solves it, what is the value in saving a customer? Marketing or Sales can give us a figure, and we now have a dollar ROI from upgrading human capital skills. If it is a combination of better skills and better communications, perhaps we can see that it was more of one than the other and simply report that the dual action solved the problem.

Go back and briefly look at the other three problems and consequences:

1. *Late Filings and Penalties.* What could cause the finance or legal functions to be late in filings with the government? It's not likely that there is a skill problem. We're relying on highly trained professionals here. It must be some combination of slow assembly of required data, a flawed process, lack of commitment to on-time performance, a computer software bug, or something else. So what is the remedy? When we fix the problem, the value is obvious. We save the late fees and penalties previously imposed. What is the human component's contribution?

2. *Missing Material and Late Delivery.* It is not uncommon for this to happen. Sometimes the problem rests within

the purchasing or procurement function. Sometimes it is the fault of the person requesting the item or the vendor supplying it. What can cause purchasing to delay processing a material or equipment requisition? It could be insufficient staff for the workload. It could be an inefficient process, wrong instructions to the vendor, or an error on the requisition. If we fix the problem, we know that material shortages will not cause future delays or missed opportunities. The value of getting to market on time with a new product or serving a customer can be computed. What is the human component's contribution?

3. *Late Work Order and Inconvenienced Staff.* This could be a trivial or a serious problem. The path of analysis is similar to the purchasing case. An internal process fails to deliver on time. Is it a failing due to human skill or motivation? Is it a miscommunication? Is it workload or timing of the work order? Are priorities straight? What is the effect? Is it only an inconvenience, like a burned-out lightbulb? Or does it affect the ability to work, like a power outage? Is it a safety issue? Does it adversely impact employee productivity? The value of the solution is directly proportional to the seriousness of the shortcoming. What is the human component's contribution?

In all these examples, time converts to cost or savings. When there is an insufficient quantity produced for the amount of resource invested, the service or product cost can be excessive. If the problem is one of errors or defects in performance, recycling of the process adds cost. Lost customers obviously cost money. Any way you cut it, if you want to have a valid and reasonable idea of the value of the human effort, you have to convert the problem to cost increase or decrease and ask what the human component is. Sometimes it is very specific and clearly all attributable to investment in human capital. Other times it is a combination of human and structural capital investments.

> If you want to have a valid idea of the value of human effort, you have to convert the problem to cost increase or decrease and ask what the human component is.

Either way, the process value analysis method makes clear the visible, measurable values.

Summary

Organizations are collections of processes. Processes run across business units, making for a complex management problem. Because they are so pervasive and complex, we might need to view them in a different light to find better ways to manage them. Keen offers us such a perspective when he talks of business processes as either assets or liabilities. Processes that contribute to enterprise goals are at least potentially assets. Those that are purely compliance based are liabilities. Most approaches to process improvement overlook the nature of processes as real capital. Clearly, a process consumes resources and should be assessed from that standpoint. In short, economic value added is the best measure of process worth.

Ashton offers some important insights from another angle.[9] He supports the notion of linking process to organization and valuation by pointing out that effective process measurement is driven by the principle of continuous improvement against critical success factors and performance goals. There are different dimensions or levels to measurement, from strategic to operational to task detail. Systemic deployment of goals, targets, and indicators is the key issue. Processes must be planned and managed from an integrative perspective. Finally, Ashton suggests that the integration of process measurement with business planning and management is a critical success factor in itself.

Processes offer five points for adding value. The first is setting requirements. By giving clear, complete instructions, we reduce the probability of misinterpretation leading to costly mistakes. The second is interference from outside the process. Through partnering with the other units that impact the process, we can ensure that things arrive on time and in proper condition. The third point is the person performing the process. Training, communication, supervision, and incentives help the person perform at an appropriate level. The fourth is feedback. Prompt, accurate information on outcomes reduces errors and shortens time to correct deviations from acceptable levels. The fifth point is the consequence. By delivering rewards or corrective actions in a fair and timely manner, we teach the performers the value of meeting or exceeding expectations.

Value is all around us. We only have to look for it. Every time we find value added, we can ask and answer these two questions: Did the person add value by improving his or her performance through training or other personal inputs? Did the person add value by leveraging the tools that were provided by the organization? With a little practice, the answers become evident.

Improving a process typically yields multiple values. This is because when we save time, we save money. When we eliminate or reduce errors, we cut costs. If we increase the output from a given input, we decrease the cost of a unit of product or service. And when we satisfy customers, we keep them and help them buy more, and they refer others to us. Fixing a process generally yields two or more of these values. The process value analysis guides us in isolating the source of a problem and leads to the logical, value-adding solution. It shows us how the internal components of the process have changed and produced an improvement in service, quality, or productivity. This is then translated into external market and financial values. Throughout the analysis, we can see the qualitative and quantitative effects of human capital investments.

Finally, all business units should maintain a set of metrics that describe their ongoing efficiency. Periodic reports of cost, time, quantity, error, and reaction act as both an early-warning signal and a signpost indicating the source of the problem. Clearly, finding the effects of human capital is not a mysterious task. It just takes dedication to the belief that people are the primary profit lever.

References

1. Thomas A. Stewart, "Yikes! Deadwood Is Creeping Back," *Fortune*, August 18, 1997, pp. 221–22.

2. Peter G. W. Keen, *The Process Edge* (Cambridge, Mass.: Harvard Business School Press, 1997).
3. Geary A. Rummler and Alan P. Brache, *Improving Performance* (San Francisco: Jossey-Bass, 1990), p. 47.
4. Marc J. Epstein, and Bill Birchard, *Counting What Counts* (Reading, Mass.: Perseus Books, 1998).
5. Richard P. Feynman, *"Surely You're Joking, Mr. Feynman!"* (New York: W. W. Norton, 1985), pp. 127–28.
6. Peter Pipe and Robert F. Mager, *Analyzing Performance Problems: Or You Really Oughta Wanna*, 3d ed. (Atlanta: Center for Effective Performance, 1997).
7. James W. Cortada and John A. Woods, *The Quality Yearbook* (New York: McGraw-Hill, 1997), pp. 410–11.
8. Scott Adams, *Seven Years of Highly Defective People* (Kansas City: Andrews and McMeel Publishing, 1997), p. 37.
9. Chris Ashton, *Strategic Performance Measurement* (London: Business Intelligence, 1997), p. 136.

4

How to Measure Human Resources' Value Added

"Measuring more is easy, measuring better is hard."

—Charles Handy

Intellectual capital can be described as the intangible asset that stays behind when the employees leave, whereas human capital is the intellectual asset that goes home every night with the employees. Measurement of the return on human capital starts with an understanding of the tasks involved with managing human capital from the workforce planning stage onward. Many measurement projects fail for one of two reasons: They start in the middle of the process, or they don't take into account how all the elements of the process interact. Figure 4-1 is the human capital management star. It displays the six tasks involved in managing the most important and the most elusive entity of the organization: the human capital.

> Intellectual capital is the intangible asset that stays behind when the employees leave; human capital is the intellectual asset that goes home every night with the employees.

Collectively, the six management activities encompass the work conducted within a typical human resources function, with the following exceptions: Human resources information systems produce the data needed to conduct the activities and to evaluate performance. As such, that function can be judged

Figure 4-1. Human capital management star.

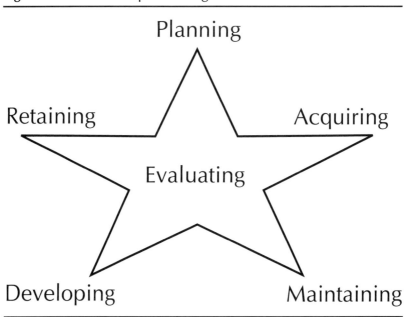

internally in terms of its ability to provide specific, accurate data on a timely basis. Measures of cost, time, quantity, and quality can be established for practically any human capital management activity. Some human resources executives supervise functions such as security, medical, cafeteria, and even janitorial and groundskeeping. When that is the case, we are looking not at human capital issues but at general administration of corporate services. This is not the focus of our study.

In the center of Figure 4-1 resides the task, or challenge, of evaluating the effectiveness of managing human capital. This is the least practiced of all six tasks. Human resources departments and line managers must hire, pay, develop, and keep human talent. They don't have to plan and evaluate, and for the most part, they don't. There is a long list of excuses for ignoring planning and evaluation. But the central, irrefutable truth is that without the data that flow from planning and evaluation, a manager is at best an unconscious competent.

Evaluating

Evaluating the management of human capital is not a separate task. It is integral to the efficient and effective exercise of the other five. There are ample opportunities to evaluate those five. The only question is, What is worth measuring? Assessment is most effective when it is built into the process. I will delve deeply into how to do this later in the chapter. At this point, I list just a few of the basic indicators that can be applied to each of the five task areas.

Planning

Before there is effective action in an organization, there must be some amount of planning for human capital. Workforce and succession planning was widely practiced until the mid-1980s. Then, with the onslaught of corporate downsizing, the idea of planning for the acquisition of talent found no support. In 1990, an article I wrote appeared in a personnel journal. I claimed that the major challenge of American companies in the latter years of the decade would be the acquisition of talent. Those who bothered to comment thought that the idea was ludicrous. In fact, a panel discussion of human resources concerns printed in the same issue gave only the fleetest consideration to the future.

At that time, companies were in a rush to get rid of people. Very few human resources professionals looked beyond their daily problems to when the economy would pick up and large numbers of people would have to be hired. It was not that I was smarter than they were. I was just paying attention to what was already happening behind the daily problems. A check of workforce demographics at the time revealed diverging curves of economic growth and shrinking birthrates. An expanding economy and a declining birthrate told a chilling tale. No one could have foretold the rate and scope of expansion that we experienced in the last decade of the twentieth century, but even modest growth would have outstripped the available talent. Today, with the economy still

booming, typical convenient excuses are lack of time and market uncertainty. Some claim that the market is moving too fast
to plan for skilling and reskilling the workforce. The obvious
alternative is to wait until the ship starts to sink and then
begin to bail like crazy. In the meantime, the more insightful
and diligent competitors will have sailed past, seldom to be
seen again, except from the rear.

The good news is that a few people are looking through
the economic maelstrom to tomorrow's needs. As we enter the
new millennium, workforce planning is resurfacing. A small
and slowly growing number of managers are working with
human resources to project human capital needs into the next
decade. They've even come up with a new name for it. They're
referring to it as *workforce management* or *readiness*. By any
name, it is a good sign.

Effective workforce planning or management can be evaluated along a couple of lines. One of the more common is to
look at the percentage of jobs that have been filled from the
existing employee population. Goals can be set up to fill a certain percentage of jobs from within. Most companies loudly
proclaim an internal promotion policy without the ability to
support it. The main reason that it doesn't occur is that there
is no ongoing development program preparing people to step
into new jobs. This is the first example of how different functions—planning and development—need to coordinate to be
effective. Planning and acquiring obviously must feed each
other. Information from employee relations should feed development and compensation. Development, in turn, can let
staffing know about skill levels encountered during training.
The combinations are many, and we will see how intricate the
cost-effective management of human capital is.

Acquiring

After there is a workforce projection for either the short or
long term, the human capital must be acquired through hiring
or renting from an agency or contracting with individuals di-

rectly for part-time or full-time work. Traditional hiring sought people who wanted full-time, permanent work. Late in the 1990s, the term *permanent* was dropped, as companies would no longer claim to offer permanent positions. In its place, the term *regular* was introduced to designate hires that were intended to be continuous for the foreseeable future, but with no guarantee of permanence. Eventually, the labor pool developed a subset that has come to be called the *contingent* workforce. This group represents people who are purposely hired for a short term. These are temporary and contract workers. They might fill in for a day while someone is sick, or they might work for more than a year on a project. A new body of labor law is emerging regarding the point at which a so-called temporary worker legally becomes an employee.

Different sources report different data on the size of the contingent workforce. According to the Bureau of Labor Statistics' records, part-time, temporary workers grew from less than 10 percent of the working population in the 1980s to over 13 percent by 1997. In 1993, Bank of America announced that it was converting 1,200 full-time employees to part-time. Bank executives were quoted as predicting that by the end of the decade, 60 percent of the staff would work less than twenty hours per week and receive no benefits. Another example in support of the trend comes from economist Jeremy Rifkin, who pointed out in 1993 that the federal government claimed that 1.2 million jobs had been created in the first half of the year but failed to mention that 60 percent of them were part-time or contract work.[2] Nollen and Axel state that no one knows for sure, but "a decent guess" is that contingent workers account for 20 to 25 percent of the workforce.[3] The belief among most executives in the placement industry is that the level is clearly above 20 percent and growing.

No matter their status, regular employees, temporaries, and contract workers have to be found to fulfill the promise of the strategic business plan. There have always been a number of people who worked part-time for a variety of reasons. Some did not want full-time, permanent jobs. Others could not find permanent positions and settled for temporary work in the hope of landing a permanent slot as it became available. We expect that the talent shortage will be solved through a combination of actions.

- More home-bound people will be hired via telecommuting.
- Older, able workers and early retirees will come back in part-time jobs ranging from consultants to clerks. An example is the McDonald's campaign to hire what it calls McSeniors.
- The practice of accommodating and hiring persons with disabilities will increase.
- Vocational training is already surging. Many people aged 20 to 50 with limited formal education have entered computer and electronics schools.
- Immigration will help, but it will not provide masses of technically skilled personnel.
- Some work will be outsourced offshore.

The bottom line is that there are people available, but they might not be the traditional types.

Some companies have been their own worst enemies in hiring. An ongoing study of the high rate of job-offer rejections shows that the process is the chief problem. Applicants come to a company because they want to work there. Sometimes the hiring process is not friendly. Interview appointments are broken, interviews are poorly conducted, communication breaks down, mixed messages are given, time lags between contacts expand. By the time offers are made, applicants are sick and tired of the way the company has treated them. They often remark, "If this is the way they treat applicants, how must they treat employees?"

Effective recruitment is most often assessed in terms of hiring costs and time to fill jobs. The quality of hires can also be evaluated, although it is more difficult. The volume of hiring activity vis-à-vis the resource commitment is an obvious measure. Finally, the satisfaction of the hiring manager can be surveyed. Staffing or recruitment is affected by internal factors, such as company growth, separation rates, and development programs, and externally by the labor market.

Maintaining

Once the precious human asset is in-house, it must be maintained. This is done principally through pay and benefits—the remuneration system. Nonmonetary reward and recognition is more of a retention and motivational effort than a maintenance program. From a hierarchy-of-needs viewpoint, people seek basic safety and security first from their employers. Paying a fair wage and providing a reasonable degree of security through benefits programs are accepted as de rigueur for maintaining a skilled workforce. After that come the frills.

With the national shortage of talent, so many incentive payment programs have been adopted that it is difficult to tell which are for maintenance and which are for retention. Sign-on bonuses have become a popular tool for acquiring talent. In 1998, 12 percent of the companies reporting in the Saratoga Institute's *Human Resource Financial Report* gave out sign-on bonuses. Furthermore, approximately 40 percent of new supervisors got bonuses for their autographs on the offer letters. Over 75 percent of executives received sign-on bonuses. This is purely a reaction to the talent shortage. You can be assured that whenever the supply-demand ratio changes, sign-on bonuses will be promptly extinguished.

Notwithstanding that, to keep talent today, stock options, profit sharing, gain sharing, and other forms of cash payouts are becoming common at much lower levels than ever before. Many start-ups are giving stock and stock options to all employees in the hope of keeping them. Whatever the motivation, there are methods for assessing the prudence and value of

> The indiscriminant, reactive throwing of money at job applicants is panic management.

monetary payments. The indiscriminate, reactive throwing of money at applicants is panic management. If companies looked ahead and developed and retained their human capital, they would not have to spend nearly so much to get talent and keep it. I discuss this in more detail later in this chapter.

Measures of maintenance effectiveness naturally focus on money spent. Wage and salary levels, pay and benefits as a percentage of revenue or expense, and average compensation for nonexempts, supervisors, managers, and executives are all captured and published by different sources. Operationally, we want to know what effect changes in compensation programs have on productivity and separation rates. This is a complex question, but there are answers for managers who are willing to commit time to studying it.

Developing

Having acquired and maintained a viable workforce, the next step is to develop it to its fullest potential. Human capital is unique, in that it is the only asset that can be developed. You can send a bicycle to training classes forever and it will never learn to fly.

American industry spends over $62 billion annually on employee development, according to *Training* magazine.[4] And that includes only formal training that the human resources development group has a role in or can identify. Human capital development is accomplished through various forms of education and training and by on-the-job experience. It is fair to state that the best development comes from on-the-job experience. Some would claim that employee development is another form of acquiring talent. This has an element of truth in it, but the talent has to be acquired first. Before a company can decide to "make" rather than "buy" talent, it has to have the raw material in-house. The make versus buy decision is a lot easier if you have data on the relative costs of acquiring, maintaining, and retaining a given set of skills. Useful data include cost per hire, average compensation expense, and the rate and cost of turnover.

Development takes many forms. Every action from supervisory coaching to self-paced training to formal classroom courses to job rotation to external programs is a form of development. The irony of development programs is that nine times out of ten, their payback is virtually unknown. The foremost source of training evaluation methods and data is Jack Phillips of Professional Resources Organization. He has developed and tested a valid and reliable process for measuring the effectiveness of all types of training interventions.[5] Another method is the process value analysis model we looked at in Chapter 3. It was originally designed and tested by a consortium of thirteen companies that wanted a generic model for measuring the ROI of any type of human development intervention. The effect was described in *Training* magazine.[6]

The value of training and development goes well beyond cost payback. If you spend time and money helping people learn and grow, you make a deposit in their loyalty bank. It is true that for a small percentage of people who are totally self-absorbed, helping them seldom generates any gratitude. If they leave, you should be thankful. Let's focus on the 95 percent who are unselfish, loyal individuals. They notice and appreciate how an organization goes about helping them attain their goals. This includes fair pay, security through benefits, and, most important, assistance in career develop-

> The attitude that training simply helps people find other jobs is stupid, shortsighted, and self-centered.

ment. The attitude that training simply helps people find other jobs is stupid, shortsighted, and self-centered. It is the classic Theory X attitude that undermines all good management practices. If someone in my company used that as an excuse for not developing his people, I would help him find new opportunities outside.

Training effects are measured best through changes in trainee job performance and the ensuing improvements in productivity, quality, or service. Asking people how they felt about the training after the fact has value only in terms of program modification and instructor ego. The company invests in development programs to achieve business goals, not just to make someone feel good.

Retaining

The last step in the human capital management game is to retain talent. Employee-relations programs, attitude surveys, and various other means are used to learn what it takes to keep talent in the organization. Improving retention generates several values:

- Reduced recruiting costs
- Reduced training costs
- Less supervisory time required
- In public contact jobs, maintenance of customer service
- Referrals by satisfied customers, thereby reducing marketing cost
- Referral of job applicants by long-term employees, reducing recruitment costs

Many organizations conduct exit interviews with employees who have quit in the hope of learning the reasons behind their decision to leave. In-house exit interviews rarely yield the truth. Extremely disgruntled employees and persons who have won the lottery or inherited a bundle are the only ones likely to reveal the real reason. People are smart enough not to burn their bridges. They know that it might come back to haunt them. Only when an external service conducts the interviews and maintains ex-employees' anonymity can the organization hope to find the truth.

The essential question is, Before you lose someone, what can be done to keep the person in the company and in a productive state of mind? Many of today's workers at all levels have personal obligations and desires that were rare a generation ago. Broken and separated families and single-parent situations are driving people to seek more social support at work. Higher levels of drug and alcohol abuse, increasing elder care demands, exalted career and income expectations, and balance of work and life affect how people view their workplace. People who have family or personal problems cannot be productive. They go through the motions, worrying about what they are facing outside. Anyone who has gone through a divorce, sickness, financial problems, or death of a loved one knows what I am talking about. The annual report in *Fortune* magazine of the best companies to work for gives us an idea of what people want from their employers. Companies are being compelled to take on the roles of neighbor, family, church, and community at a much more intense level than ever before.

Clearly, the main measure of retention efforts is the separation rate. Beyond the raw percentage, the key questions are, Who is leaving? Why? At what point in his or her career? What drove the person to consider employment elsewhere? and Where is he or she going? Finally, the most intriguing question is, What in a competitor's offer appealed to the former employee that he or she thought was unavailable with us? If you want to get someone's attention regarding turnover, the answers to these questions will help. But the pièce de résistance is showing what it cost to lose a valued employee. We'll go through that calculation later.

Given all of the above, we know now the issues and some key trends that affect our human capital from an asset management standpoint. Within these five activities we can find ample data on which to act. Once we have taken action, we will also have plenty of data to measure and evaluate the return on our investment.

Human Capital Performance Evaluation

As you saw in Chapter 3, all performance can be evaluated using a matrix. We have been applying this matrix at the Saratoga Institute for both internal performance assessment and external market impact for nearly twenty years. We have yet to find a case in which a performance measurement and reporting system couldn't be built around the matrix. Figure 4-2 shows the components of the matrix when it is applied to four core human resources activities: acquisition, maintenance, development, and retention.

Figure 4-2. Human capital performance matrix.

	ACQUIRING	MAINTAINING	DEVELOPING	RETAINING
COST				
TIME				
QUANTITY				
ERROR				
REACTION				

The Matrix Metrics

Cost

Cost is the one variable that always gets management's attention. It is direct. You can usually count business issues in monetary terms. People talk readily about the cost of serving a customer, the cost of rework, and the unit cost of a product. Management always seems to want to manage cost first. In one sense, this is good news, because it is the easiest metric to understand, present, and describe.

As the matrix shows, we can track the cost of individual services and programs. The cost of hiring can be broken down into its major elements to understand where the opportunity for reduction lies. We have developed and tested a formula for cost analysis that severely reduces the effort needed to track the ongoing cost. Six elements account for 90 percent of the cost of hiring, plus or minus 1 percent. The elements and a typical breakdown by percentage is as follows (plus about 10 percent for all other related activities):[7]

Advertising:	23%
Agency fees:	21%
Referral bonus:	2%
Travel:	4%
Relocation	21%
Recruiter cost:	20%

These were the averages for 891 companies in 1998. Obviously, in any given situation they can change radically when relocations are involved. The point is that you can set out on a new staffing strategy or employ a new tactic and track your ROI by element or in total. This tells you which is the most cost-effective method for selected job groups.

Costing processes in compensation and benefits management is relatively easy. We have conducted studies of the cost of processing paychecks and found tremendous differences among companies. The range was from one dollar per check to over twelve dollars. Clearly, in the latter cases there is a considerable unnecessary expense. But so long as no one traces it, the money will be wasted. Benefits administration has focused much more on the cost of processing claims and other benefit program transactions. Most companies consider the provision of benefits as a necessary expense that should be conducted at as low a price as possible.

When we move to other activities, such as those involving employee relations, the history of cost management is somewhat spotty. Granted that most programs are budgeted, but not many are reviewed for ways to reduce cost without losing the value of the service. Employee assistance programs are usually outsourced, and costs are monitored in the contract. Recognition events and ad hoc problem counseling are usually managed only from an overall cost standpoint. Some companies track the cost of counseling employees as well as the effects. This was detailed in my book *How to Measure Human Resource Management*.[8] Basically, a simple grid can be constructed that shows the number of counseling sessions conducted by topic and the total amount of time spent on counseling. This tells us where the counseling time is being spent if we track it by department or level. Those data are a signpost pointing to the business units with problems. Today's computer programs make tracking anything a much easier task than it was twenty years ago. With demographic sorting capability, three-dimensional analysis is as easy as dragging and dropping the demographic variable.

Turning to the last two columns—developing and retaining—in Chapter 3 we saw how to measure the ROI of a training (employee development) intervention. We can also measure the cost of turnover (or lack of retention). There are four costs associated with turnover: termination, replacement, vacancy, and productivity loss. The costs are calculated like this:

1. *Termination.* Typically, someone must process out the departing employee. This may take a few hours to collect badges, keys, and company equipment. The person must also be taken off payroll and any security lists. There may be benefit program extensions involved. In total, the cost is usually

about $1,000 to $1,500 in staff time to process the termination.

2. *Replacement.* In most cases, the departing employee must be replaced. The cost of hiring and orientation for a nonexempt employee, according to Saratoga's 1999 *Human Resource Financial Report,* was a little over $1,100. For an exempt person, the cost was close to $9,000 on average. Obviously, there is a great range across different situations.

3. *Vacancy.* Assuming that all jobs add value or we would not have them, we incur a loss of revenue for every day a position is vacant. The amount of loss depends on the position. A cost can be determined in the following manner: Take the total annual company revenue per employee and divide it by the number of workdays in the year—usually around 240 to 250, depending on vacation and holiday programs. Multiply this number by the number of workdays that the job is vacant. Subtract the cost of pay and benefits for those workdays (they weren't paid out), and you have the cost of vacancy.

4. *Productivity.* The new employee is seldom as productive as the departing one, so there is a denigration of performance for some period until the new person's productivity at least matches the former's. You can get very detailed on this measure or just develop a rule of thumb. The detailed route involves calculating the revenue per employee per day and then deciding how many days it takes to reach the level of performance of the previous incumbent. During that time, there is some productivity or value. The question is how much. Our experience over hundreds of cases is that the absolute minimum loss is the equivalent of three to six months' pay and benefits. For professional positions, it is more likely a year's worth. Other research has shown that the true cost of losing a salesperson is as high as $300,000.[9]

At Taco Bell, it was found that the 20 percent of stores with the lowest employee turnover yielded double the sales and 55 percent higher profits than the 20 percent of stores with the highest turnover rates. So the full effect of turnover, counting all four elements, is easily in excess of the equivalent of one year's pay and benefits.

Time

Time has become more important as the pace of life and business has increased. With pagers, e-mail, cell phones, and computers, we can do things faster, but we are also expected to respond more quickly. To paraphrase an old cliché, time truly is a surrogate measure for money. Managers manage response time, cycle time, delivery time, and many other times. Like cost reduction, if you can do something faster than your competition, you have a differentiating competitive advantage. The race may not always be won by the swiftest, but it is seldom won by the slowest.

Time has other effects as well as direct costs or savings. Delays frustrate people. They affect morale and thereby negatively impact productivity. Delays in filling jobs can put extra stress on the incumbents. Failure to deliver information on time can stop the wheels of productivity of a whole function. Taking too long to fix an employee performance problem can cause other employees to despair and quit. The hidden effect of time lost can be devastating.

Quantity

Quantity is the third most common metric. It is easy to deal with, because you can physically count the items under consideration. Whether we want to know how many applicants were hired, customers or employees served, paychecks or medical claims processed, or people trained, there are many ways to tally it up. To me, one of the more ironic facts is that although many computer programs in human resources departments automatically count the number of items processed, human resources professionals almost never use that capability to understand even this simplest performance indicator. Consequently, when they go to management to ask for more resources, they can't tell how much they are doing, much less what it costs or the average cycle time of the current process. By itself, knowing the quantity processed is not very useful. But it is the starting point for asking the important question, What difference did it make that we produced this much with a given amount of resource input?

Error

Error and defect rates became popular with the advent of the quality craze of the early 1980s. Thanks to Deming and Juran, American business learned how to measure quality.[10] An error or defect is simply something that did not meet expectations or requirements. With the publicity around quality programs, consumers began to demand better product and service quality. Eventually, employees picked up the chant inside their companies. Employees expect the company to make fewer errors as it relates to their records, benefits claims, training requirements, and communications needs. Acceptable error rates are a very individual issue. Some people would like perfection. For them, life must be an unending series of frustrations. What constitutes an error or defect is sometimes a subjective issue. One person may feel that something is "good enough," whereas another individual flies into a tantrum over the same level of treatment. Having spent many days and nights as the recipient of earnest attempts by airline, hotel, and restaurant personnel to please, my observation is that a good spanking early in life might have given the adult customer brats a more tolerant viewpoint.

Reaction

Human reaction refers to the physical, psychological, or emotional response of individuals to events around them. Here, we drop into the purely subjective realm. Some people are more demanding, have higher expectations, want more of something, or just have a bee in their breeches. These folks tend to react more negatively than the average bear. Customers and employees have values and attitudes that determine their reactions to services and products. These are measurable through a wide variety of tools, from galvanic skin responses and blood pressure readings to psychological tests, survey questionnaires, interviews, and focus groups. Scores can be produced and sorted by any demographic set we need. The most important issue is response. If we don't want to deal with what people tell us, then we shouldn't ask them. The worst and most common mistake is for companies to poll employees about something and then fail to acknowledge the responses or act on them.

■ ■ ■ ■ ■ ■

In summary, the five indices of change give us ample opportunity to monitor, measure, and report change. These apply to personal and organizational issues within any functional unit. They can be used for establishing internal measurement and reporting systems and for benchmarking outside entities. The first, last, and only important question is, Is the change for the better? That is, did it add value? To answer that, we need a context. The primary context is the immediate effect on internal service, quality, or productivity levels. The secondary and more critical context is the effect those internal improvements had on key external success factors such as customer retention. The final context is the economic value added to the enterprise.

> Is the change for the better? Did it add value?

Figure 4-3 shows examples of human capital management measures using the matrix. These are a small sample of the many ways that staffing, compensation, benefits, development, and retention can be viewed from an objective perspective.

Change Measurement

In organizations, measurement is usually about the degree or amount of change. Managers don't measure absolute points so much as they manage change. They monitor the amount of change that takes place from one instance to another—hour by hour, month by month, quarter to quarter, and year to year.

Figure 4-3. Human capital performance matrix examples.

	ACQUIRING	MAINTAINING	DEVELOPING	RETAINING
COST	Cost per Hire	Cost per Paycheck Cost per EAP Case*	Cost per Trainee	Cost of Turnover
TIME	Time to Fill Jobs	Time to Respond Time to Fulfill Request	Cost per Trainee Hour	Turnover by Length of Service
QUANTITY	Number Hired	Number of Claims Processed	Number Trained	Voluntary Turnover Rate
ERROR	New Hire Rating	Process Error Rate	Skills Attained	Readiness Level
REACTION	Manager Satisfaction	Employee Satisfaction	Trainee Responses	Turnover Reasons

*EAP = employee assistance program

That being so, the most important thing about measurement is to be consistent. Pick a methodology, define your terms tightly, and do it over and over using the same process. Seldom in management do we have to prove anything. In the more than two decades I have been presenting performance measures to executives, I can count on one hand the number of times someone has asked me for statistical data—and still have four fingers left over. One CEO, one time, asked for the standard error in a survey, and he was an engineer. What is more common was the side comment of a CEO during a presentation on the results of an employee survey. The tables and graphs went on endlessly, and he finally turned to me and whispered, "This is why I never talk to these guys." Management simply wants to know:

- How are we doing?
- How does this compare with someone else or with a previous period?
- What can we do to get better?

Human Capital Scorecard

The arrival of the balanced scorecard model has opened a new path to organizing and monitoring human capital information. We can take the concept behind the balanced scorecard and create a human capital version. The human capital scorecard consists of four quadrants, each devoted to one of the basic human capital management activities: acquiring, maintaining, developing, and retaining. Planning is not part of the scorecard, since it is not practical to monitor the effects of planning on a regular basis. By its nature, planning deals with the future. The human capital scorecard is focused on recent and current events. There are no generally accepted accounting principles that must be ad-

> We can take the concept behind the balanced scorecard and create a human capital version. It has four quadrants: acquiring, maintaining, developing, and retaining.

hered to at this point. In fact, the scorecard concept was developed to deal with factors that are ignored in standard financial statements. It was realized that standard accounting was not sufficient for presenting data that were necessary to manage large organizations in times of great change, intense competition, and rapid growth.

Figure 4-4 is an example of the types of metrics that can be used in the scorecard. Ideally, the choices made should provide a basic yet thorough look at the investment and utilization levels of human capital. Each of the quadrants should contain cost, time, quantity, and quality measures to the extent practical and possible. Across the bottom, a base can be added to cover reaction factors. The reactions of managers and employees to human resources programs are important. A measure of manager satisfaction is useful for the human

Figure 4-4. Sample human capital management scorecard.

ACQUISITION	MAINTENANCE

Cost per hire
Time to fill jobs
Number of new hires
Number of replacements
Quality of new hires
	Total labor cost as percentage of
	  operating expense*
	Average pay per employee
	Benefits cost as percentage of
	  payroll
	Average performance score
	  compared to revenue per FTE

RETENTION	DEVELOPMENT

Total separation rate
Percentage of voluntary
  separations: exempt and
  nonexempt
Exempt separations by service
  length
Percentage of exempt separations
  among top-level performers
Cost of turnover
	Training cost as percentage of
	  payroll
	Total training hours provided
	Average number of hours of
	  training per employee
	Training hours by function
	Training hours by job group
	Training ROI

Job Satisfaction	Employee Morale

*Includes contingent labor cost.

resources department. An employee morale measure can be added to the base if it is carefully crafted and deemed useful.

Acquisition

The first activity after planning is to acquire human capital for the organization. This can be done with a combination of three tactics: hiring, renting, and developing. Developing is accomplished through any number of activities, from daily supervisory coaching to expensive outside educational ventures. Our focus in the acquisition quadrant is on the results of hiring or renting. The term *renting* is a catchall for contingent workers. It includes paying an agency or a person directly for a period of work without the person's being on the company payroll. This form of human capital is, in effect, being rented or leased and then let go after the requirement is satisfied. The rental period can be anything from a few hours to fill in for someone who was delayed one morning to as long as a year or more to complete a project. The legal and ethical question of when a "rental" really becomes a "buy" is not at issue here. We are only concerned at this point in factors such as cost, time, quantity, and quality.

Maintenance

This function covers a broad base of activities focused primarily on paying salaries and providing benefits. Any asset needs to be maintained in good condition in order for it to retain its value and, in the case of a human being, continue to contribute value to the goals of the organization. Pay and benefits are monitored through a combination of cost ratios. This section does not deal with salary surveys, which are designed to provide external benchmarks for decisions regarding pay levels of various jobs. In our case, we want to monitor the effects of managing salaries and wages. Therefore, we can look at pay in terms of average pay of employees, distribution across levels, cost as a percentage of operating expense, or other macro measures. The decision of what to put in the maintenance quadrant is left to the user.

Development

Tracking and monitoring the development of human assets or capital is the most difficult of the four quadrants. It is a complex problem. First, what is training or development? We have already noted that it can be anything from daily coaching to external formal programs. Where do we start and stop? Second, from a practical standpoint how do we capture the costs? So much of development is invisible and even unrecognized that it is truly impossible to know the total cost. Most accounting systems do not easily capture formal training expenditures. To make the situation even more perplexing, everyone realizes that some portion of so-called external training expenses is a surrogate for other expenditures. We know that in some cases, training trips simply mask rewards for exceptional performance or are used for purposes outside of the sphere of human development. Having said all that, this topic is too important to ignore. We must create a set of measures that give us some general sense of resources being committed in the name of development. It is a practical matter in which something is better than nothing.

Retention

Keeping talent will always be an important activity. Even in the severest times, when a company plunges into a negative earnings position, it still must retain a critical talent core. In a merger or acquisition, human capital is a key issue. By far the vast majority of mergers and acquisitions pay scant attention to the talent of the organization. Typically, only in the highest technical buys does the acquirer focus on key talent in the acquired company. I lived through an acquisition in which the buyer poured half a billion dollars into the game before writing it off as a failure. It was largely a case of letting the wrong people go and bringing in people who were ill suited to the task. Quite often, technical expertise is assigned to the task when the real skill needed is organizational and people management. Experience has proved time and again that when people and people-related issues such as culture are ignored, the potential for failure is well above 50 percent. It follows that separation rates and costs are important and must be part of any human capital scorecard system.

The metrics selected act as a platform for measuring the human effects within tasks and processes, the next stage in the data-to-value cycle. As we view how well we are designing, making, selling, and servicing products and services, the cost, timely acquisition, and quality of the human elements are some of the factors that go into process evaluation. The others are commitment of equipment, facilities, materials, energy, and the overarching financial capital invested.

At this point, employee-relations staff members may be wondering where their work fits. The effects of their work are found most often in retention. Through employee assistance and social and recreational programs, they contribute to keeping employees. Beyond that, they also make contributions to all other quadrants, since they are constantly moving about the organization working with employees on personal and interpersonal issues. As such, when they are functioning as they should, they are an intelligence unit that contributes to the plans and designs of many human resources programs. Ultimately, their work affects employee productivity.

Human Capital Accounting

In 1965, Roger Hermanson proposed a method for determining the value of a human being to an organization. This, along with work at the Institute for Social Research at the University of Michigan, became the foundation for what was then called human resources accounting (HRA). The first attempt by a public company to publish pro forma financial statements that included human assets was the R. G. Barry Corporation, a small manufacturing company in Columbus, Ohio. Interest grew slowly through the early 1970s, and in 1975, Flamholtz published the seminal text on the topic.[11] As more people became involved, articles appeared in various personnel and accounting journals. However, it gradually became apparent that this was a very complex problem requiring expensive long-term research, without any assurance that the problem could be solved. Over the next decade, interest waned and waxed until the topic finally withdrew in favor of more pressing business issues.

The principal failure was an inability to agree on how to put a monetary value on people. Several models were proposed but never widely adopted. Accountants are never comfortable with something they cannot "buy" or "sell" at a given price. To put a value on a person within a business organization, one has to be able to calculate the variability of a person from four perspectives:

1. Productivity
2. Promotability
3. Transferability
4. Retainability

The human resources value depends on the value of each of the four factors during a fiscal year. The likelihood of an individual being in any of those positions—or service states, as they are called—is subject to the law of probability. Flamholtz argued that by using a *stochastic rewards valuation* model, one could determine the following:

1. The mutually exclusive states a person might occupy
2. The value of each state to the organization
3. A person's expected tenure in the organization
4. The probability that a person will occupy each state at specific future times
5. The expected discounted future cash flows that represent their present value

As intriguing as this problem is, so far, there has been no support from business or professional groups to take it on. To my mind, the problem has been attacked from the wrong angle. I would even be willing to grant that the problem could be worked out. But it is just too esoteric and complex for executives who are charged with achieving current financial objectives.

The first issue is that we can't know the value of a person based on efforts to be made in the very uncertain future. Right there, it turns an interesting model into an impractical solution. Business is too variable, not to mention people. As a person who started his own company and ran it for almost two decades, I can testify that the true value of any tangible asset is unknown until someone gives you money for it. You can forget the so-called value that is carried on the books. Everyone knows that this is nothing more than an agreement. Depreciation and amortization are artifacts of the deliberations of the Financial Accounting Standards Board, and God does not sit on the FASB. A more practical angle is to look at what really happened, as accounting does, and then calculate the value added by human effort after the fact.

> God does not sit on the FASB.

I can tell you with a reasonable degree of accuracy what it costs to hire, train, and lose an employee. I can also calculate the average value per employee based on sales and net income before tax. You saw it in the human capital value added and human capital ROI formulas in Chapter 2. Admittedly, these are gross numbers, but they are factual as opposed to probable. Business executives are held accountable for results. Only the most enlightened and secure are going to fund complex research. This is regrettable but true.

As of late 1999, there was a growing groundswell of calls for the reform of standard accounting, such as including nonfinancial data and reporting in "real time." There are calls for the Securities and Exchange Commission to open its mind to a parallel system that will evolve over the next decade into a system that reflects the realities of 2000 and beyond rather than 1930.[12] Fresh initiatives are under way at the Brookings and Hoover Institutions, among others, to find an answer to the human capital valuation problem. These will build on the work of Flamholtz, Baruch Lev, and others and will advance our knowledge and ability to value human capital. The Saratoga Institute has worked on this issue for two decades. The human capital profit-and-loss statement is one of its latest contributions to that effort.

A Human Capital P&L

Granted, the accounting establishment has not yet accepted human capital accounting. This is not surprising, since dramatic changes and new methods seldom come from within the establishment. None of the mainframe computer makers came up with the personal computer. None of the airlines or railroads originated next-day delivery of small packages. None of the big-three automobile companies developed the Volkswagen Beetle or the Honda Civic. AT&T did not open up new telecommunications opportunities. Innovation almost always comes from outside the established institutions. This is because institutions concentrate most of their energy on fighting a rearguard action to protect their *assets*. Since our assets are considerably smaller and need less attention, we can dare to suggest that there is another way to think about this issue. Figure 4-5 is an example of a human capital profit-and-loss (P&L) statement for the fictional Megacorp (based on a real company).

In Megacorp, we can see that there is a potential for cost savings from either improving the hiring process or reducing the level of turnover. In this simple case, we can see the relative value of each move. The point is not the actual numbers, but rather that it is possible to put an economic value on human capital management using familiar accounting concepts.

Megacorp has data on revenue as well as expenses related to its human capital. To improve either its top or bottom line, there are several feasible actions open to its management team. They are the following:

1. *Reduce cost per hire.* If cost per hire can be reduced from its present rate of $2,305 to the average of the top tenth

Figure 4-5. Human capital P&L.

MEGACORP
HUMAN CAPITAL INCOME STATEMENT
1999
(in millions)

REVENUE
Human capital value added $2,665   Revenue less "nonhuman"
                                        operating expense

DIRECT EXPENSES
Acquiring   15   Cost of hiring
Maintaining   1,128   Pay and benefit cost
Developing   12   Cost of training

GROSS INCOME $1,510

INDIRECT EXPENSES
Vacancy   126   Revenue lost for days jobs unfilled
Learning curve   438   Revenue lost for partial productivity
                                        during first year of employment

NET INCOME (before tax) $ 946

percentile of companies reporting in Saratoga's 1999 *Human Resource Financial Report* ($725), it would reduce direct expenses by $10 million and increase in net income by 1 percent.

2. *Reduce time to start.* If time to start can be reduced from fifty-nine days to the average of the top tenth percentile of companies (forty-three days), it will increase revenue and pay, sales per position filled, and pay given to incumbents. Since jobs are filled sixteen days sooner, this decreases indirect expenses by shortening vacancy time and adds $51 million to net income (5.4 percent).

3. *Reduce turnover.* If turnover can be reduced from 29.7 percent to the average of the top tenth percentile (7.2 percent), it will increase revenue owing to fewer lost days and less of a

learning curve loss. It will also reduce expenditures for hiring and increase pay through fewer vacant job days. Gross income and net income will increase $820 million (87 percent).

These are startling numbers, which assume several things. One is that Megacorp can reach the top tenth percentile, which is a formidable task that, by definition, only 10 percent of the industry attains. It also assumes that the quality of people is constant—that is, productivity and quality are unchanged. But that type of assumption is no different from any business projection, since all projections are based on the ceteris paribus principle. Again, the point is not the numbers but the process, which demonstrates an ability to calculate the relative value of human capital management activities. Now, that didn't hurt much, did it, FASB?

Human Capital Management Consortia

Since it is important to know how well we are doing in key success areas, it is also useful to be able to compare our performance with that of other companies. The popular term for this is *benchmarking*. Traditionally, a benchmark is a point of reference, but in common business parlance, it has come to mean any type of comparative activity. Benchmarking or performance comparison can be accomplished through a variety of methods and sources.

The range of benchmarking models runs from informal, short-term networks to formal, long-term consortia. In the latter, groups can be set up whereby participating companies agree to share certain information on a regular basis. Members of these groups might be in the same industry, or they might constitute a domestic benchmarking group that crosses several industries. Increasingly, international networks are being formed to share metrics and practices in search of world-class practices. This is being driven by the increase in multinational operations. The draw to join a consortium is usually a topic of common interest, such as how to become an employer of choice. The criterion for membership could be a common operating issue such as extremely fast growth, knowledge management, or system globalization. A number of these groups are always in operation. They come and go, but some have been around for decades.

The central issue in any benchmarking or data-sharing program is the guarantee that data definitions, data quality, and terminology are reliable and valid. It is a good practice to look for a program that has produced consistently valid and useful data over a number of years. A one-short survey by a consulting firm designed primarily to open the door to its predetermined solution seldom yields anything of value and can even be misleading.

Best-Practice Reports and Other Fairy Tales

When the topic of "best practices" comes up, the question focuses on what difference these practices made in an organization. Did they help reduce operating expense and thereby product cost? Did they shorten the cycle time of an important process? Were people able to do more with less through this method? Was the number of errors or defects reduced? Is

> The vast majority of so-called best practices are never subjected to stringent quantitative analysis.

a customer or an employee more satisfied than before? The vast majority of so-called best practices are never subjected to stringent quantitative analysis. A close study shows that most reports evade the issue or dance around it with simplistic, partial, and inconsistent measures.

A typical example is to state that a certain method significantly reduced the cost of hiring and shortened the time to fill jobs at a given site. Are there hard numbers to prove it? And what about related issues? Has this process improved the quality of hires? Has it positively affected separation rates? And, most importantly, was it a flash in the pan at only one site, or did it work over a protracted period at several sites? In short, is it a generalizable practice, or is it workable only under very specific circumstances? An incident that is not repeatable is not a generic best practice and should not be called that. One should never take a best-practice report at face value. It should be checked with the author for logic and demonstrable data. Adoption of an unverified practice can be embarrassing or worse.

Truly Effective Practices

There are several practices that the most effective companies exhibit in the management of their human capital.

Planning

Workforce planning has begun a slow comeback in a new form. A small but growing number of organizations are launching new workforce *management* projects. At this point, these projects are more prevalent in very large industrials and in government, which are more stable organizations than fast-growing, constantly changing technology-driven companies. In these latter companies, the future is too unpredictable and short term to make planning useful. In the former cases, the methodology has not changed very much from the previous generation of workforce planning. But many of the examples of the new generation of workforce analysis focus on competency development rather than planning. They often take on a workforce management aura, although they are not recognized as such. In those situations, competencies are being identified in relation to business plan projections. This approach puts less energy into manning tables and more into developing a cadre of personnel with certain skills. The more common model for the study of planning practices has been that one large firm sponsors and bears the expense of inviting others of similar size to join a short-term project. Our experience with such projects at the Saratoga Institute is that they produce a relatively small amount of useful and valid data.

Staffing

Some people believe that costing staffing is not useful, since the most important issue is the quality of talent attracted. It is true that quality is the prime issue. However, our experience shows that those who manage cost also obtain better quality. The reason is that they are truly managing the process, not just responding to job orders. By monitoring cost sources, they also monitor quality simultaneously. Their basic tool is source analysis, in which the staffing manager reviews the cost, time, quantity, and quality for each source of applicants. Traditional and experimental sourcing is analyzed. The questions are:

- What is the most cost-effective source for a given job group? Is it advertising in a local newspaper, a professional journal, or a Web bulletin board?
- Which agencies are best, and how do they compare on cost, responsiveness, volume, and quality of applicants?
- How effective is an employee referral program?

At the end of the day, the staffing manager knows which source produces the most cost-effective applicant flow. By including all views—cost, time, quantity, and quality—the company is assured of an excellent return on its staffing investment.

One of the more effective methods outside of forming a consortium is to start by identifying organizations that have a reputation for excellence in staffing. This information is not easy to find. Periodically, someone will write an article in a human resources journal, but these need to be verified, since performance claims are often exaggerated. Consulting firms are a good source of firsthand knowledge from a number of companies. If you have a relationship with a consulting firm, you can ask for nominations, but such firms will not volunteer names to anyone who calls in. It takes time and resources to locate practices that are truly effective. Then, contacts have to be made and discussions held to determine whether there is a good match. At that point, visits can be scheduled. I describe how to carry out an effective benchmarking project in Chapter 7.

Compensation

Pay programs can be set up in response to the market, or they can be configured as a strategic tool. In general, the distribution of pay between top and bottom performers is barely differentiated. Everyone knows it, and the salary increase scales prove it. I believe that viewing pay as an investment to motivate performance needs a good deal of work. In a diverse, highly competitive market, we need more flexible pay programs. We have to stop being afraid of losing poor or even mediocre performers and concentrate on rewarding the performance we ask for.

Rather than viewing pay as an ongoing process, we recommend that the pay of all employees above entry level be more flexible both upward and downward. Paying for exceptional performance requires a reliable measurement system and a new look at the effects of individual human effort on business outcomes. A study by Interim Services showed that employees want more differentiation in pay.[13] They have little tolerance for ineffective coworkers and resent the organization that harbors them, paying them nearly as much as productive people. Experience proves that productive people would rather be rid of the nonproductive and pick up the extra work themselves rather than have the poor performers around.

Effective pay practices are very idiosyncratic. Unique and often sensitive internal forces drive them. Management philosophy, ability to pay, competitor's actions, organizational structure, and other factors come into play in establishing compensation programs.

Benefits

Employee benefits are background. No one thinks of them except when they need them. Traditional benefits such as

health care and 401(k) programs should be outsourced. There
is no value to be added by keeping administration of them in-
house. Remember what Keen said about processes as either
assets or liabilities. So long as someone manages the vendor
and responds to employee problems promptly, the benefits
program will yield what it was meant to: security at a reasonable price. Other benefits such as child care, recognition
events, and those programs having more immediate daily effects should be kept inside and managed closely. These can
make a big difference in productivity and retention.

Development

Paradoxically, employee development is one of the most
important issues for the foreseeable future and one of the
worst managed. In fact, it would be an overstatement to claim
that it was badly managed. Our experience is that it is unman-
aged. No one knows how much money and time are spent on
even formal training programs. And very few have any idea of
their ROI. ROI in training can be calculated with a sufficient
degree of accuracy, as the value analysis case in Chapter 3
demonstrated. Despite this fact, our surveys have consistently
shown that less than 5 percent of America's $62 billion train-
ing effort is evaluated. When cost and effectiveness are unknown, how can anyone claim that training is managed?

Retention

In the latter half of the 1990s, managers became sensitive
to the need to retain talent. The most effective method is to
start with an ongoing analysis of the employment processing
and job offer system. This tells us why people apply to our
company, what they experience in the selection process, and
why they walk away from our job offers. We can learn a great
deal about the attractiveness of our company and how we
treat people who approach us. Later, after we have the people,
we need to communicate with them.

There are points in a person's career when he or she is

most susceptible to the siren call of the outside opportunity. About two years in, at four to five years, and again at seven to eight years of employment, people see themselves as prized commodities. These are the points when we should be especially attentive to their career needs. Over 70,000 exit interviews have proved that the principal reason people leave a company voluntarily is the behavior of their supervisors. The secondary reason, principally for professionals, although it can apply to anyone who intends to stay for a long time, is perceived lack of growth opportunities. Accordingly, effective retention programs focus on supervisory training and career management. Finally, when we lose a person, a systematic, thorough exit interview conducted by a firm specializing in that can be extremely illuminating.

The point is that there are management practices that are truly "best," in the sense that they are generalizable. These so-called world-class practices have proved themselves through quantitative analysis. They show us how to manage a function and demonstrate cost-effectiveness in hard dollar terms.

Summary

ROI begins with the processes and elements within human capital management. This requires starting with workforce management and proceeding through staffing, compensating, developing, and retaining people. Significant changes in costs, time cycles, volumes, error rates, and human reactions flow through the organization. In most cases, these changes are absorbed downstream within the organization's processes. Because they are submerged, they are unseen. Accordingly, the unenlightened tend to ignore or discount emerging signals.

However, when the cost of hiring decreases, the volume of human resources' output over input increases, or employees acquire practical new skills, that is a value added. Factors such as the quality of new hires and the satisfaction of hiring supervisors can also be tracked. These are first-level returns on investment in human resources' programs. If you need a detailed description of the pros and cons of human resources department measurement, I suggest my book *How to Measure Human Resource Management.* It contains over fifty formulas and many graphic examples taken from my experience managing human resources in three companies. By developing a human resources department measurement system and monitoring changes monthly or quarterly, the ROI of initial human capital management becomes clear. These become part of the mix when customer service, product quality, or unit costs are measured later. It is only through the actions of these human capital assets—people—that anything happens downstream.

The performance matrix is the basic assessment model that can be laid on any business operation. It is as applicable to the administrative units of human resources, accounting, and information services as it is to manufacturing. When evaluation problems are encountered, it is usually because the objective of the process is unclear. Quite often, people or units are given objectives that are specific in terms of delivery date but nonspecific in relation to cost or quality. The best measures are those that incorporate as many of the five indices of change as possible. Failure to look at all of them leaves the producers vulnerable to criticism that they didn't get the most important factor right. The lesson is obvious: Know exactly what the outcome should look like, and be able to specify it in terms of desired amount of change in service, quality, or productivity.

Saratoga's research over the past fifteen years has generated an educated estimate that only about 20 percent of the firms in America manage their human capital with any systematic, proven, evaluative methods. For the most part, they run a continual series of stimulus-response exercises, hoping to respond as quickly as possible to the latest unplanned-for event. The real culprit is not the human resources manager but the CEO—the person who sets low expectations and accepts suboptimal performance as the mode. Top executives fool themselves into thinking that they have an effective management program when, in actuality, they have no idea what they have or what one looks like. Their criteria for an effective human resources function seem to be file and smile, come quickly when I call, and keep me out of trouble.

Consider for a moment that total labor costs typically consume anywhere from 10 percent to 50 percent of sales revenue (depending on the industry)[14] and that the productivity of human capital is the only profit lever. Doesn't it make you wonder when top management will catch on to the lost opportunity cost and the profit potential that exists? The objective of this book is to give managers a model that they can apply to draw a better ROI from their expensive and valuable human capital.

References

1. Jac Fitz-enz, "Getting and Keeping Good Employees," *Personnel Journal*, August 1990, pp. 25–28.
2. Jeremy Rifkin, *The End of Work* (New York: G. P. Putnam's Sons, 1995), p. 167.
3. Stanley Nollen and Helen Axel, *Managing Contingent Workers* (New York: AMACOM, 1996), pp. 9–10.
4. *Training*, annual survey, October 1999, pp. 37–81.
5. Jack Phillips, *Return on Investment* (Houston: Gulf Publishing, 1997).
6. Jac Fitz-enz, "Yes, You Can Weigh Training's Value," *Training*, July 1994.
7. *Human Resource Financial Report* (Santa Clara, Calif.: Saratoga Institute, 1999), p. 335.
8. Jac Fitz-enz, *How to Measure Human Resource Management*, 2d ed. (New York: McGraw-Hill, 1994).
9. Frederick F. Reichheld, *The Loyalty Effect* (Boston: Harvard Business Schools Press, 1996), pp. 102–3.
10. W. Edwards Deming, *Out of the Crisis* (Cambridge, Mass.: MIT, 1986); Joseph M. Juran, *Juran on Quality by Design* (New York: Free Press, 1992).
11. Eric Flamholtz, *Human Resource Accounting*, 2d ed. (San Francisco: Jossey-Bass, 1985).

12. Stephen Barr, "Back to the Future," *CFO,* September 1999, pp. 42–52.
13. *The Emerging Workforce* (Fort Lauderdale, Fla.: Interim Services, 1998, 1999).
14. *Human Resource Financial Report,* pp. 74–78.

5

End-to-End Human Capital Value Reports

"I believe our present ways of understanding organizations are skewed."

—Margaret Wheatley

To this point, you have seen how to measure the value of human capital at three levels, from the enterprise- or corporate-level targets down through the functional business unit processes to the activities of the human resources department. You've seen how management of human capital supports functional processes in pursuit of enterprise goal fulfillment. Now it is necessary to bundle all the components together in one cohesive system so that you can see the connections and interdependencies. As you might presume, this is a complex package that requires some degree of concentration.

Although there is a general pathway from human capital investment to enterprise value, there are many routes that are somewhat specific to each organizational function. As with any asset, whether material, equipment, facilities, or energy, there is a multitude of links and drivers that vary with each case. Figure 5-1 shows the basic pathways. Within each cell there are measurable actions and results. Starting at the bottom of the diagram, the result of an action in hiring, paying, training, or keeping talent affects the activities and outcomes of the functional units for which the provider (usually but not

Figure 5-1. Pathways.

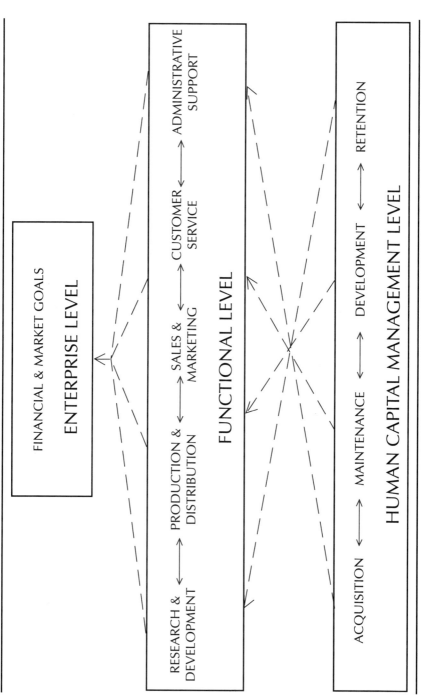

FINANCIAL & MARKET GOALS
ENTERPRISE LEVEL

RESEARCH & DEVELOPMENT ←→ PRODUCTION & DISTRIBUTION ←→ SALES & MARKETING ←→ CUSTOMER SERVICE ←→ ADMINISTRATIVE SUPPORT
FUNCTIONAL LEVEL

ACQUISITION ←→ MAINTENANCE ←→ DEVELOPMENT ←→ RETENTION
HUMAN CAPITAL MANAGEMENT LEVEL

always the HR department) is performing the human capital management service. In turn, since organizations are collections of processes, the work within one functional unit affects the ability of related functions to fulfill their commitments. Whereas objectives run vertically through an organization, processes run horizontally and diagonally. The collective outcome of all functions largely determines the level of enterprise performance. So a positive or negative action in one function or process can ripple throughout the organization. And it all starts with and is dependent on the behavior and talent of people. Such is the power of human capital.

I realize that an organization, be it a commercial business or a not-for-profit institution, is not a closed system. In a commercial situation, management can screw up and still beat its competition if the competitors screw up even worse. It can also go the other way. That is, superb performance does not always guarantee goal achievement, because the actions of other stakeholders—most of all the customers—can change. If the economy takes a sudden downturn, even the best-run company may not be profitable in the short term because customers stop buying. All that notwithstanding, the pathways outlined in Figure 5-1 essentially describe a valid, tested model.

Note that there are arrows running horizontally within the functional and human capital processes. These are an illustration of the natural interaction among groups and activities. I called it *collaboration* in my study of the practices of exceptional companies. The top performers achieve their preeminence through internal partnering in a common cause. Collaboration is one of the many platitudes that the mediocre espouse but don't practice. For the best of the best, it is not a platitude.

Pathways

We'll look at three examples of enterprise goals and how human capital management links with and supports the functional processes that achieve those goals. Most improvement programs focus on cost reduction. That is too simple a challenge. Many turnaround specialists, including the archetype slash-and-burn master Al Dunlap, have showed how fast one can cut out waste. I would not begin to make a case for Mr. Dunlap. However, he probably picked on the wrong people to start. He should have fired the board of directors, which hired him, for letting the enterprise it was supposedly directing devolve to such a horrible condition. Not being able to do that, he attacked the problem at the next set of culpables, top management. Then came the massive employee layoffs and asset sell-offs. That didn't take a lot of intelligence. If you cut out extra employees and sell off assets, your income statement and balance sheet are bound to look better—for a while. Any first-year MBA student learns that. In the end, I don't think people condemned him for doing the job he was hired to do. But as with everything else in life, it was the way he did it that ticked us off. Cold-blooded arrogance is not an endearing attribute.

Overall, American businesses did a credible job of reducing their size and improving their efficiency during the 1990s. Downsizing, total quality management, and reengineering all contributed to general cost reduction and competitiveness. Unfortunately, less attention was paid to the revenue-generating side. Eventually, managers looked around at the aftermath of reductive efforts and asked what they could do next. Obviously, the pathway was through people—the only asset that can add value. Customer service came into fashion in the middle of the decade. This was one of the first signals that management had discovered the value-generating capability of employees. It led to the popularity of employer-of-choice programs. It finally seems to have sunk in that people—customers and employees—are the drivers of successful businesses. I accept that the investment bankers can manage mergers and acquisitions to create synergies, some of the time. Their record is rather spotty, in that more than half of all acquisitions fail to achieve their initial financial projections. Nevertheless, after the new management team is in place and the palace coups have run their course, someone has to do the damned work and keep the beloved customers happy. Business is, in the final analysis, a people game. The path to long-term success is through effective management of internal human capital, which in turn finds, services, and retains customers.

Beyond cost reduction, there are many pathways we can trace from the enterprise goals downward through organizational functions to human resources. When the human resources department is truly supporting the enterprise instead of just filing and smiling, it becomes the host of human capital. It leads management in acquiring, maintaining, developing, and retaining the precious commodity without which nothing happens. I deliberately use the word *lead* to emphasize that human capital management is not the sole responsibility of the human resources department. It is everyone's job from top to bottom in the organization. Human capital investment is optimized only when all parties from the board of directors to first-line supervisors and the employees themselves play a role.

> When the HR department is truly supporting the enterprise instead of just filing and smiling, it becomes the host of human capital.

Staff departments such as information services, finance, or human resources presumably develop systems, design processes, and offer services aimed at supporting corporate goals. It would be absurd and wasteful for them to do otherwise. However, in all my years in and around staff groups, I have often found it difficult to locate the connections. Most often, it is a case of a general enterprise goal and a general staff response void of direct, verifiable, point-to-point links. This is okay if you want average returns on your staff investments. That is what probability theory predicts—general response and average results. In our case, we are building direct, visible links all the way up and down the pathway from the enterprise level to the human resources–led response and back up again. With direct links it is possible to assess results in explicit terms and thereby make improvements that yield above-average results.

So let's look at three examples of specific pathways between enterprise goals and human capital management. The cases I've chosen are important issues for any commercial endeavor. They are also points on which government and education should focus. Moving more quickly, serving the constituents, and operating in a more flexible and humane way internally would be a great improvement for many public institutions. The three key issues are:

1. Time to market
2. Customer service
3. Employer of choice

Each has a different focus: time, service, or employee retention. They represent the basics that give us a number of different angles from which to understand the multitudes of connections along the pathway. Figures 5-2, 5-3, and 5-4 display the pathways of the three cases that follow. They reveal only a small number of the many connections between human capital management outputs and various functional units. They show a mix of activities and possible measurable outcomes. Space (and mental exhaustion) precludes showing all the possibilities of all three cases. It would be overkill. By applying your experience with each of the line and staff functions listed, you will be able to think of many more relationships. Of course, the outputs from the functional units relate to and support the specific enterprise imperative.

Cases

CASE 1: ENTERPRISE GOAL: IMPROVE (SHORTEN) TIME TO MARKET

Value: Being in the market ahead of the competition enables us to stake out a position and gain market share before competitors preempt the space.

Imperative: Each function—line and staff—must focus on the primary issue of timeliness within its arena without negatively affecting cost, quality, or service.

Human capital management applies the time criterion to acqui-

(text continues on page 138)

Figure 5-2. Sample human capital-to-enterprise pathway for time to market.

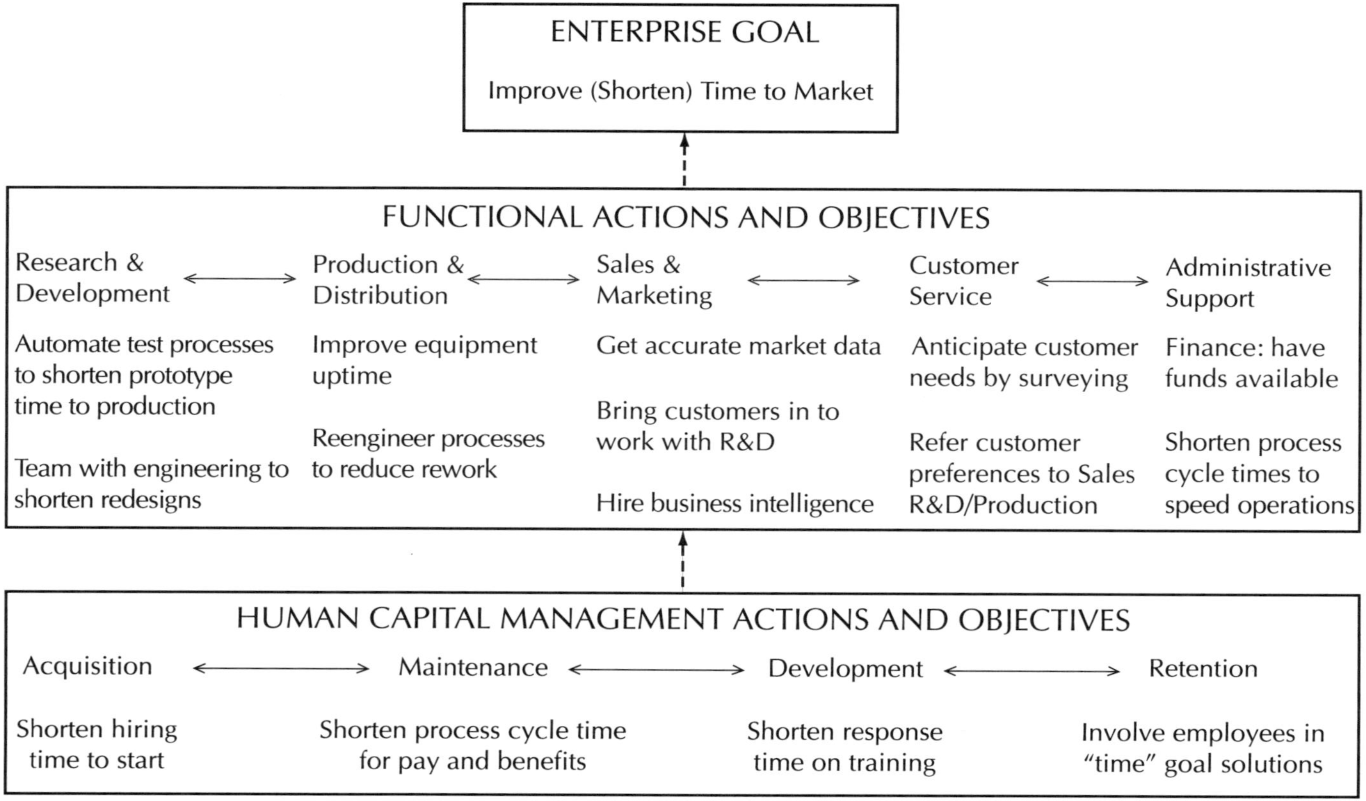

ENTERPRISE GOAL

Improve (Shorten) Time to Market

FUNCTIONAL ACTIONS AND OBJECTIVES

Research & Development ⟷ Production & Distribution ⟷ Sales & Marketing ⟷ Customer Service ⟷ Administrative Support

Automate test processes to shorten prototype time to production

Improve equipment uptime

Get accurate market data

Anticipate customer needs by surveying

Finance: have funds available

Team with engineering to shorten redesigns

Reengineer processes to reduce rework

Bring customers in to work with R&D

Refer customer preferences to Sales R&D/Production

Shorten process cycle times to speed operations

Hire business intelligence

HUMAN CAPITAL MANAGEMENT ACTIONS AND OBJECTIVES

Acquisition ⟷ Maintenance ⟷ Development ⟷ Retention

Shorten hiring time to start

Shorten process cycle time for pay and benefits

Shorten response time on training

Involve employees in "time" goal solutions

Figure 5-3. Sample human capital-to-enterprise pathway for world-class customer service.

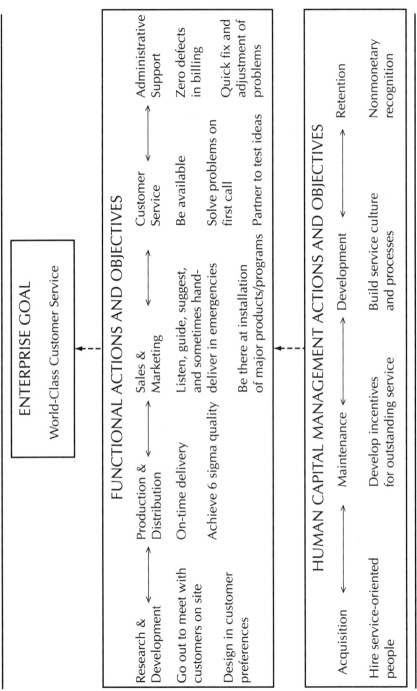

ENTERPRISE GOAL

World-Class Customer Service

FUNCTIONAL ACTIONS AND OBJECTIVES

Research & Development ⟷ Production & Distribution ⟷ Sales & Marketing ⟷ Customer Service ⟷ Administrative Support

Go out to meet with customers on site — On-time delivery — Listen, guide, suggest, and sometimes hand-deliver in emergencies — Be available — Zero defects in billing

Design in customer preferences — Achieve 6 sigma quality — Be there at installation of major products/programs — Solve problems on first call; Partner to test ideas — Quick fix and adjustment of problems

HUMAN CAPITAL MANAGEMENT ACTIONS AND OBJECTIVES

Acquisition ⟷ Maintenance ⟷ Development ⟷ Retention

Hire service-oriented people — Develop incentives for outstanding service — Build service culture and processes — Nonmonetary recognition

Figure 5-4. Sample human capital-to-enterprise pathway for employer of choice.

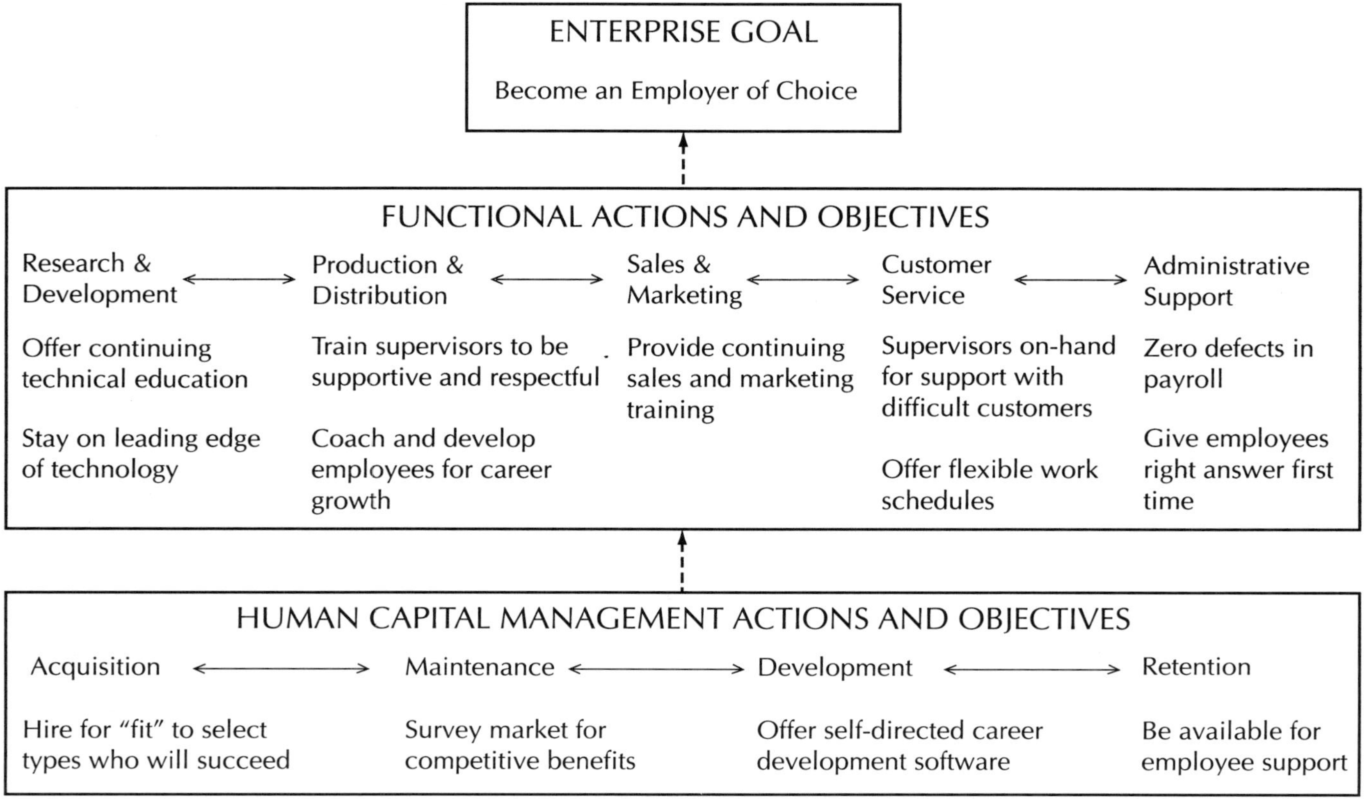

ENTERPRISE GOAL

Become an Employer of Choice

FUNCTIONAL ACTIONS AND OBJECTIVES

Research & Development	Production & Distribution	Sales & Marketing	Customer Service	Administrative Support
Offer continuing technical education	Train supervisors to be supportive and respectful	Provide continuing sales and marketing training	Supervisors on-hand for support with difficult customers	Zero defects in payroll
Stay on leading edge of technology	Coach and develop employees for career growth		Offer flexible work schedules	Give employees right answer first time

HUMAN CAPITAL MANAGEMENT ACTIONS AND OBJECTIVES

Acquisition	Maintenance	Development	Retention
Hire for "fit" to select types who will succeed	Survey market for competitive benefits	Offer self-directed career development software	Be available for employee support

sition, maintenance, development, and retention of human assets (employees):

- *Acquisition.* Reduce the number of days required to obtain a quality hire for the requesting department. Ensure that jobs are filled promptly and production is not adversely affected. *Measure:* Average number of days for time to start. You can assume that quality is constant or periodically test for it.

- *Maintenance.* Improve process efficiency in compensation, benefits, and payroll so that it does not interfere with operating imperatives. Processing salary increases and benefits claims promptly supports employee morale and reduces time wasted by employees tracing their missing pay or unpaid claims. *Measure:* Average time to complete selected key processes. You can also track employee satisfaction with pay and benefits processing.

- *Development.* Shorten time to respond with appropriate training, development, or consultative services. Upgrade skills, enabling employees to produce at the required level. *Measure:* Time to deliver program. Later, measure the effect of the acquired skill on business unit performance to validate the program's value.

- *Retention.* Involve employees with the enterprise time imperative through communication and counseling programs (quickly), thereby bonding them to it. *Measure:* Time to implement the programs. Later, assess the impact on employee commitment to timeliness.

Summary

If human capital services are provided as outlined above, quantitative connections can be made between some of the human capital management results and the outcomes of the affected functional departments. One way to do this is to apply the process value analysis model described in Chapter 3. As we move from one imperative to another (e.g., time to service), the question becomes, Which is more important? Treacy and Wiersema argue that companies have to have one primary imperative: product leadership, customer intimacy, or operational excellence.[1] Their position is that no one can be number one in all three areas. Companies must choose their primary competitive edge and do the best they can in the other two. Not everyone agrees. Many argue that a company can eagerly pursue two or three simultaneously. Yet the evidence is relatively consistent that most great companies are great because of one of the three imperatives. In its heyday, IBM dominated the market with service, even though competitors offered equal or better technology. Hewlett-Packard was always the engineer's company. Its products were top of the line. Wal-Mart's initial rise came out of operating excellence, specifically inventory management. This is an argument with no winner, although it seems in the end that one imperative will eventually emerge as the prime driver.

CASE 2: ENTERPRISE GOAL: INCREASE CUSTOMER SATISFACTION

Value: Customer satisfaction can be assessed through surveys and interviews. More important, it can be measured through customer retention, account penetration, and account profitability indices.

Imperative: Management realizes that the customer truly is king. Competition—domestic and international—has forced all firms to focus employees on customer service.

Human capital management applies the service criterion to human resources department services:

- *Acquisition.* Develop a hiring profile to identify applicants who have a service mentality and value system. *Measure:* Service-oriented interviews and questionnaires can be scaled to yield scores that tell how closely we are hiring to the desired profile.
- *Maintenance.* Design incentive programs for excellent customer service. For example, in units that have an impact on customer satisfaction and retention, monetary incentives can be offered. *Measure:* Satisfaction and retention-level improvements can be weighed against the amount of incentives paid.
- *Development.* Determine the elements inherent in a service-

oriented culture. Communicate that to other human resources units and to managers and supervisors by incorporating it into all training programs, no matter the topic. *Measure:* In time, employee surveys will tell how far the culture has moved in the desired direction. This is a slow-moving, long-term change.

- *Retention.* Design nonmonetary recognition programs for excellent customer service. Also, support development's culture program through employee counseling and supervisor coaching. *Measure:* Track the number of persons who receive recognition awards and the effects of the improved customer service.

Summary

Human capital management is critical to sustained customer service excellence. Incentives typically yield short-term effects. It is necessary to inculcate service into the workforce as everyone's primary responsibility. This is directed by customer service management and supported by human resources programs. The system starts with service of internal customers. Since processes flow horizontally through organizations, the output of one department is the input of another. In effect, every department has internal customers. Measures of customer satisfaction can be taken across the company as well as externally. One way of promoting good internal service is to put cross-functional teams together. These teams not only get work done but also teach everyone on the team, by personal experience, the value of collaboration. Organizations that practice good internal customer service become highly efficient and set themselves on the road to becoming employers of choice. This is one of many human capital management truisms that most people know intuitively but forget to practice daily. It's also another example of the interaction among organizational activities and functions.

Case 3: Enterprise Goal: Become an Employer of Choice (EoC)

Value: The ability to attract and retain top talent is reflected in organizational effectiveness and eventually in financial performance.

Imperative: The talent shortage in America is not going away. Population demographics prove it. Those who wish to be in the top echelons of their industry must focus on making their workplace as attractive as possible.

Human capital management focuses on the issues that drive persons to apply to, join, and stay with an organization. This is a more complex problem than the previous cases. Since EoC is a multifaceted, idiosyncratic issue for each organization, no single, direct service or program will achieve the goal. In essence, you are looking at culture change. EoC is more than pay, special benefits, and recreational programs. It demands actions on the part of all employees from the CEO down to entry level.

- *Acquisition.* Conduct research to learn what makes an employer attractive to the type of talent your organization seeks. Most employees share common basic interests, but once you move beyond those there are diverse needs. A fast-paced versus a stable environment, a technological versus a marketing orientation, a cooperative versus a competitive atmosphere, company size and location, degree of flexibility, and many other variables attract different types of people. Profiles can be drawn and a staffing strategy launched to draw your type. An efficient and empathetic hiring process tops off the program. *Measure:* Degree to which you are attracting the people who score high on your profile.

- *Maintenance.* Survey people regarding their benefit needs. Day care, work-hour flexibility, telecommuting, recreation, and health care plans all have their customers. Selecting a flexible set of benefits that people can choose from to fulfill their needs helps the recruiting and retention process. *Measure:* Surveys of employee needs, focus groups, and interviews yield satisfaction data.

- *Development.* Offer career development services. Professional-level employees are very interested in career paths. Lower-level employees can also be shown that there is no ceiling for ambitious types. Self-administered career planning software and counseling follow-up is a cost-effective way to show people that you care about them. *Measure:* Promotion rates, performance scores, and turnover rates are all prime indicators of how employees are moving through the organization and how they see the organization as a place to work. Measures of diversity also indicate how attractive your organization is to all segments of the workforce.

- *Retention.* Survey general employment needs. This can be anything from pay to supervisory support, corporate leadership, advancement opportunity, tolerance for change, coworker relationships, physical work environment, and so forth. *Measure:* Degree to which the organization can comply with the needs expressed in the survey.

Summary

All visible actions are susceptible to measurement. The only question is, How deep do you want to go? An EoC program is not a single profile. As this book goes to press, there is a need for large-scale, longitudinal studies of what EoC really implies. The prime question is, Does EoC mean the same thing across industries and geographic regions? Is it the same profile in an economically depressed area as it is in a hotbed of commercial activity? Another question that has yet to be answered definitively is, How does it affect financial results? This type of research cannot yield definite answers in six months. It may need a year or more before we can say that we truly understand this phenomenon's complexity.

An Integrated Reporting System

Now that we have established the pathways, you understand how to move deductively from the enterprise level down to functional objectives and human capital management responses and move inductively back up the levels. Assume for the sake of example that you have set up such a process. Now, you can track selected high-priority activities and watch the change in the metrics at each level. The bad news is that when you stretch such a system across a total organization, monitoring the outputs can become an onerous chore. You need to proceed with caution. Having set up measurement systems around the world for over twenty years, I can tell you that there are three things that eventually kill them:

1. The amount of work involved in collecting the data on a timely basis
2. Finding a way to report the data that makes them easy to understand
3. Sustaining management's commitment to the system

Taking these in order, the only way to solve the first problem is to computerize. We do not have a scarcity of data, but we do have difficulty collecting it easily. Fortunately, there are a number of data extraction tools coming on the market that will greatly reduce the manual labor involved in data collection. That will be the first blow in breaking through the wall of apathy around data management for staff functions.

Second, automated reports have to be designed that are simple and explicit and focus the readers on the key issues without burying them in mountains of secondary data. Again, available data is not the problem. Cutting the mountain down to bedrock is the challenge. Graphics are helpful, so long as they are used wisely and not as a substitute for focus. A graph that is irrelevant is no help. Fortunately, new methods of data display are coming out all the time to help us. Displays are important, because at heart, we are all still impressed with color and movement. Software programs now use color to signal tolerance levels. These displays are typically called a *dashboard*. There are many variations on the layout, but the principle is the same. If performance is within tolerable levels, the light on the dial is green. If it is moving a bit in the wrong direction but is not too far off, the light turns yellow. And if the performance level is way off, the light goes to red. Furthermore, the latest extraction tools give us the ability to instantaneously hop from one set of variables to another and show us in green, yellow, and red when the results have moved from acceptable to unacceptable levels.

Finally, top management has a short attention span for anything that is not tightly focused and explicitly displayed.

This is understandable, since the higher one goes in the organization, the more entities one has to manage and the more complex are the issues. This puts a premium on specificity and brevity. To maintain management's support for human capital performance metrics, we need to show managers issues that are important to them and not bury them in data for the sake of data. Consistently, I see reports coming out of human resources departments that are waaaaay too big. Since human resources people prefer narrative over numbers, they tend to publish a volume of text with a minimum of quantitative displays. It must go in the opposite direction: lots of graphics with a minimum of annotation. I always caution clients to publish only the most important aspects of the most important issues. If the audience wants more, it will tell you.

> Top management has a short attention span for anything that is not tightly focused and explicitly explained. We need to show them issues that are important to them and not bury them in data.

Figure 5-5 is an example of the dashboard idea. Using the time-to-market example, I have laid in a model of three blank metric lines and circles per function. The lines represent the metric title, and the circles need a color indicator. I am not prescribing three metrics for each function. Every company is different, and imperatives change over time, making it necessary to add or remove certain metrics. Essentially, this is a sample template that needs filling in.

Dashboards can be set for monthly or quarterly snapshots by using the lighted dial method. For progress reporting against targeted objectives, a thermometer-type graphic can be designed. You can even run the thermometer horizontally if that suits you better. The choice of graphic representation depends on the preferences of the readers.

Looking Ahead: Leading Indicators

Assuming for now that we have a workable system for measuring the impact of current human capital management on in-

Figure 5-5. Enterprise dashboard template.

Enterprise Goal: Shorten Time to Market by 12 Months

Functional Objectives

R&D	Production	Distribution	Sales	Marketing	Customer Service	Information Services	Accounting
1. ─ ○	1. ─ ○	1. ─ ○	1. ─ ○	1. ─ ○	1. ─ ○	1. ─ ○	1. ─ ○
2. ─ ○	2. ─ ○	2. ─ ○	2. ─ ○	2. ─ ○	2. ─ ○	2. ─ ○	2. ─ ○
3. ─ ○	3. ─ ○	3. ─ ○	3. ─ ○	3. ─ ○	3. ─ ○	3. ─ ○	3. ─ ○

Human Capital Objectives

Acquire	Maintain	Develop	Retain
1. ─ ○	1. ─ ○	1. ─ ○	1. ─ ○
2. ─ ○	2. ─ ○	2. ─ ○	2. ─ ○
3. ─ ○	3. ─ ○	3. ─ ○	3. ─ ○

termediate functional objectives and the ultimate enterprise goals, what about the future? Given the rate of change in today's market and the continual increase in competition, windows of opportunity open and close rapidly. By definition, financial measures are lagging indicators of an organization's state. Looking backward through accounting lenses is not sufficient, since they restrict our view to internal happenings of the past. It is imperative that we have some sense of how prepared we are to meet the challenges of the future. Part of being prepared is to have flexible policies and structures that can be shifted rapidly to meet emerging customer demands and exploit the opportunities of the marketplace. Another way to prepare is to have a workforce that is skilled and stable and can move quickly. There are enterprise, functional, and human capital metrics that can be developed and monitored to give management an idea of how well the enterprise is prepared for the unforeseeable.

Enterprise Futures

The future of the enterprise is the sum of the future of the functional and human capital levels. Top management can set future goals, but if the future capability doesn't exist below it, this will be an exercise in frustration. An element of the future was embedded in Figure 2-3 when I presented the corporate human capital scorecard.

The two principal enterprise-level futures are shown in the financial column. They are human economic value added (HEVA) and human capital market value (HCMV). First, if the company's balance sheet (economic value added is balance sheet–oriented) is in a free fall, we are in a heap of trouble. Our ability to fund short-term emergencies or long-term growth from borrowings will be severely if not totally diminished. Lenders will tell us by withholding funds that they doubt our ability to sustain a viable business. Our ability to offer commercial paper will be diminished, and our bond ratings will sink. If this goes on long enough, the operative word is *bankruptcy*.

Second, if our market to book value is dropping precipitously, the market is telling us that it is losing faith in our ability to perform in the future. The stock market is the biggest gambling table in the world. Smart gamblers (read investors) are not investing based on what we did last year or last quarter; they are betting on the next turn of the economic wheel. Which way will the economy go? Which way will the stock market go? And which way will our performance go? If they don't like the looks of the future, they don't bet, and our stock loses its luster. As our stock price falls, the value of stock option incentives declines, and their employee holding power diminishes. Typically, the top managerial, sales, and technical talent has stock options. The loss of those people can seriously undermine a company's ability to meet future challenges, even if it is profitable today. Income statement figures seldom display any direct links to the future unless they are in extremis, in which case they are a sign that the whole bloody enterprise is about to sink.

Functional Futures

The functional units depend on human capital to attain their objectives. As we already know, all nonhuman assets of the organization are inert (so are some of the human assets). People leverage them to achieve their mission and produce profits. Therefore, leading indicators should be focused on the characteristics of the workforce. To the experienced eye, they paint a picture of how well we are positioned for the future. The metrics cover issues such as preparedness, competence, job satisfaction, commitment, and depletion. They can be viewed on their own merit or combined with financial measures of human capital at the enterprise level to create an enterprise scorecard. This scorecard can be developed in the dashboard format discussed earlier. Figure 5-6 is a sampling of leading indicators that can be helpful on a regular or intermittent basis. Use it to stimulate your imagination and generate others.

Figure 5-6. Leading indicators.

Human Capital Competence Level
  Percentage of key employees who have met competence standards

Human Capital Readiness Level
  Percentage of key positions with at least one fully qualified person ready

Human Capital Commitment Level
  Percentage of employees expecting to stay at least three years

Human Capital Satisfaction Level
  Percentage of employees scoring in top quartile of job satisfaction survey

Corporate Climate
  Percentage of employees who indicate concern with culture and climate

Human Capital Depletion Rate and Cost
  Voluntary separations as a percentage of head count and the cost of separations

Be Prepared

There are two measures of preparedness: competence and readiness. The competence level is simply the percentage of people who have demonstrated the skill and knowledge that make them able to meet current and near-term future performance requirements in their current jobs. Competence became a much-talked-about topic in the last half of the 1990s. Since it has gained so much attention, I believe that it is useful to provide background and definition.

The concept of competence sprang from David McClellan's pioneering work for the United States Information Office in the early 1970s. He was charged with determining which were the critical competencies for the successful performance of a field service information officer, a position that functioned in a wide variety of geographic, political, and ethnic settings around the world. To make a long story short, he was able to accomplish the task by focusing on the person in the job rather than on background factors such as education or aptitude test scores. From that came the first standardized definition of the term *competency:* "A competency is an underlying characteristic of an individual that is causally related to criterion-referenced effective or superior performance in a job or situation.[2]

Criterion-referenced is a fancy way of saying that a given competency actually predicts behavior and performance. When you cut through the jargon, this is what we want to be able to do in selecting and developing people for jobs in our companies. It is logical that if we could identify competencies for key jobs, then we could test the incumbents to agree on how many are average and how many are superior. Target levels could be established and tracked.

This metric could be monitored as we work with people to bring them up to full speed. From it, we would know two things: where we stand today, and how well we are prepared for the foreseeable future. So long as there is no drastic change in the character of a job, the required competencies should not change materially.

The competencies are also precursors and requirements for the next level of preparedness measurement, which is bench strength or succession. I call this the readiness level. This is the percentage of key positions with at least one fully qualified (competent) person ready to take over now. Applying the readiness criterion to all key positions yields a picture of the organization's general human capital health. Just as vital medical signs tell us how fit a person is, and therefore how vulnerable he or she is to disease, readiness tells us how vulnerable the enterprise corpus is to the onslaught of future competitiveness. If we have people who can step in and take over at a moment's notice, we will probably experience fewer slowdowns in the event of unforeseen emergencies. This cadre of qualified personnel can also be mobilized quickly for problem solving, team projects, or new market opportunities.

For readiness, it is again a case of the percentage of people who have demonstrated their capability to step into a position above them on short notice. The future is unpredictable. We never know when a key talent will decide to leave or will need to be transferred to support another initiative. Clearly, if we have backup talent ready to step in immediately, we are more ready for the future than if we have a void for any significant period of time. The one unequivocal demand is a clear description of the required capabilities. It is no sense fooling ourselves into thinking that we are ready when we actually aren't.

The two preparedness measures—competence and readiness—are testable against a set of standards that you establish. If you detail the requirements for key jobs, it should be a simple matter to assess how close the incumbents are to attaining them.

Employee Mind-Sets

A second set of predictors deals with the veiled attitudes and feelings of our workforce. Indicators of the mind-set of the workforce are important. They uncover a hidden view of what we might consider undercurrents or background concerns. It doesn't take a great deal of imagination to foresee that dissatisfied employees or employees who have concerns about the culture are unlikely candidates for longevity awards. Very seldom do employees tell us directly that they are unsatisfied. They give subtle signals such as solemn faces, not volunteering for projects, being absent, or working at a slower pace than normal. One sure way of tapping into the mind-set of the workforce is to look around the offices and see how many people are still there an hour after quitting time. If the place is empty and the parking lot has no cars in it, we have a problem. When people are unhappy, the easiest way for them to express their displeasure is to withhold effort. High levels of absenteeism are a concrete sign that something is on people's minds. These half-hidden concerns can be turned up through surveys, interviews, or informal discussion groups. Surveys are useful because they produce structured data unfiltered by another person.

Surveys of commitment, job satisfaction, and culture and

climate yield data points that can be tracked periodically. Many companies tap this well once a year. That is usually sufficient, provided you do two things. First, during the time between surveys, keep your eyes and ears open. As you know from experience, problems don't occur overnight. There is usually a series of frustrations that build up over time. The cliché of management by walking around has a kernel of value in it if you pay attention to the subtle signs that employees are continually putting forth. The second absolutely critical requirement is that when you do conduct an employee survey, you provide prompt feedback to the respondents. If you are not committed to dealing with uncomfortable information from below, don't ask for it.

Indirect Sign

There is another two-part indicator that is not necessarily a direct leading metric but is useful to monitor and stimulate action before a major loss occurs. It is depletion rate and cost. I already discussed separation rate in Chapter 2 as part of the human capital enterprise scorecard. Now I want to take another look at it as a leading indicator. I grant you that the separation rate is an indicator of past action. The employees have voted with their feet already. But if the rate is increasing, it is a sure sign that trouble lies ahead.

Normally, departures are called turnover or separations. Bontis refers to voluntary terminations as depletions of human capital, which gives us a different perspective.[3] First, let's focus on voluntary separations rather than total separations, because totals include involuntary separations resulting from management's decision to cull unneeded or unsatisfactory labor. One could make the argument that downsizing to reduce fixed costs is depletion. But if we needed the people in order to be profitable, we wouldn't have let them go. The conclusion must be that we did not deplete our human capital capability bank.

In effect, every time the organization loses a person it

would rather keep, its stock of human capital is depleted. There are at least two ways to avoid or reduce such depletions. One is to run surveys on a regular basis and to act on the results. That is the proactive method for handling it. The other is to employ an outside professional firm after the fact to conduct exit interviews with departed employees. When these are well done, they yield a wealth of information that can be used to avoid further losses.

The best way to become motivated to do this is to calculate the cost of turnover or human capital depletion. Saratoga Institute's research has shown that the loss of a competent exempt-level person typically costs the equivalent of at least one year's pay and benefits for that position. Note that these calculations do not include effects on customers, which are potentially additional costs. The point is: At today's compensation level, if you lose ten professionals, it will cost you $1 million, plus unknown outside losses. Ask yourself this question: How much do you have to sell to produce a pretax profit of $1 million?

> If you are continually having to break in new people, there is no way that your company can be highly competitive.

The bottom line on depletion rate and cost is that unwanted turnover not only costs you today; it leaves you vulnerable in the short run for tomorrow. If you are continually having to break in new people, there is no way that your company can be highly competitive.

Competitiveness

Finally, in addition to the list in Figure 5-6, a composite metric can be developed that can be described as a competitiveness measure. Rather than give you a pat definition, let me pose a question. From a human capital standpoint, what would you have to do, have, or be to be able to claim a certain level of competitiveness? That takes a minute to establish, doesn't it?

So, what does competitiveness consist of from a human capital standpoint?

I believe that it would contain the data points listed earlier; competence, readiness, employee satisfaction, commitment, climate, compensation levels, separation rates, and perhaps something else unique to your company. If you and I were to sit down together, I am certain that we could come up with a superordinate metric that describes your ability to compete in the human capital marketplace. We could call it a competitiveness index. This type of metric shows how prepared your company is to compete in the near-term future. The last variable, company-unique factors, is yours to develop.

The individual measures of competence, readiness, employee satisfaction, commitment, and climate cannot be taken every month or even every quarter. The same is true for a competitiveness index. Separation rates are objective and can be monitored each month.

The world is a mix of the objective and subjective. Movement in any or all of these indices helps explain corporate performance trends. If we see negativism in any of them, it would probably be a precursor of problems to come in turnover, further damaging employee productivity and customer service. One of the shortcomings of accounting is that it deliberately does not include perceptual data. Accounting can alert management to impending cash shortages but not to foreseeable human capital problems, which are much more difficult to solve. We can go to the bank, borrow cash, and put it to full use immediately. It takes a good bit more effort and a much longer time line to acquire key talent, infuse them with new skills, and make them fully effective. Adding the perceptual element aids in focusing management on the more complex human side.

You could make the competitiveness index a semiannual adjunct to your human capital enterprise scorecard. Collectively, these would tell you how you were doing financially, structurally, and competitively from a human capital management standpoint. Along with that, your data from the operating processes and human resources service levels would make you more knowledgeable than your competition by a couple of light-years.

Human Capital Management Futures

At the bottom of it all are the foundation activities to support the functional units. As I pointed out in Chapter 4, the human resources department should be leading this activity. Working with its management and employee *customers*, human resources hires, pays, supports, develops, and assists in retaining the organization's human capital. There is plenty of data available, some inside and some outside, that the human resources department should be monitoring and placing on a futures board. Examples from human resources activities are as follows.

Talent Availability Trends (Acquisition Function)

The Bureau of Labor Statistics and various other federal agencies and private organizations study and publish labor trends. Unemployment level, workforce population trends, absence and turnover rates, part-time versus full-time employment ratios, visa regulations, and other indices provide a picture of what is happening and what may be coming. These types of measures could be tracked individually and then presented as an index number on the futures scoreboard.

Salary and Benefit Surveys (Maintenance Function)

Pay rate and benefit program comparisons and trends within an industry or region give you an idea of the movement of employee costs. This is factored into annual budget building, which is a crystal-ball exercise if there ever was one. With a workforce whose needs are dynamic, it behooves everyone to constantly monitor what types of benefit programs will support hiring and retention. Again, pay and benefits could be put into a single number and reported as total labor cost.

Investments in Training and Education (Development Function)

The knowledge economy demands constant learning. Hence, a company's investment in all forms of employee development is an effective predictor of future human capital capability. This includes all types of training courses, career development services, and all outside education, including tuition reimbursement benefits. Arguably, supervisory coaching, mentoring, and on-the-job experience are the most effective development processes. However, it is difficult to extract and collect the cost of these activities. It is doable, but beyond the scope of this paragraph to describe. The easiest metrics to capture are training investment as a percentage of payroll or as a percentage of revenue. Since these activities are a mix of quantitative and qualitative, they should probably be reported as two separate data points. Mentoring might be a good catch-all for the qualitative and investment dollars for the quantitative.

Workforce Values and Needs (Retention Function)

Nothing helps retain talent so much as addressing people's personal issues. Interim Services developed a standard method for assessing workforce values that was tested in two national surveys.[4] The study focused on the direction of change in employee values. It dealt with a number of variables that have a futures implication. The list includes attitudes toward loyalty, management style, job duties, performance and rewards, advancement, career opportunities, the work environment, and change, among others. As a rearguard action, exit interviews can be conducted by an objective outside party to find out why people became dissatisfied and why they eventually left. These values can be grouped into composites such as management, opportunity, or culture and climate. Since this is a new idea, you can construct it any way that suits your needs. The important point is to have a valid and reliable telescope through which to view the future.

Figure 5-7 is a cutout example from Figure 5-5, showing how the future's dashboard might look. In addition to the enterprise-level indicators of HEVA and HCMV, I've selected four of the eight functions and the four human capital arenas and put in examples of the topics that could be displayed. These are only basic suggestions to stimulate your imagination. I'm certain that you and your colleagues can come up with a set that serves your needs.

Scoreboarding Overview

Because accounting looks only backward, many managers are forced to operate more through a rearview mirror than through a windshield. This accounts for the fact that so many companies suddenly find themselves unprepared. They can't fund a response to a competitor's unexpected move, can't support new product development with people or facilities, or can't stop the outflow of talent whose stock options are suddenly underwater. The point is that the future is a lot harder to understand and prepare for than the past. That may sound like a non sequitur, but you get the point.

Of course, you can add whatever suits your special needs. We are building a new method of accountability together, and as yet, there are no generally accepted accounting principles. When we reach a point where hundreds of companies are practicing this as an essential way of doing business, a standard system will develop so that people can benchmark themselves against the marketplace. Until then, you are free to be creative without fear of violating some arbitrary standard. The FASB is unlikely to get involved so long as the attitude is that

> You are free to be creative without violating some arbitrary standard. It is better to be approximately right than precisely wrong.

Figure 5-7. Enterprise futures dashboard template.

Enterprise

HEVA $ ——— ◯   HCMV $ ——— ◯

Function

Production	*Sales*	*Customer Service*	*Information Services*
1. Readiness ——— ◯	1. Readiness ——— ◯	1. Readiness ——— ◯	1. Readiness ——— ◯
2. Commitment ——— ◯	2. Commitment ——— ◯	2. Commitment ——— ◯	2. Commitment ——— ◯
3. Depletion ——— ◯	3. Depletion ——— ◯	3. Depletion ——— ◯	3. Depletion ——— ◯
4. Satisfaction ——— ◯	4. Satisfaction ——— ◯	4. Satisfaction ——— ◯	4. Satisfaction ——— ◯
5. Culture ——— ◯	5. Culture ——— ◯	5. Culture ——— ◯	5. Culture ——— ◯

Human Capital

Acquire	*Maintain*	*Develop*	*Retain*
1. Talent Availability Index ——— ◯	1. Total Labor $ Cost Index ——— ◯	1. Mentoring Index ——— ◯	1. Management Index ——— ◯
		2. Investment $ ——— ◯	2. Opportunity Index ——— ◯
			3. Climate Index ——— ◯

Note: Except where indicated, the values would be expressed in percentages or index numbers.

if the asset isn't a piece of real estate, inventory, cash, or equipment, it can't be measured. One of the best arguments for the value of measuring intangibles comes from the early work on intellectual capital when someone said, "It is better to be approximately right than precisely wrong." Traditional accounting is precisely the wrong thing when one looks to the future.

Summary

The underlying theme of the book and this chapter is the connection between human capital management and organizational outcomes. This chapter shows the total outline, with the basic pathways from the human capital level, through functional business units, to the enterprise goals. Step by step, we see examples of how an action at the first level should have a measurable effect on business unit operations. These, in turn, contribute to the strategic goals of the organization.

The process reaches its culmination with an example of integrated dashboards and a futures dashboard template. These do not take the place of standard reports. Rather, their purpose is to provide management at middle and top levels with a sharply focused report on the state of key human capital and process goals and objectives. Since executives have a large number of units to supervise, they need a quick-look model that tells them at a glance where there might be trouble spots. By having both accounting's backward report on recent results and human capital measurement's forward view of what might be coming, management has a better sense of what to do next to develop or maintain a competitive advantage.

References

1. Michael Treacy and Fred Wiersema, *The Discipline of Market Leaders* (Reading, Mass.: Addison-Wesley, 1995).

2. Lyle M. Spencer and Signe Spencer, *Competence at Work* (New York: John Wiley & Sons, 1993), p. 9.
3. Nick Bontis, "Human Capital Valuation," Working Paper, Saratoga Institute, 1999.
4. Emerging Workforce Values Study 1997–1998, Interim Services, Fort Lauderdale, Fla. (copies available through Interim or the Saratoga Institute).

6

The Next Generation of Human Capital Valuation

Trends, Forecasts, and Predictions

In October 1996, doctors predicted that Lance Armstrong would be dead from cancer in less than six months. In July 1999, he won the Tour de France.

Prediction is a fine but dangerous art. If anyone really knew with certainty what was going to happen tomorrow, much less a year or more from now, that person's advice would be prohibitively expensive. I don't claim for a moment to know with certainty what will happen tomorrow around human capital management. But I do know something about the variables and how they interact in predictable ways most of the time. From this, we can risk projecting future events with a better-than-average degree of success.

Relationships and Patterns

You've heard the old saying: He has twenty years' experience at the company—one year repeated nineteen times. Doing something over and over does not necessarily equate with understanding the intricacies of the task. Likewise, measuring something over and over does not necessarily guarantee that anything is learned from each iteration. Often, we do tasks the same way each time simply because we give the motions no thought. There is a story that makes the point: A man observes that every time his wife prepares a roast, she cuts two inches off the end before putting it in the roasting pan and inserting it into the oven. When he asks his beloved why she does this, she replies, "My mother always did it this way." At the next opportunity he asks his mother-in-law why she did that. The lady answers, "Because I had a small roasting pan."

In that case, the wife simply followed her mother's example without ever inquiring why she did it that way. Many of us do this: unconsciously follow an instruction or example without thinking about the rationale behind it. There are several reasons for this. Among them is fear of contesting an authority figure, whether it be Mom, our boss, or a so-called expert. Another is resistance to change. It is easier to do it the accustomed way than to spend energy thinking of another way. How many times have I done something the old way rather than take the time to reset or revise the process so that I could do it more easily in the future? And if you think I am going to read the bloody manual, you're crazy. Frustration is another barrier. Maybe we tried to do it a different way and were told, "That isn't the way we do things around here." Then there is apathy. Some people simply don't care. In business, people's common retort when asked why they are doing something a certain way is, "I just work here. They don't pay me to think." As my wife has testified many times upon returning from a shopping trip, "They don't have to say it, you can see it in their attitude." Their sad but all too common retort is an example of doing without learning—and obviously without caring. If we apply that to measuring human capital performance, we learn nothing through mere repetition. There is a better way. I call it looking for patterns.

We've established in previous chapters that there is a connection, an interdependency, between and among human capital activities, between and among functional processes, and between human capital management outputs and functional process outcomes. Logically, we should expect to see correlations between and among some of the many variables inside those activities, processes, and outcomes. If we look for them, we will find them. Once these correlations have been established at any consistent rate of occurrence, we should be able to make tentative predictions.

Now comes the problem: Things are not always what they seem to be. Just when you thought I was going to be profound, I fall back on a cliché. I'm sorry if I disappointed you, but clichés are often an effective way to startle us into peering through our biases or misperceptions. As my mother once told me after I explained in great detail all the things I was learning in a psychology seminar, "It seems like common sense to me."

Fallacies in Trend Identification

In the research business, we are always looking under the covers of data for patterns. This is what we have to sell. If we can find a valid trend, we can package it and sell it to people who want to understand their company, market, or region better. This inner drive of researchers often leads them to espouse a directionality that doesn't exist. It also pushes them to infer causality that is not sustainable.

Stephen Jay Gould, a paleontologist who writes so beautifully that I read his books for the language as much as for the content, has written a marvelous treatise about data analysis that a layperson can understand.[1] An interesting side note that is relevant to my point is that Gould and Ed Purcell (a Nobel laureate in physics), both of whom are baseball fanatics, once conducted an exhaustive study of baseball streaks and slumps. They found that all such runs fell within reasonable probability except for one solitary instance: Joe DiMaggio's fifty-six-game hitting streak in 1941. According to probability statistics, it should not have happened at all. Thus, it is the greatest achievement in modern baseball, if not all sports. What few people know is that the day after his streak was broken, he started another that lasted seventeen games. Imagine a seventy-four game streak! Before that, he had a sixty-one-game hitting streak in the minors. Thank you, Joltin' Joe. I am indebted to Gould for the following dissertation on the complex but fascinating issue of data analysis, to which I have added my views.

Finding Meaning

We are prone to read patterns into sequences of events because we are looking for meaning in our lives. Yet to the untrained eye, there is little sense of how often a pattern will or should emerge from random data. Gould illustrates this with coin flipping. Since the probability of heads is always one in two, or one-half, the chance of flipping five heads in a row is $\frac{1}{2} \times \frac{1}{2} \times \frac{1}{2} \times \frac{1}{2} \times \frac{1}{2}$ or one in thirty-two flips. This is rare, but it happens occasionally simply through randomness. No one can predict when that rare sequence might occur, but when it does, we might think that we are on a "hot streak" if we are betting heads against the flipper. If, after a couple more trials, the flipper produced a run of five tails in a row, we would think that the person was cheating somehow, even if he wasn't. As Gould points out, people have been shot over such innocent occurrences.

Another fallacy about trends is perpetrated when people correctly discover a directionality in events but then assume that something else moving in parallel must be the cause or the effect. Mixing correlation with causality is the stuff of the naïve, of charlatans, and of demagogues. Politicians, religious fanatics, and consultants are masters at this. As my consultant friend Gus Bigos says, "Anything that is not provably wrong is arguably right." In any system there is variation. The apparent trends can be nothing more than random expansions or contractions of the natural variation within a system. Nothing runs in a straight line, or along a predictable curve, for long. To add even more unpredictability to the mix, two things running in the same system will occa-

> Mixing correlation with causality is the stuff of the naïve, of charlatans, and of demagogues. Politicians, religious fanatics, and consultants are masters at this.

(text continues on page 178)

sionally coincide for no apparent reason. This is why we cannot ever *prove* anything. Even in the controlled atmosphere of the laboratory, we don't try to prove our hypothesis. We only try to disprove the null hypothesis—that is, that the effects we observed are apparently not caused by forces other than our treatment 95 percent of the time (.05 level of confidence). This is as close as we try to get in the lab. So imagine how much less proof there is available in the field, the so-called real world, where nothing is controllable. (I must add that in medical or pharmacological research, which deals with matters of health, the level of confidence must be much higher—in the neighborhood of 99 percent or greater during repeated trials.)

Over the years, I have witnessed the arrival and departure of many products in the business market that allegedly claimed correlations, if not also causation. One of the most popular exercises has been the attempt to correlate employee activity and human resources programs with financial results. The best-practice craze lent support to the search for this Holy Grail—namely, the value of people in business. Published stories of isolated events claimed to be revealing generalizable paths to financial performance. Not a single one of them has ever been proved to work.

The latest flawed attempt at validity centers on gathering management attitudes toward a set of mixed, arbitrary, often overlapping, subjective issues, simultaneously ignoring quantitative performance records, and then promising to draw correlations with creation of shareholder value. This is one of the more blatant ruses I've seen. Even if a set of opinions about programs, employees, applicants, systems, and what have you did correlate to some degree with the movement of shareholder value, it is ludicrous to claim more than coincidence. Finally, carrying this ruse to the ridiculous, to take one sample in time and make claims of general validity is almost criminal. There are so many reasons why this is bogus that I won't even attempt to list them. Opinions do not correlate with anything other than the opinion-giver's own biases. So, let's call it what it is: a very thinly veiled attempt to sell consulting services.

Business Applications

Taking business events as examples of correlations and causation, there are a multitude of variables that coalesce in sales, operating expense, and profitability. All the people and things inside the enterprise plus the people and things outside of it that can affect sales, expense, or profit are in constant movement. At any moment, there can be an aligning of two variables, such as increasing pay and increasing sales. Although both might be moving in the same direction—correlation—there may be absolutely no causality involved. Sales can rise for many reasons that have nothing to do with the incentive pay plan for salespeople. To infer that the new pay plan caused sales to increase is premature until we check out and eliminate the other possible causes. Among those other drivers that must be examined are our product compared with the competition's in terms of price, performance, reliability, deliverability, and service, plus the personal relationships of seller to buyer. The movement of any single variable or combination of variables could affect sales in either direction.

Congratulating the sales force without checking other possibilities can cause problems. We might even go so far as to give an extra bonus for outstanding performance only to learn later that the increase was due to a competitor's inability to deliver after its plant burned down. Suppose the competitor subcontracts production to a third party and next month is back in business, perhaps with an even more reliable product, and our sales decrease accordingly. If we didn't take the time to research the cause, our conclusion might be that the salespeople were coasting after receiving a big bonus. Having spent nearly ten years as a salesman and sales manager, I have personally witnessed this type of executive disappointment many times. The typical response is, "They're not as hungry as they used to be." This is the classic rationalization of executives who won't incur the time and expense to understand what is really happening. As a result, they continue to make the same mistakes over and over in sales and other functions as well.

An example in another direction is the way in which we set standards of performance. Nearly everyone dislikes having to do performance appraisals. We know that accurately judging another human being's performance is an extremely difficult task filled with room for error. In an attempt to reduce the error rate, we set supposedly objective standards of performance. For the simplest tasks, this is not too difficult if we have enough observations of a given performance. For example, assume that we want to know how long it should take warehousemen to move a number of boxes a certain distance in the warehouse by hand. This would allow us to forecast how many workers we will need as the volume of boxes increases with increasing sales. If we observe the one-time movement of one 10-pound box that is 2 by 2 by 1 foot a distance of 20 feet, we can say that it takes 7 seconds (Ellen, my wife, just timed me doing it). So, we set the standard at 7 seconds. What are the variabilities: my strength, agility, motivation? Am I the model for all men? (Ellen has a ready comment on that.) What if the box size, shape, and weight change? What if the material in the box varies? If the box is filled with paper and the humidity is very high, the weight of the box can change dramatically. What about the fatigue factor, boredom, and breakage if we have to move 200 boxes versus 20? Forecasting performance is a subtle and complex task.

To make a long story short, you can see how complicated it is to set standards of performance for even the simplest tasks. When we move to the work of salespeople, systems analysts, loan officers, nurses, or a hundred other professional occupations, you get the point. So, how do we rate and forecast human performance if we can't step away from our prejudices and sometimes flat-out mistaken notions? Obviously, if it is important, we have to study the variables within the system to reduce our estimation errors. To end with another cliché, you get back what you put in. If we want to understand the correlation and causation of our business in pursuit of competitive advantage, we have to put some effort into it or continue to follow the pack. To use a graphic model for being in the pack: If you are not the lead animal in a sled-dog team, you spend your career looking at the rear end of the guy ahead of you.

We are indebted to W. Edwards Deming for showing us how to reduce variance and set valid performance standards in factories. After he explained it, we could see that it made sense and was comprehendible by the average person. Carrying the same concepts into other areas such as human capital management greatly reduces the mystery and exposes true correlation and causation.

Data Sensors: Forecasting and Predicting

There is a phenomenon I call *data sensors*. These are data that tip you off to the emergence of a problem or opportunity. They are early-warning signals. The following are examples drawn from my experience:

1. An increase in absenteeism is often a sign of unrest among employees. Employees are telling management that they are unhappy by staying off the job. If this signal is ignored, it is highly predictable that turnover will begin to rise in about six months.

2. Increases in processing errors of any type are a precursor of employee and later customer dissatisfaction. Employees respond to their unhappiness by slowing down their productivity, turning out sloppy work, and staying home. Customers respond by complaining and eventually finding another supplier.

3. Reductions in any voluntary activity, from suggestion programs to company picnics, are signs of employee unrest. People are signaling with their abstention.

4. Sharp increases in employee requests for transfer, even when there is no problem with the current supervisor, might be a sign of general malaise or boredom.

5. High levels of employment-offer rejections tell us that we are not treating applicants properly. Offers are seldom

turned down for pay reasons. More often, it is due to the employee's perception that this is not a good place to work.

6. A change in any metric presages effects in others. Increasing turnover means more hiring and training to come. More employees coming to talk to employee-relations staff indicates problems with supervision, which leads to quits. Decreases in attendance in training usually signal employee frustration or supervisors who won't let employees take time to be trained. Either one will lead to requests for transfers or quits.

All the above negatively affect productivity, quality, and customer service.

So, what can we predict with some degree of confidence? What leads to what? This was implied in Chapters 2 through 4. I claimed that there were clearly predictive connections between the human capital management tasks of acquiring, maintaining, developing, and retaining employees and the outcomes of the various functional unit processes. To quickly review linkages, consider the following: If human resources, in collaboration with the hiring supervisor, delivers a high-quality candidate faster than normal, the business unit supervisor should be able to maintain or even increase productivity. Hence, there is probably a correlation between time to fill jobs and productivity, all other things being equal. But as Hamlet said, "Ay, there's the rub."[2]

The nonbelievers have a standard objection: What if this or that happens during the same time period? What about all the things in the environment that pop up and affect the outcome? The obvious answer is that when you change the circumstances or an intervening event occurs, you get a different result. That is why the only way you can judge or forecast anything, in any function, at any time is to assume that surrounding conditions are constant (even if they aren't). This principle is called ceteris paribus, or other things being equal. This constraint is not unique to social science. It applies to all attempts at evaluating and predicting. Budgets, sales plans, and production schedules are based on ceteris paribus assumptions.

In effect, we say, if things go according to our assumptions about the cost of goods, competitor actions, product development, the weather, customer tastes, and so forth (ceteris paribus), the following should be attained (probability).

If something happens during the course of the study, we can identify it and account for it. In Chapter 3, we played out the process value analysis model and saw that at step three, the impact stage, we would be able to account for significant external events and make statements of apparent correlation, if not causality. This can be done without running a field experiment. At the very least, using that model would allow us to be more confident of our conclusions than most managers can be of theirs. So, let's get on with it.

The following is a set of examples of actual problems, actions, and events and their predictable results compiled over the past fifteen years.

Issue	Result
Time to fill jobs increasing	Productivity and/or customer service in the hiring departments negatively affected at a predictable level
Absenteeism increasing	Turnover will increase within six months
Introduction of flextime and telecommuting	Turnover will decrease while applicant pool increases
Introduction of employee-referral bonus program	Quality of candidates improves, and cost per hire decreases
Employees cite poor support and/or communication from supervisors in exit interviews	Incidence of employee-relations problems and absence increases, performance decreases, then turnover and customer dissatisfaction increase in public contact units
Introduction of employee assistance program	Absenteeism decreases, performance increases, eventually cost of health care benefits decreases
Training increased	Internal replacement pool increases, and turnover decreases

Issue	*Result*
Training staff and budget cut	External applicant pool shrinks as market learns we have reduced development support; eventually, voluntary separations increase
Consistent college recruitment program with internships	Higher job-offer acceptance rate, lower cost per hire, improved hire quality, increased longevity

Over time, you will see patterns that are common, as well as ones that are unique to your situation. The more you study your data, the more your predictive capability will improve. The key to improving that capability is to ask yourself, Why? when you see any phenomenon. What could have caused this: problems with people, material, process, equipment? People can be employees, supervisors, managers, and even executives. Here is a true story that makes the point of predictable results.

Company X had a very successful year. The following February, the CEO assembled everyone through an electronic town-hall setup. He went on at great length about what had occurred last year and what was coming this year. In the next month, morale dropped like a lead balloon, turnover started to increase, and customer service slipped noticably. What happened at that meeting? If we knew, what would we have predicted?

> The key to improving your predictive capability is to ask yourself, Why?

The CEO's remarks can be boiled down to two statements.

1. "We had a great year last year with record profits (read between the lines, I got a hell of a bonus)."
2. "This year will not be as good, so we are cutting the salary increase budget in half."

Do you have any idea why the people responded as they did? Could you have predicted their behavior after that communication? Of course you could. These things happen, and people—managerial personnel, especially—have to think ahead to the predictable response. Most important, they have to get out of their skin and put themselves in the place of their audience with *its* values, needs, and viewpoints. As an example, a single parent, male or female, who is barely making ends meet has a different view of life than does a high-income male executive. In the end, you can watch data over time and begin to improve your forecasting capability. You can also view planned actions and suggest probable responses of customers and employees.

Toward a Human Capital Financial Index

Indexes are a common and effective trending mechanism. They provide an effective base from which to risk predictions. Since it usually takes a good deal of study, definition, and consideration of variables and relationships to set up an index, we can count on its reliability.

The only caution we need to observe involves semantics. Calling something an index doesn't make it one. Sometimes the term is applied to any unconnected set of data. Making an alleged random selection of variables into an index because they "feel right" is invalid. The dictionary offers several definitions of an index. The one that most closely suits our situation is "something that serves to direct attention to some fact, condition, etc."[3]

Underscore the word *fact*. I think of true indexes as a valid and reliable set of data that is focused on a given concept and is maintained over an extended period. It must have internal validity as the central point. This means that it represents a true relationship among components. The most familiar examples of long-standing, reliable indexes are the cost-of-living index and the consumer price index. These are well-established data sets that give us a good idea of how these two issues are moving. The government does not claim perfection, and through criticism and modification, it has improved the indexes over time. An index doesn't purport to *prove* anything. Rather, it gives us a consistent, legitimate view of a complex phenomenon.

If we study the components of an index, we can understand what drove the index number up or down. Then, if we understand what affects each component, we can look into the future and plan accordingly. For example, if the cost-of-living index is rising and we see that one of the components, the price of petroleum products, is rising more than other components, how can we react? Turning to the commodities market, we can look at the futures contracts for petroleum and decide for ourselves whether the price is likely to continue to rise for the next twelve months. Then, we can look at long-range weather forecasts for the Middle West (if that is where we live) to learn if we are in for a cold winter. Coincidentally, if the weather is going to be unseasonably cold, the cost of heating oil will rise even more. This leads to a decision about adding insulation to our homes to preserve ambient heat.

In business it is useful, if not vital, to know trends. Trends offer the astute an opportunity to view the future with a bit more certainty than their less insightful competitors. That's what separates the winners from the also-rans—a slight incremental advantage time after time. We read about the great leaps in results of great companies, but we don't see and hear about the daily decisions that, individually, are a bit better than those of their competitors and that, collectively, blow them away. Managing a large-scale business is not a walk in the park. It requires great attention to detail. This means having reliable data and knowing what they truly mean. Indexes offer an advantage over single, unconnected data points, in that they provide the collective result of a set of related variables. This gives us a broader view. Inside the index, we can look at the component movements.

The first hurdle in developing a human capital financial management index is the lack of longitudinal, quantitative, business databases. To the best of my knowledge, the only one that has been around in a consistent, validated, large-scale form is the human resources financial database at the Saratoga Institute. We started the annual publication in 1985. The original objective was to develop a standard model for measuring quantitative results of human resources programs and human capital activity. It was somewhat of a validation exercise for the human resources profession. The goal was to give human resources people a base on which to stand to demonstrate the effects of their work beyond the morale-building stage. Fifteen years later, data from nearly 900 companies yield norms on sixty topics. Figure 6-1 is a list of the benchmark metrics included in the 1999 report.

Over time, our focus has shifted from proving human resources' value to managing human capital. Typically, the human resources department budget represents about 1 percent of the operating expense of the enterprise. Obviously, that is not the thing to worry about. Instead, we want to know how the human capital of the enterprise is responding to investments of money and management time. We spend a good deal of report space explaining the interactions between human capital investments in hiring, paying, developing, and keeping talent and the ensuing financial results. The institute does not claim that there are direct, one-to-one correlations in all cases. Nevertheless, we believe and state that fifteen years of observation have shown consistencies that are more than coincidental.

In 1999, in an effort to extend and share the knowledge gained in the *Human Resource Financial Report,* we published the Saratoga Institute human capital financial index. In its first iteration, it covered the years 1989 through 1997. The index focuses on three human capital phenomena: revenue, cost, and profit (see Figure 6-2). The indexes are defined as follows:

- *Human Capital Revenue Index (HCRI):* revenue per full-time equivalent (FTE) employee. Revenue includes all sales and service income. FTE employees include all persons on payroll plus all contract, temporary, and other workers not on

(text continues on page 178)

Figure 6-1. Saratoga Institute 1999 benchmarks.

1. Organizational Effectiveness
   Revenue Factor — Revenue ÷ Total FTE
   Expense Factor — Operating Expense ÷ Total FTE
   Income Factor — (Revenue − Operating Expense) ÷ Total FTE
   Human Capital Value Added — Revenue − (Operating Expense − [Compensation Cost + Benefit Cost*]) ÷ Total FTE
   Human Capital ROI — Revenue − (Operating Expense − [Compensation Cost + Benefit Cost*]) ÷ (Compensation Cost + Benefit Cost*)

2. Human Resources (HR) Structure
   HR Expense Percentage — HR Expense ÷ Operating Expense
   HR FTE Ratio — Total FTE ÷ Total HR FTE
   HR Exempt Percentage — HR Exempt FTE ÷ Total HR FTE
   HR Investment Factor — HR Expense ÷ Total FTE
   HR Separation Rate — HR Separations ÷ HR Head Count
   HR Structure Breakdown — HR FTE by Category ÷ Total HR FTE

3. Compensation
   Compensation Revenue Percentage — Compensation Cost ÷ Revenue
   Total Compensation Revenue Percentage — (Compensation Cost + Benefit Cost*) ÷ Revenue
   Total Labor Cost Revenue Percentage — (Compensation Cost + Benefit Cost* + Other Labor Cost) ÷ Revenue
   Compensation Expense Percentage — Compensation Cost ÷ Operating Expense
   Total Compensation Expense Percentage — (Compensation Cost + Benefit Cost*) ÷ Operating Expense
   Total Labor Cost Expense Percentage — (Compensation Cost + Benefit Cost* + Other Labor Cost) ÷ Operating Expense

Compensation Factor — Compensation Cost ÷ Workforce Head Count

Supervisor Compensation Factor — Supervisor Compensation Cost ÷ Supervisor Head Count

Supervisor Compensation Percentage — Supervisor Compensation Cost ÷ Compensation Cost

Executive Compensation Factor — Executive Compensation Cost ÷ Executive Head Count

Executive Compensation Percentage — Executive Compensation Cost ÷ Compensation Cost

4. Benefits

Benefit Revenue Percentage — Benefit Cost ÷ Revenue

Benefit Expense Percentage — Benefit Cost ÷ Operating Expense

Benefit Compensation Percentage — Benefit Cost* ÷ Compensation Cost

Health Care Factor — Medical and Medically Related Benefit Cost ÷ Covered Employees

Workers Compensation Factor — Workers Compensation Cost ÷ Workforce Head Count

Benefit Cost Breakdown — Benefit Cost by Category ÷ Benefit Cost

5. Separations

Separation Rate — (Voluntary Separations + Involuntary Separations) ÷ Head Count

Voluntary Separation Rate — Voluntary Separations ÷ Head Count

Involuntary Separation Rate — Involuntary Separations ÷ Head Count

Voluntary Separations by Length of Service — Voluntary Separations by Length of Service by Category ÷ Voluntary Separations

6. Staffing

External Accession Rate — (External Add Hires + External Replacement Hires) ÷ Head Count

Internal Accession Rate — (Internal Add Hires + Internal Replacement Hires) ÷ Head Count

College Accession Rate — (College Add Hires + College Replacement Hires) ÷ Head Count

(continues)

Figure 6-1. (Continued).

External Add Rate	External Add Hires ÷ Head Count
Internal Add Rate	Internal Add Hires ÷ Head Count
College Add Rate	College Add Hires ÷ Head Count
External Replacement Rate	External Replacement Hires ÷ Head Count
Internal Replacement Rate	Internal Replacement Hires ÷ Head Count
College Replacement Rate	College Replacement Hires ÷ Head Count
External Cost per Hire	(External Hiring Cost × 1.1 Factor) ÷ External Hires
Internal Cost per Hire	(Internal Hiring Cost × 1.1 Factor) ÷ Internal Hires
College Cost per Hire	(College Hiring Cost × 1.1 Factor) ÷ College Hires
External Cost per Hire Breakdown	External Hiring Cost by Category ÷ (External Hiring Cost × 1.1 Factor)
Internal Cost per Hire Breakdown	Internal Hiring Cost by Category ÷ (Internal Hiring Cost × 1.1 Factor)
External Time to Fill	External Days to Fill ÷ External Hires
Internal Time to Fill	Internal Days to Fill ÷ Internal Hires
External Time to Start	External Days to Start ÷ External Hires

Internal Time to Start	Internal Days to Start ÷ Internal Hires
External Hires Offer Acceptance Rate	External Offers Accepted ÷ External Offers Extended
College Hires Offer Acceptance Rate	College Offers Accepted ÷ College Offers Extended
Sign-on Bonus Percentage	Total Hires Receiving Sign-on Bonus ÷ Total Hires
Supervisor Sign-on Bonus Percentage	Supervisor Hires Receiving Sign-on Bonus ÷ Supervisor Hires
Executive Sign-on Bonus Percentage	Executive Hires Receiving Sign-on Bonus ÷ Executive Hires
Sign-on Bonus Factor	Sign-on Bonus Cost ÷ Total Hires Receiving Sign-on Bonus
Supervisor Sign-on Bonus Factor	Supervisor Sign-on Bonus Cost ÷ Supervisor Hires Receiving Sign-on Bonus
Executive Sign-on Bonus Factor	Executive Sign-on Bonus Cost ÷ Executive Hires Receiving Sign-on Bonus

7. Training and Development

Employees Trained Percentage	Employees Trained ÷ Total Head Count
Training Cost Factor	Total Training Cost ÷ Employees Trained
Training Cost Percentage	Total Training Cost ÷ Operating Expense
Training Investment Factor	Total Training Cost ÷ Total Head Count
Training Staff Ratio	Total FTE ÷ Training Staff FTE
Training Cost per Hour	Total Training Cost ÷ Total Training Hours
Internal Staff Training Hours Percentage	Internal Staff Training Hours Provided ÷ Total Training Hours
External Staff Training Hours Percentage	External Staff Training Hours Provided ÷ Total Training Hours

*Pay for time not worked must be subtracted from benefit costs since it is included in compensation cost.

Figure 6-2. Human capital financial indexes.

	Revenue HCRI		Profit HCPI		Cost HCCI	
1989	$185,742	100.0	$100,489	100.0	$73,512	100.0
1990	$195,409	105.2	$102,365	101.9	$79,060	107.5
1991	$205,878	110.8	$ 94,767	94.3	$81,092	110.3
1992	$212,639	114.5	$101,899	101.4	$79,554	108.2
1993	$201,570	108.5	$112,675	112.1	$76,752	104.4
1994	$215,970	116.3	$106,557	106.0	$83,845	114.1
1995	$219,434	118.1	$111,400	110.9	$81,624	111.0
1996	$227,467	122.5	$115,745	115.2	$84,039	114.3
1997	$239,506	128.9	$116,342	115.8	$84,204	114.5

payroll (termed contingent). It does not include the personnel who work for outsource program providers. That human effort is considered to be part of general purchased services.

■ *Human Capital Cost Index (HCCI):* total labor cost per FTE employee. Human capital cost includes pay and benefits of persons on payroll, contingent worker cost, and the cost of absence and turnover. The latter two are generally ignored in calculations of labor cost. However, it is logical and obvious that absenteeism and employee turnover are a cost of labor.

■ *Human Capital Profit Index (HCPI):* revenue less purchased services per FTE employee. Profit attributable to human capital investment is total revenue less all nonhuman expenses (everything except pay and benefits), divided by FTEs. The numerator is a standard form for calculating value added. This shows the leverage of human effort that resulted in profit. This is one of two metrics developed by the Saratoga Institute in the mid-1990s that showed ROI in human capital. The other divided the numerator above by pay and benefits. That produces a profit leveraged from employee pay and benefits. It is termed human capital ROI and was shown in Chapter 2 in Figure 2-3 and in Figure 6-1.

Figure 6-2 shows the index data for 1989 through 1997. It gives the dollar-value trends plus the index-number trends for each of the three indexes. There is slightly more year-on-year variation in our figures than in the federal government's, since our sample size is smaller and more susceptible to random fluctuation. Nevertheless, by including other variables not included in federal numbers and by mapping our sample against the national profile, we believe that we offer a useful index. All figures are in *deflated dollar terms*.

One of the most revealing aspects of the cost figures is that they are relatively flat over the years 1994 through 1997. It tells us that the cost of people has tracked almost on top of the inflation rate. In short, job for job, there has been very little real dollar increase. This is one of the reasons why the American economy through 1999 has been so robust. The cost of human capital, one of the two major costs of most companies, has barely risen.

> The cost of people has tracked almost on top of the inflation rate. Job for job, there has been very little real dollar increase. This is one reason the American economy has been so robust.

The other interesting and surprising point was that human capital–leveraged profit did not track with revenue. Whereas there was an increase in revenue per FTE of nearly 29 percent over nine years, profit per FTE over those nine years increased only 16 percent. This says something about the effects of the massive downsizings and technology investments during the 1990s.

The value of having a human capital financial index is the ability to uncover and understand the real story of human value in organizations, devoid of media or government hype. Given our knowledge of what has affected the trend, and looking ahead at those factors, we can begin to understand what the near-term future might look like. From there, we can do a much more effective job of planning a path to profitability. If we add to this type of index a human economic value added index, we would understand in depth how much value, if any, was being added to the national economy by human capital as opposed to equipment and facilities. If a company spends $XX million on computerizing the workforce, how much does productivity rise, and therefore what is the leverage on that investment? Productivity is a human issue. Investment in sophisticated equipment does not guarantee productivity improvement. Strassmann has written extensively about the relationship of information technology and knowledge creation. He has shown that, generally speaking, the true cost and ROI of software, in particular, are largely unknown or miscalculated.[4] When management fails to follow up information technology investment with training, process improvement, and, most important, sound strategic moves, there is seldom economic value added.

Index Exercise

Using the data from Figure 6-2, what could we have learned to make us more effective in managing our human capital? Take revenue per employee (FTE) and ask yourself how your company compares and what the drivers of your results were. Key questions might include:

1. What contributed most to our sales and service income?
2. What was the ratio of investment in equipment, facilities, and people?
3. What hard data evidence is there that each investment improved productivity?
4. Were there visible interactive effects among the three?
5. What is the competition doing to improve human capital productivity?
6. How did the competition manage the ratio of contingents to regular employees, and how should we manage ours?

On the cost side, ask these questions:

1. What is the average compensation of our employees—pay plus benefits—in critical job groups (salary surveys do not disclose average pay, only pay ranges).

How does that compare within our industry or to other human capital competitors (companies that hire away our people)?
2. What is the ratio of benefits to payroll, and how is it changing?
3. What are our absence and turnover rates, and where are they concentrated?
4. How does our rate of compensation growth compare with revenue, productivity, and profitability?
5. What is our leverage factor on human capital investment? (See human capital ROI in Figure 6-1 for a definition.)

For the profit side, ask these questions:

1. How many dollars of profit per employee are we generating?
2. Is profit per employee growing at the same rate as revenue per employee? If not, why not?
3. How does our economic value added (EVA) look compared with that of competitors in our line of business? (EVA is not included in the index at this point, since we do not have access to longitudinal individual corporate EVA.)

It should be clear that if you have the answers to these questions, you can do an effective job of forecasting.

Data Sources

Your efforts at prediction are strongly supported by the availability of public data. North American businesses are blessed with a plethora of data. In both the United States and Canada, the governments support extensive databases of population, economic, and business information. A few of the U.S. federal government sources include:

Congressional Budget Office
Department of Commerce: Bureau of Economic Analysis
Department of Labor: Bureau of Labor Statistics
Economic Reports of the President
Economic Research Service
Economic Statistics Briefing Room
Federal Reserve Board
Social Security Administration
U.S. Census Bureau
U.S. Government Printing Office

FEDSTATS is a Web site for quick searches of these and other federal agencies with annual research and publication budgets in excess of $500,000. It lists over a hundred federal government data sources. Many states also have research services. If you are new to this type of research, you can get guidance from your local public library research section.

In Canada, Statistics Canada is an excellent central source of national population, workforce, economic, and commercial data. In addition, the Canadian Conference Board conducts and publishes ongoing business research.

A few of the commercial sources of quantitative business data include magazines such as *Business Week, Forbes, Fortune, Industry Week, Information Week, CIO,* and *CFO,* among others. They provide both hard data and articles on trends and effective practices.

Prominent research organizations are:

American Productivity and Quality Center
American Society for Training and Development
Bureau of National Affairs
Corporate Leadership Council
Dun and Bradstreet
National Association of Manufacturers
Prentice-Hall
Saratoga Institute
Society for Human Resource Management
The Conference Board
U.S. Chamber of Commerce

Plus there are many industry watchers, of which the Gartner Group of Connecticut is representative.

Internationally, there are the several United Nations bureaus; the Organization of American States in Washington, D.C.; and the *World Competitiveness Report* published by IMD in Switzerland, which provides data on forty-seven countries and lists over fifty other sources of data worldwide.

Finally, the Internet is spawning information Web sites faster than we can keep up with them. By merely listing a keyword, you are likely to find several sources.

There are other sources too numerous to mention. The point is that there is a great deal of information available from which to identify trends, build forecasts, and even attempt prediction. Just be ready to modify your original estimates with periodic updates. The marketplace is so volatile that today's truth is tomorrow's anachronism.

Summary

The business of data management is maturing. We have moved from a reliance on accounting as our primary source of business information to literally hundreds of government and commercial sources of objective and practice databases. Some require membership, but most are available to the public either free of charge or for a fee. The trick is to learn how to interpret the data and use them to look forward as well as backward.

Success will accrue to those who can see patterns and relationships among data. The objective is to turn data into information and ultimately intelligence. This takes experience and practice. Through trial and error, anyone who has the energy to stay in the hunt can learn to improve his or her forecasting ability. There are four levels of data. One level is the general marketplace,

> The objective is to turn data into information and ultimately intelligence.

which offers everything from international demographic and economic data to industry and technology data. Internally, there are data at the enterprise, function, and human capital management levels. These naturally interact and are interdependent. Actions at one level drive activities and outcomes at the others. Businesses are complex and dynamic environments. The wealth of data generated by business activity can be overwhelming. We must learn how to identify the factors and forces that make a difference.

Take care not to fall prey to the natural desire to draw correlations where they do not exist. Data from one activity may be moving in parallel with those of another. However, this may be more coincidence than correlation. It very seldom shows causation. Isolated, one-time events are rarely generalizable to a different population or situation. It is useful to understand the intention behind the publication. Is it a desire to share useful information, or merely a thinly disguised attempt to sell you something beyond the data?

Forecasting and predicting are difficult but not impossible. All attempts at explaining the future are made under ceteris paribus conditions. That is, other things being equal, if one applies our assumptions, the following will have a high probability of occurring. Skill can be built and estimations made more accurately if one practices looking behind the extant data to what might be driving them. Indexes are valid bases from which to practice forecasting. A well-designed index offers a number of components that are inherently related. This simplifies the task of prognostication. But just because someone calls a data set an index does not make it one. Look into it and ask yourself whether the alleged connections are logical and consistent. Caveat emptor.

References

1. Stephen Jay Gould, *Full House* (New York: Harmony Books, 1996).

2. William Shakespeare, *Hamlet*, act 3, scene 1, line 56.
3. *American Collegiate Dictionary* (New York: Random House, 1998)
4. Paul Strassmann, "The Value of Knowledge Capital," *American Programmer*, March 1998.

7

How to Value Improvement Initiative Results

"Son, you can't find new ways of doing things by looking at them harder in the old way."

—My father

Evolving to a New Order

Although few people recognized it at the time, American business began a revivification in the 1970s. Coming out of World War II, the productive capacity of Europe and Asia was in ruin. As a result, America ruled the world market for the next ten years. However, by the 1960s, the new European and Asian factories, their relatively low wage rates, plus their motivation to recapture market share brought fierce new competition. Only after we lost large segments of major consumer product markets did Americans wake up.

Our initial response was the productivity movement of the mid-1970s. This led to the first rebuilding of our manufacturing structure and the first cutbacks in staff. Two of the more prominent productivity service organizations that started in that period were the American Productivity Center (APC), launched by Jack Grayson, and Productivity Inc., founded by Norm Bodek. APC obtained seed money and sponsorship from a number of major corporations. The center's express mission was to carry out research and share information on productivity methods. Productivity Inc. ran productivity improvement seminars and conducted study trips (read *benchmarking*) to Japan to learn better manufacturing methods. A number of other organizations jumped on the bandwagon as American business sought to regain market share.

That laid the foundation for the quality movement, which was initiated by a television white paper titled, "If Japan Can, Why Can't We?" that aired in 1980. It featured the work of W. Edwards Deming, an American whose statistical process control methods had been rejected in America but adopted with great success in Japan. From this came the "quality is free" work of Phillip Crosby and the 6 Sigma programs popularized by Motorola. Toward the end of the decade, the first major downsizing of companies began. By this time, everyone was aware of the competitive nature of the marketplace. Nevertheless, some still didn't comprehend that it was the end of the nineteenth-century manufacturing model, the Industrial Age, and the beginning of a new order.

Eventually, we came to recognize that we had entered the Information Age, a system dominated not by factories and hard goods but by computers, communications systems, and information services. Gradually this new era came to be accepted as more executives stated with conviction, "People are our most important resource." What had long been a platitude was finally coming to be the mantra of management. This brought us to the threshold of the new generation of human capital management.

Measuring the New Human Capital

As I pointed out in the first chapter, I am not trying to determine the intrinsic value of humanity. I am confining my ambition to methods of assessing, evaluating, or measuring— whichever term you prefer—the effects of human behavior on organizational processes. In short, I am looking for valid and reliable procedures for determining what difference people make in the pursuit of organizational goals.

The first attempts to evaluate services in this brave new world were crude. They tried to apply manufacturing process measurements. This worked for routine administrative trans-actions, but it wasn't suitable for professional work that was varied and whose output was often more qualitative than quantitative. Methods had to be found to measure white-collar work on its own terms. I had encountered this problem in 1969 when, after ten years in sales, I went to work for Wells Fargo Bank as a management trainer. I found almost immediately that the personnel and training function was not valued be-cause it didn't know how to express its value added in financial terms. The function was viewed strictly as an expense center to be minimized and largely avoided. In fact, the people doing personnel work didn't think of themselves as value generators. Over the next decade, at the bank and later at a computer com-pany, I tried various assessment methods and eventually dis-covered the processes and rules that have been described throughout this book. Today, we are faced with a different chal-lenge. It is how to evaluate the major management imperatives driving businesses worldwide as they try to reposition the new cohort of human capital for the Information Age.

The following examples are chosen from the most preva-lent initiatives undertaken by management in general and by human resources (HR) specifically. They involve restructur-ing, outsourcing, managing contingent workers, mergers and acquisitions, and benchmarking projects. Each is different, yet all share common needs and can apply a consistent meth-odology to tease out the value added by the program. I outline some of the processes and experiences from each of these ini-tiatives and then point out ways in which you can quantita-tively evaluate the effectiveness of the endeavor.

Restructuring: Back to the Beginning

Call it what you will, restructuring is one of the oldest man-agement gambits. I remember a quotation from a famous

Roman general who said, in effect, "every time we are finally prepared to act, we reorganize." As organizations have come under the gun to restructure themselves for greater competitiveness, all units inside have had to do the same. Typically, restructuring in manufacturing companies starts with production processes. Quite often the marketing and sales functions come along shortly thereafter and bring the customer service departments into the game. Eventually the principal staff units—finance, information technology, and human resources—join in.

There is a continual flow of studies regarding various aspects of restructuring in general and of human resources in particular. Most of them are annual surveys conducted by consulting firms. The principal value of these is a general knowledge of trends. Unfortunately, they carry admonitions of what HR should be doing and descriptions of what is typical. They seldom lead to self-directed restructuring, for obvious reasons. The publishers want to help you with consulting services, and there is nothing wrong with that. Typical of such reports was one by PricewaterhouseCoopers reported in the *International HR Journal.*[1] Sixty-nine multinationals were surveyed in the second of what was intended to be an annual series. It focused on:

- Planning and policy making
- Sourcing and selection of employees
- Rewards and retention programs
- Development and coaching
- Knowledge sharing
- Administration and information management

A summary of the findings showed that for most HR departments, a new service delivery model was needed that simultaneously improved customer service, provided strategic consulting to line businesses, and reduced the costs of HR administration. The survey discovered that many departments have yet to fully automate, outsource, or shift administrative and transactional responsibility to employees and managers. To move toward the new model, more than two-thirds are planning to install new HR information systems. Thirty-eight percent have outsourced benefits administration. Seventy-seven percent have outsourced administration of 401(k) plans. One-third have outsourced both management development and skills training. Eighteeen percent have outsourced payroll. All these figures are up from the previous year. On the knowledge management side, little organizational knowledge is systematically captured. Although 88 percent noted that knowledge management is extremely or very critical, 85 percent rated their performance in knowledge sharing as average to poor.

Two of the more broad-based and representative studies are *Transforming HR to Support Corporate Change,* by Business Intelligence in England,[2] and *Restructuring the Human Resources Department,* by the Saratoga Institute and the American Management Association.[3] Between the two, they cover just about all the major questions touched on by the other studies. In doing so, they answer the three principal questions of restructuring: Why? What? How?

The Prime Question

Usually the first question in restructuring is, What should be redesigned? I submit that the first question should be, Why are we considering redesigning anything? In this, all studies tend to find the same rationale. Restructuring is undertaken to gain competitiveness by:

- Lowering cost structures
- Improving service
- Taking advantage of technology advances

In the course of doing this, companies typically:

- Downsize
- Reengineer processes
- Shift controls by centralizing or decentralizing
- Outsource some noncore functions

On the surface, this is what happens to HR departments as well. However, underlying those activities is a more long-established and deep-rooted issue. It is the basic question of human resources' raison d'être.

The Lost Profession

For more than three decades, the question has been, What is HR's role in the organization? If we don't know the purpose of the HR function, maybe it shouldn't exist. HR is the only function that has been asking this question. All other units seem to know why they exist. But since this is the case, it seems imperative that we ask why human resources exists before we talk about restructuring it. When there is no consensus on who we are or where we're going, any road will take us somewhere, but when we arrive, we will still be asking, Where are we? I volunteer an answer to both questions so that we have something on which to base decisions.

The basic reason that any function exists is to add value. That is unequivocal. No one opens a department simply to spend money. Since we have an HR function, there are two basic questions for starters:

1. Do we need one at all?
2. If we do, what value can it add?

The answer to the first question is up to you. If you can run your enterprise just as well by assigning all human capital management work to line managers or outside vendors, then I say, dissolve HR. It is HR's first imperative to demonstrate that it can do the work better, faster, and cheaper than any other source. If it can't, dump it!

> It is HR's first imperative to demonstrate that it can do the work better, faster, and cheaper than any other source. If it can't, dump it!

It is not my responsibility to make the case for HR in this book. I believe that it has a valid role when it shows that it adds value. I also believe, based on more than 500 presentations to

HR groups in twenty-five countries from 1978 to date, that well over 50 percent of the HR departments in the world don't come near to fulfilling their potential. But hold on! Before we dump them—or nuke them, as Stewart suggested in his controversial *Fortune* article—let's remember who hired them and gave them their marching orders: the CEO.[4] I estimate that only 20 percent of HR managers take hold of the job and proactively show top management how they can add tangible value. I will focus on how these 20 percent go about restructuring their departments to meet changing circumstances.

Restructuring Issues

There are a small but critical number of issues that are central to any restructuring plan:

- Service expectations: What are we supposed to accomplish?
- Control: Where will control and accountability reside?
- Competencies: Are we prepared to deliver?

All other questions and answers, problems and solutions, devolve from these three.

To make good decisions, it helps to know the landscape. Externally and internally, what are the forces at play? In short, what happened or will happen that has caused someone to launch this restructuring drive? Starting on the outside, there are several marketplace factors and forces that have driven us to believe that we need to change our organizations. In no particular order, they include the availability of talent, the productivity of our workforce, advances in technology, plans and actions of our competitors, mergers and acquisitions, entry into new markets, and, in some cases, the state of the national or regional economy. Each of these can be a complex issue with many ramifications. Suffice it to say that some combination of them is the most common external factor driving restructuring.

Internally, our studies uncovered eight factors that drive most HR department restructuring. Figure 7-1 shows the rela-

Figure 7-1. Reasons for restructuring the HR function (%).

Service improvement	96
Cost reduction	88
HR director's vision	77
Benchmarking	69
Update methods	58
Downsizing	54
CEO's vision	50
Merged/acquired	35

tive weight of each. Service improvement, cost reduction, and the vision of the HR director were the main drivers. Quite often, we found that CEOs decided that HR needed to be run differently. Those executives hired new HR directors with the charter to change HR into a value-adding function.

Success Factors

Studies of over seventy-five restructurings in the United States and England uncovered a set of six factors that separated the successful from the unsuccessful. The magic six are as follows:

1. *Business Focus.* First, and most important, there must be a compelling business reason for the change. This requires an awareness of the vision, values, and mission of the organization. Along with that is implied a detailed knowledge of the workings of the organization. HR needs to be familiar with the operating processes of its internal clients. This leads to an understanding of the needs of the clients—both employees and management.

2. *Planning.* An effective plan includes several components. This generates a clear strategy for carrying out the change, along with an explicit set of goals and performance targets. A communication plan must be in place to articulate the reasons for the change and the values to be obtained. An often neglected point is how the change will be phased in. In

addition, there should be a program for dealing with the effects restructuring will have on the HR department and its corporate customers. Finally, there needs to be a method for assessing and evaluating the outcomes.

3. *Communication.* This is so essential that it cannot be overemphasized. The best companies believe that you cannot communicate too much. This is doubly true in the time of upset, which is what a restructuring is. Power shifts, control changes, processes are redesigned. Almost nothing is untouched. People must continually be kept up-to-date about what is happening. Failure to communicate breeds fear, and fear leads to dysfunctional behavior.

4. *Teamwork.* Large-scale change requires involvement. Very few organizational projects are done by individuals. Teams make most of the restructuring happen. Since restructuring affects everyone who is served by HR, as well as everyone who inputs data to HR, there must be a great deal of teamwork. Collaboration with persons outside the department builds support for the change, a sense of shared ownership, and perseverance through the difficult days of implementation.

5. *Commitment.* Top management must actively and visibly show support for and personal commitment to the change. When it doesn't, people believe the restructuring to be just another management game. Project leadership is absolutely critical. The organization must commit a superior individual to lead the project. This is someone who is respected, wants the job, and is creative, hard-driving, and influential with others.

6. *Benchmarking.* Three out of four companies reported that they engaged in some amount of external benchmarking before launching their projects. Ideas, cautions, and effective methodology come from a sound benchmarking exercise. Both practices and metrics can be studied and incorporated as appropriate. The caution is to make certain that whatever learning you adopt you adapt to your circumstances.

Human Resources Changes

The Saratoga Institute's study found that restructuring resulted in one of two quite different results. In the first case, the department found new ways to manage transactions and develop and administer programs. Value was usually found in cost reduction and ease of administration. In some instances, the restructuring also made it easier for employees to interact with the HR function. The second result shifted the department into a new modus operandi. Instead of being principally a service provider, it moved toward being more of a business partner to its management clients.

Some of the signs of change were that in about one-third of the cases, the staffing function underwent a major overhaul. Some recruitment and placement functions were outsourced to placement firms, some were delegated to line management, and others went into shared service centers. All this helped shift HR staff attention to strategic business matters. The other HR function that was severely impacted was training. Only about one-quarter of the responding firms planned to retain training in its present form. Corporate universities, self-study systems, and telecommunications networks are coming into vogue. Overall, the training function is slowly moving out of HR in favor of decentralization and utilization of contract trainers and consultants. Outsourcing of benefits, payroll, and some employee-relations programs is increasing. This is releasing transaction work and embracing strategic partnering.

Restructuring's ROI

When all is said and done, we need to know whether we have achieved our restructuring goals. Obviously, in order to assess that and measure the ROI of the project, we have to have clear objectives at the outset. The basic question that assessment answers is, What did we set out to improve: service, quality, productivity, ease of administration, cross-functional processes and relationships, or what? Quantitative data can be obtained before and after the restructuring to determine whether we achieved those objectives.

Figure 7-2 is an outline of the elements in a spreadsheet report that provides an overview of how we are doing. The key points are:

1. Issue
2. Baseline performance at the time the restructuring started
3. Target performance level
4. Quarterly progress points

Plotting the results of the restructuring stimulates people to persevere. People need feedback on their efforts. They need reinforcement that says, You're making it, or, You need to do better. With this method, they can see how fast and how far they have gone. Some changes will occur quickly; others will take time. For example, requisitions per recruiter will not change until you have had time to reengineer the recruiting process and perhaps install an automated applicant tracking system. As you see the changes from quarter to quarter, you

Figure 7-2. Performance measures of restructuring.

Issue	Baseline	Target	Progress per Quarter			
			First	Second	Third	Fourth
Service (hours)						
Response time	72	24	60	54	48	36
Cost ($)						
Exempt per hire	18,786	12,000	15,150	13,300	12,500	11,900
Nonexempt per hire	1,300	800	1,190	924	890	810
Per trainee hour						
Efficiency (number)						
Exempt requisitions per recruiter	18	30	28	28	26	20
Nonexempt requisitions per recruiter	35	50	35	38	39	45
Customer satisfaction (%)	70	95	85	90	90	94

can calculate the values. In the case of the recruiter-to-requisition ratio, if you reduce the number of recruiters needed for a given requisition load, you are saving staff time to apply toward more value-adding work in HR; you can transfer the recruiters to other jobs or downsize the function. With cost issues, it is easier to see value added, because there is a direct reduction in the targeted hiring costs. Improvements in service to employees obviously helps morale, which in turn should positively affect productivity and turnover. It may take six months or more for the effect to be felt and acknowledged by the employees. So long as you have a tracking system to monitor your progress, you will be able to show the return on time and money invested in restructuring.

In summary, by studying restructuring projects, we can clearly see the focus shifting from HR specialties to business-centric services, from HR department management to human capital management, and from process and policy activities to planning and operating management.

Outsourcing: The Latest Panacea

Outsourcing has become a popular management gambit in the past decade. It can be described as having a third-party vendor furnish administrative services for an activity that would normally be carried out by internal staff. Two staff functions that have adopted outsourcing in a big way are information services and human resources.

Although there was outsourcing of some administrative tasks as far back as the 1960s, it didn't become a common tactic until the 1990s. A useful strategic baseline from which to start to understand and later evaluate the effects of outsourcing is a ratio of work done inside to work done outside. In effect, an outsource ratio is the ratio between the cost of employee pay and benefits, plus the cost of absence and turnover, and the cost of outsourced and contingent labor. This general ratio can be modified to focus only on HR staff and programs.

You notice that I added the cost of absence and turnover

to the inside cost. Ignoring it is to understate the real cost of work done internally. As we will see later, another hidden expense item is the cost to supervise. It can be calculated, but seldom is, based on the claim that one also has to manage the outsource provider. This is true, but if the contract is well written and the vendor is effective, much less time is devoted to monitoring vendor performance than to managing the staff of a processing function on a daily basis.

There are two sides to the outsourcing question. Books have been written about them, so I won't go into the opposing arguments. Nevertheless, I am suggesting that there is value in tracking how much of total labor cost is being spent on outsourcing and on contingent labor working in-house. Contingent labor is a form of outsourcing. I have not seen many companies take this holistic view of labor cost. In the end, there is no *right* ratio. Still, it behooves management to know exactly where its labor dollar is going. Outsource ratio and depletion rates are two metrics that go beyond standard views of human-financial metrics. Together, they provide a benchmark for monitoring labor costs against a target budget.

Rationale Supporting Outsourcing

The argument for outsourcing centers on core competencies. Whether it is or isn't a core competency in a given situation, people strategy should be a core competency of the HR function. However, people administration is not a core competency according to *HR World*.[5] There is little chance for the average HR department to keep up with the changes in payroll, labor law, expatriate regulations, and the like. The best it can do is hope to hold the errors to a minimum while devoting a large amount of resources to it. This is why outsourcing is growing at a steady rate.

Unfortunately, the success rate of outsourcing is rather mixed. The American Management Association (AMA) conducted a survey in the late 1990s to determine the rate at which goals had been met through outsourcing. Three of the most common goals for outsourcing were cost reduction, time saving, and quality improvement. When companies were asked what percentage of these goals had been realized in full, the average response was just under 20 percent, or one program in five.

Figure 7-3 combines the results of two surveys into a list of reasons commonly given for adopting outsourcing, along with their success rates. Quite often, outsourcing is approached as a tactic rather than a strategy. When viewed simply as a way of getting rid of daily administrative tasks, the result is seldom value-adding, except as a cost-reduction scheme. My experience is that outsourcing is almost always launched as a cost-cutting tactic. There is nothing wrong with this, but it is a suboptimizing approach. The most important question is, How do we positively manage human capital to optimize value added?

> Outsourcing is almost always launched as a cost-cutting tactic. This is a suboptimizing approach.

Outsourcing inevitably entails significant organizational change. This change affects process management, employee security, and employee service. In one case, the Saratoga Institute convinced a client to think about how it could best affect the enterprise goals in terms of payroll and benefits processing. Once the client raised its eyes from the mundane cost per transaction issue to the potential for impacting employee morale and productivity, the executives felt like they were business managers rather than transaction administrators.

There are a number of advantages and disadvantages to outsourcing. Figure 7-4 shows the most common opportunities and pitfalls of this scheme. The lesson is that outsourcing is a complicated maneuver with much promise and a more than adequate amount of risk.

Trends in Functional Outsourcing

Having seen the rationale and success rates for the outsourcing of various functions, the next question is, What is most often outsourced? Studies are consistent in showing which human capital management programs are most often and least often outsourced. Generally, with the massive down-

Figure 7-3. Two surveys of reasons for outsourcing and success rates.

Reasons for Outsourcing	Met Objectives (%)	Did Not Meet Objectives (%)	Too Soon To Tell (%)
Improve cost-effectiveness	82	5	13
Reduce administrative costs	75	8	17
Capitalize on technological advancement/expertise	82	7	11
Improve customer service	70	19	11
Redirect HR focus toward strategy and planning	66	15	19
Allow company to focus on core business	63	21	16
Reduce corporate overhead	82	9	9
Provide seamless delivery of services	47	38	15
Lack of sufficient staff	69	27	4
Increase level of participant satisfaction	54	27	19
Improve response time to requests	59	29	12
Control legal risk, improve compliance	53	29	8
Increase flexibility in handling special needs	41	38	11
Increase level of accuracy	49	41	10
Make administrative costs more definable	45	44	11
Implement total quality management	17	71	12

Source: 1996 Outsourcing Survey, Hewitt Associates.

Rationale for Outsourcing (%)	
Most Common Reasons for Outsourcing	
Improve HR service delivery or quality	91
Access to technology	74
Access to expertise/innovation	70
Secondary Reasons for Outsourcing	
Predictable HR costs	36
Increase flexibility	34
Reduce administrative head count	31
Criteria Least Important for Outsourcing	
Reduce risks	44
Redeploy and refocus HR resources	42
Reduce administrative head count	41
Top Criteria Incorporated in Service Agreement	
Predictable HR costs	76
Improve HR service delivery/quality	70
Access to technology	54

Source: 1999 Outsourcing Survey, Saratoga Institute and Andersen Consulting, V. Yeh, editor.

Figure 7-4. Advantages and disadvantages of outsourcing.

Advantages	Disadvantages
Usually the cost of providing the service is reduced	It is not a panacea; sometimes it doesn't work due to poor planning or selection of a vendor that can't perform to expectations
Don't need to make large capital investments in computers and software	
Easier to hire a vendor than prepare to deliver the service from in-house	Lose control and contact with employees
	Some HR personnel usually lose their jobs
Cut space and equipment needs	Inadequate vendors cause employee morale problems
Give the work to an organization that has the core competence to handle it	Need to hire an attorney to review the contract and possibly handle contract negotiations
No need to hire and manage scarce, highly paid experts	Risk fines if the vendor does not comply with government regulations

sizing and restructuring of American business, several HR functions are turning to outsourcing.

I noted in the earlier discussion of restructuring that outsourcing was one of the methods applied when redesigning or reengineering HR. Benefits was the first function that dealt with outsourcing. This goes back to the late 1960s. I outsourced benefits administration when I ran an HR department in the mid-1970s. As more regulations spewed out of Washington, D.C., companies found it easier to contract for administration rather than try to keep up with the changes internally. Pension plans, 401(k) plans, and profit-sharing plans are most often outsourced.

Payroll has long been an outsourcing candidate as well. A large group of payroll processing companies has developed over the past couple of decades. ADP, Ceridian, Paychex, and some banks provide payroll processing for clients. In a survey conducted by the Saratoga Institute in 1997, we found that the cost per paycheck varied tremendously, from as low as just over one dollar per check to as much as twelve dollars. Some companies chose to keep a costly payroll department inside because they believed that employee service was more important than cost. Others didn't even know what their cost per paycheck was. This is a classic example of managing to a gross budget rather than to a unit cost.

Staffing began to seek outsourcing help as the labor market dried up. Many large corporations have brought vendors onto the corporate campus to act as a source of temporary and, in some cases, permanent employee recruitment. In these instances, the vendor's operation looks just like the internal staffing department. This trend could well turn into a permanent change in recruitment strategy.

Training has recently become a prime target for outsourcing. Well over half of the training departments contacted in recent surveys report some degree of outsourcing. There are two reasons for this trend. One is to reduce fixed costs of training staff and facilities. The other is a response to a perceived lack of value added. Mary Cook, whose text is the most thorough explication of outsourcing to date, reports an extreme case of training outsourcing.[6] At Conoco, owing to complaints from managers, the training function was reduced from twelve employees to one. The sole survivor acts as an adviser to managers needing training. This person helps determine the specific need and finds a vendor that can provide the best solution. Outside trainers deliver all the company's training under the direction of the internal training adviser. Thus, fixed costs have been reduced by over 90 percent, and the company is getting the training it needs—and no training for the sake of training.

Some parts of the employee-relations (ER) functions are being outsourced. ER has long been the kitchen sink of human resources. Any dirty dish that did not have staffing, paying, or developing written on it was dumped into ER. Many benefits programs turn to ER to monitor or administer them. Employee assistance programs are typically outsourced and monitored by ER. Some of the recreation and day-care benefits are outsourced under ER's direction.

One of the last functions to be outsourced is the HR information system. Although more companies are deciding to outsource their information technology functions, not as many are willing to put HR information systems in the hands of a systems company. However, it would not surprise me to see the systems outsourced and selective access given to persons inside the company.

Viewed strategically, outsourcing is one way that HR is releasing transaction work and embracing strategic partnering.

Success Factors

The Outsourcing Institute conducted a survey of its membership in 1998 on the factors necessary for carrying out an outsourcing program.[7] Figure 7-5 shows the responses in order of importance.

Note that the first two factors on the list have nothing to do with outsourcing directly. They are focused on the enterprise and its environment. Throughout this book I have been pounding away about how everything starts with the enterprise's goals, not with the process in question. Here is corroboration.

Figure 7-5. Top ten factors for successful outsourcing.

1. Understanding company goals and objectives
2. A strategic vision and plan
3. Selecting the right vendor
4. Ongoing management of the relationships
5. A properly structured contract
6. Open communication with affected individuals/groups
7. Senior executive support and involvement
8. Careful attention to personnel issues
9. Near-term financial justification
10. Use of outside expertise

The middle-range factors revolve around and depend mostly on communication—communication with the vendor, with individuals affected by the outsourcing, and with senior management. All stakeholders need to be considered and involved. It is only at the end that financial justification was noted. This is ironic, since almost all outsourcing programs start with the idea of cutting expenses.

Exult

One of the more interesting recent developments has been the formation of Exult, Inc. Headquartered in Irvine, California, Exult is focused on providing Global 500 corporations with the complete spectrum on business process outsourcing (BPO) services for the human resources management (HRM) function and affinity shared services processes. Exult's mission is to help its clients achieve service-level improvements, cost savings, and tangible business benefits by assuming complete management, ownership, and accountability for the entire HRM process. Its services include design, implementation, operation, management, and administration of all key HR functions and e-enabled HR processes. This comprehensive approach to HRM is a new force in the management of human capital.

Exult is bringing more than a set of transaction services to a client. It aims to transform the paradigm of human resources departments into a range of human capital management support services. We might think it is a hard sell to a CEO to replace an entire function. However, within a year of its formation, it has already signed a contract for $600,000 million with a major multinational corporation. I believe we are seeing the first light of a new era in human capital management.

Outsourcing ROI

To know what to measure, we have to go back to the question, Why are we considering outsourcing? As always, measurement starts with an assessment of the current situation. What could or should be done better? Is it a matter of deciding between upgrading our internal capability versus turning over a noncore function to an outsider? If it is, then we have to start by asking which path best leads to the enterprise's goals. The rationales and the advantages and disadvantages displayed in the preceding figures give us a set of questions we can ask as they relate to our enterprise goals and our internal capability. The following is a pathway that you might find helpful.

1. Start by listing the enterprise's key goals.

2. Next to each goal, put down how this task or process potentially affects that goal. Without calculating it, you can simply state cost, timeliness, employee morale or productivity, customer service, or whatever fits. Often there are multiple effects, so stay with the main one or two.

3. Then state the current level of performance. This can be in terms of unit cost, time to process, error rates, number of employees committed to the process, or how happy you are with the process and result. If you don't have baseline data, how will you know what, if anything, you have accomplished?

4. List alternatives for solving the problem if the performance or cost is not satisfactory.

- One option is to invest in staff and equipment. What would be the cost of that, and how long would it take to bring the capability up to speed?
- Another choice would be to transfer the responsibility to another department that does similar work and perhaps gain economy of scale while avoiding additional capital expenditures.
- You could just stop doing it. Drop a program. It has been done. What would be the savings and the potential downside?
- And, of course, you could outsource it. What would that cost? How long would it take to get it up to speed? What would be the effect on employees?

5. If you choose to outsource, you already have an analysis of the cost and potential performance effects. These form the basis for your ROI or cost-benefit analysis. You know your present performance indices. You know how much improvement is necessary to support the enterprise goals. As the program unfolds, you can track your progress against time to implement, unit cost of the service, process times, error rates, and satisfaction of your internal customers—employees and management.

Contingent Workforce Management: The New Human Capital Challenge

The temporary workforce has grown so dramatically in the past ten years that we had to invent a name for it. That name is contingent. The dictionary defines *contingent* as "dependent for existence, occurrence, character, etc. on something not yet certain; conditional." I'm sure that is the way a lot of contingent workers feel: not yet certain.

The rationale for the swing to a larger contingent workforce is flexibility. Management can rather quickly increase or decrease the workforce without having to go through massive recruitment campaigns or uncomfortable layoffs. After ten years of large-scale and continual downsizing, most people were tired of the stress this put on everyone—survivors, staff, and those terminated. The argument goes that using contingent workers is a less painful way to manage the workforce and ultimately save the company money. However, not everyone agrees with that. Jeffrey Pfeffer, an outspoken Stanford professor, argues:

> If competitive success is achieved through people—if the workforce is, indeed, an increasingly important source of competitive advantage—then it is important to build a workforce that has the ability to achieve competitive success and that cannot be readily duplicated by others. Somewhat ironically,

the recent trend toward using temporary help, part-timers, and contract workers, particularly when such workers are used in core activities, flies in the face of the changing basis of competitive success.[8]

Logically, he has a point. However, no matter its logic and validity, economics will rule, as it always does. So long as executives don't know how to measure the economic value of people, they will continue to treat them as an expense, not as a value-generating force, and to believe that they are saving money by using a large percentage of contingent workers. An interesting fact is that few have carried out systematic, longitudinal studies of the point of diminishing returns when using contingent workers. So again, without data, what do we think we are managing?

> Few have carried out systematic, longitudinal studies of the point of diminishing returns when using contingent workers.

Reasons for Growth

The figures on the size of the contingent workforce are muddled for several reasons. First, there is no consistent definition of what is included. The possible components are part-time on-payroll employees, temporary on- and off-payroll workers, contractors, and self-employed individuals who run their own businesses. Until there is a consensus or at least a common definition, we cannot speak reliably about the size of the contingent workforce. The figures vary from slightly over 10 percent in the middle of 1999 to claims of as much as 25 to 30 percent as early as 1993. As was mentioned in Chapter 4, the best estimate at this point is that, excluding self-employed persons who run small businesses employing others, about one in five people works on a contingent basis.

The contingent segment will likely continue to grow, perhaps reaching one-third sometime early in the first decade of the twenty-first century. Barring any trauma in the economy, companies will continue to fill current needs with contingents. This growth will be driven in part by the growth of the

service economy. Since the mid-1970s, services as a percentage of the total economy have almost doubled. Services cannot be stockpiled for later delivery, so service workers have to
be available as demand waxes and wanes. Restaurants cannot
produce meals for a week and then put them in the refrigera-
tor awaiting patrons (although in some cases the food might
taste like it). There is a natural flow of patrons three times a
day, with lulls in between. This calls for a flexible workforce.

White-collar workers now represent over 60 percent of
the workforce. Since much of white-collar work is still viewed
by many as more cost than value, contingents will be an attractive cost management option.

Downsizing programs of the 1990s eliminated many
older workers who are now coming back as contingents to
work part-time. Some like making additional money to supplement their retirement incomes. Others just want to stay
busy and feel that they are still contributing members of society. Companies like these older workers because they are de-
pendable and are already familiar with the business world and
can step into full productivity immediately.

Finally, more people are opting for less money and more
time for family or avocations. They enjoy working on projects
for several months and then having time off for other things
in their lives. During the period they work, their average pay
is sometimes more than they were making as regular employees, so in the long run, they are doing well enough financially.
This is especially true for people with computer and other
high-technology skills. In short, like it or not, contingent work
will remain a significant segment of the workforce.

Intelligent Use of Contingents

Nollen and Axel make the point that without strategy, we
cannot decide on the most effective structure.[9] Absent a business and marketing plan, there is no efficient way to determine how to use contingent workers. Because short-term
financial reporting drives many executives, they overreact to
market swings. Downsizing is often carried out with an ax

rather than a scalpel. This often leaves the corporate corpus hemorrhaging and incapacitated, requiring the company to bring back some of the laid-off workers or employ other outsiders in core competency areas.

As illustrated many times in this book, everything must start with the enterprise's goals. Although this might sound unduly cumbersome and inhibiting, it is exactly what we found in our study of the top performing companies. Everything rests on a commitment to a long-term strategy and market position. You may choose to be the high-price, high-quality leader or the low-margin, high-volume merchant. Whatever position the company wants to occupy in the marketplace dictates every decision. The commitment to position then drives a certain corresponding culture. The culture dictates how closely people work together, how much risk taking is condoned, and how communication takes place. The underlying ethic is the company's view of its employees. That ultimately influences how contingent staff will be used.

Advantages and Disadvantages

There are two sides to every question. For every advantage, there is often a corresponding disadvantage. So it is with the use of contingents. Figure 7-6 is a short list of the two sides. Use of contingent workers calls for more management skills than might initially be assumed.

Probably one of the most difficult problems with a large contingent workforce is the split workforce. With some people enjoying a degree of job security and receiving benefits working alongside others who have neither, there are bound to be problems. Issues of inclusion in everything from corporate information to parties and picnics drive a wedge into the work process. Professional contingents go home at five o'clock or get paid for extra work hours. Regular professionals are expected to work more than eight hours a day. Self-esteem, jealousy, fear, selfishness, and even greed affect productivity and coworker relations. In Saratoga's study of voluntary terminations, coworker relations was an important issue.

Figure 7-6. Advantages and disadvantages of using contingent workers.

Advantages	Disadvantages
Allows for flexibility in sizing the workforce.	Limits the pool from which to draw tomorrow's managers.
Reduces fixed costs for employee pay and benefits.	Brings in people unfamiliar with company culture and policies.
Reduces hiring, laying off, and record-keeping work and expense.	May require special security precautions.
Reduces risk of violation of employment regulations.	Does not engender loyalty and motivation.
Reallocates regular staff toward value-adding functions (e.g., sales, production).	Creates a divided two-tier workforce.
Gives access to special, high-cost skills on an as-needed basis.	Requires judicious use to avoid "creeping contingents" who ultimately cost more than regular staff.

How to Measure Cost-Effectiveness

To measure cost-effectiveness, you need to gather data on pay, benefits, training, supervision, and productivity.

Pay

Regular full-time employees might have a higher hourly or monthly pay than contingent workers doing the same job, because they have been on the job longer. There are exceptions to this rule. If contingents stay for an extended period, they usually get raises. In addition, if contingent workers come from an agency, the agency marks up pay to cover its costs and a profit margin. So, in the end, an agency person can cost as much as or more than an employee.

Benefits

Regular full-time employees get benefits that part-timers might not receive, depending on the number of hours they work. Contingents may get benefits through their agencies.

Training

Regular employees usually get some amount of training, but each person has to be trained only once. If a new employee comes in or a contingent worker arrives, there may have to be additional training. In the case of a contingent worker, the cost of the training is lost once the person finishes his or her assignment. When the next contingent comes in, the cycle repeats itself.

Supervision

New regular employees and contingents need more supervision than do long-standing regular staff. How much depends on the individual, but in general, the new or contingent worker will absorb more supervisor time for at least the first couple of weeks, if not longer.

Productivity

It is not possible to claim a productivity differential between the two groups. A case can be made for either type of worker. Long-term employees should be more productive since they know the job and the culture and are supposedly committed to the company. Or they may be bored or angry and deliberately perform below their capabilities, but not poorly enough to be terminated. Contingents may see the job as simply a meal ticket, or they might work hard, hoping to impress management and be offered a regular position. A large part of the difference depends on how both types of workers are treated by their supervisors.

■ ■ ■ ■ ■ ■

To determine the costs of each factor, you need to track expenses and productivity levels. In cases of higher-level technicians or professionals, hard performance data might not be easy to establish. In the simplest example, the calculation looks like this:

$$\frac{\text{Pay + Benefits + Training + Supervision}}{\text{Units produced}} = \text{Cost per unit}$$

In cases of professional work, productivity measurement is more subjective. Professionals most often have to work with others on a team project as well as perform their own tasks. So, the productivity or, more appropriately, the value added is a function of several behaviors. When judging a contingent professional, you can observe how much the person did in a given time and determine whether that is as good as your average regular professional staff person. Ask these questions about contingent workers:

- Did they finish projects, and were they finished as fast as you expected?
- What was the cost from beginning to end of the project for their pay, training, and supervisory time required?
- How did the quality of their work compare with that of your regular staff?
- If they were in contact positions, were there any complaints or compliments from customers, coworkers, or staff from other departments?

All these will help you make a judgment as to the cost-effectiveness of contingents versus regular staff.

Mergers and Acquisitions: Buy versus Make

M&As, as they are called, are daily occurrences. Many companies have found that it is faster, cheaper, and potentially more sensible to merge with or acquire another company rather than try to build capability from scratch. However, several studies have shown that more than half of all M&A deals fail to achieve their intended goals. The reasons for this are the same as the reasons for most business failures: neglecting preparation, ignoring warning signals, and looking at only part of the picture. During the 1970s and 1980s, I was employed by companies on both sides of acquisitions. About half of them worked well enough, and the other half were costly failures. In the case of the failures, it was because the acquirer did not understand the dynamics of the organization it was acquiring or refused to see or hear the danger signals, which were glaring.

The good news is that things are improving somewhat although the success rate is nothing to rave about. In 1997, Mercer Management Consulting (MMC) conducted a survey that showed that M&As of the 1990s were doing better in financial terms.[10] It looked at 215 transactions valued at $500 million-plus. The data showed that 52 percent of the 1990s deals were achieving above-industry shareholder returns, compared with only 27 percent of the 1980s deals. MMC found no correlation between premiums paid and value created. Its conclusion was that higher rates of return were due primarily to postmerger management.

Human resources has a central role to play in every stage of a merger or acquisition. Yet, in most instances, HR doesn't come into the picture until after the deal has been pretty well decided. There are a couple of reasons for this. First, most deals are finance or marketing driven. In either case, it would seem that HR does not have much to offer in the preplanning stage. This is not true, or should not be true. In any deal,

> Many HR people have only a surface knowledge of their own company's business and marketing plans.

people are an important part of the purchased value. Everyone has read about deals that drove top talent out in short order, leaving a much-depreciated asset for the acquirer. This happens so often that in many mergers there is less value six months after the deal than on the day of the close. The second reason that HR is not in the front end of deal negotiations is that HR people don't understand the dynamics of M&As. To start with, many HR people have only a surface knowledge of their own company's business and marketing plans. The technology of the business is a foreign language. The strategy is not well-known. The short-term and long-term drivers are a mystery. In such a situation, why would HR be invited to the table? Clemente and Greenspan confirmed this deficiency in a survey of 370 companies that had been involved in an M&A within the past eighteen months.[11] Only 19 percent of the respondents believed that HR had the technical knowledge of an M&A to support the acquisition strategy development.

Critical Success Factors

From preplanning to postdeal integration, Clemente and Greenspan offer ten critical success factors that are HR based.[12] Attention to these factors greatly enhances the probability that a merger or an acquisition will go off without a hitch.

1. Address HR issues during strategy development. By knowing industry practices regarding incentive compensation, the acquirer can structure the offer with equity incentives that retain key personnel.

2. Involve HR in target company examinations. Intelligence gathering in the market can uncover problems that don't show up on balance sheets but can affect operations and sales afterward.

3. Include HR factors in predeal contracts. Allowing HR access to employee records and people can help identify potential problems, as well as highlight key personnel to be retained after the deal.

4. Focus HR's due diligence on cultural compatibility. Beyond policies and practices, the acquirer must understand the culture of the firm to be merged. Culture clashes have highlighted some of the great deal failures of the past.

5. Include HR at the table for integration planning. HR often has a better feel for how to integrate people than does marketing or production, whose focus is not people-centric.

6. Avoid hasty decisions on postdeal downsizing. In a hurry to cut costs to pay for the acquisition, the dominant party often lays off large groups of people that it will need later to make the transition.

7. Conduct employee sensing throughout the course of the integration. It is tempting to take the employee pulse once and assume that everyone is comfortable with and knowledgeable about what is happening.

8. Design training to support the merged objectives. In some cases, people from each side will be dealing in operational or sales issues originating from the other side. Both need training in the new procedures or products.

9. Pick the best people for the new positions of leadership. Avoid the temptation of thinking that "to the victor belong the spoils" and awarding all top jobs to the acquirer.

10. Maintain ongoing employee communications. Failure to conduct ongoing communications can hamper integration efforts. People need their questions answered and need to be kept up-to-date through the entire postdeal integration.

Risk Management

Deal makers are great assumers. Many investment bankers who devote much of their careers to putting deals together feel that they understand and have accounted for all contingencies. Usually they are correct. Still, after the smoke of the deal has cleared and most people on both sides are smiling again, seemingly innocent moves can blow up in the acquirer's face. Such was the case of the First Union acquisition of Signet Bank in 1997.

First Union had made a number of acquisitions similar to its deal with Signet Bank without any significant problems. In this case, as was its standard practice, First Union liquidated $250 million in investments by 5,000 Signet plan participants in eight different options. It shifted the funds to four of the seven investment options available in the First Union plan. The problem surfaced when shares in the former Signet investments in Capital One tripled after the liquidation. In addition, First Union began charging employees administrative fees that it did not require some of its corporate clients to pay.

It was another case of management myopia, wherein senior executives enjoyed the attitude that they could do things that affected employees without any fear. When First Union announced its intention to make the change, the former Signet workers claim that they tried unsuccessfully to make their case for keeping their investment in Capital One. First Union spokespeople allegedly stated with an arbitrary and condescending attitude, "We don't feel it's wise for you to have so much invested in a single stock." The people of Signet did not go along with that condescension and filed a class-action lawsuit on behalf of the 5,000 former Signet workers. The claim was for the $150 million difference between the Capital One performance and the First Union fund performance, plus unspecified "millions of dollars" for administrative fees charged by the bank for managing the employee investments.[13] Win or lose, First Union executives have changed their attitude about arbitrary decision making.

Key Issues to Address

There are many important issues to address in the merging of two companies. They include:

- Structural issues related to how the various functions will be combined or not
- Compensation, which is always a key concern of everyone involved
- Product lines that often have to be revamped or merged
- Reporting relationships, which are or can become sensitive matters
- Technologies to be learned or adapted

Any of these issues can be sources of lingering or explosive problems, but there are three issues from which all others seem to arise: communication, culture, and morale.

Communication has been discussed previously, because it is the most pervasive of all human activities. It is at the heart of everything we do with other people. In our research of top performing companies, their passion for communicating with employees was evident. They stated, "You can't communicate too much."

Culture is another enveloping factor. It is everywhere and nowhere. Sometimes it is so strong that you can see it being played out over and over. Other times it is so subtle that you kind of feel it but can't actually describe it. But make no mistake, it is the signature of an organization. It is what makes it different from all others. Trying to buck the tide of the culture is like swimming up rapids.

> Trying to buck the tide of the culture is like swimming up rapids. Ignoring culture has drowned many mergers.

Culture is a powerful force flowing in one unequivocal direction. Positive or negative, it is there. The cultures of both parties must be understood in their own terms and in terms of each other if there is to be a successful integration. Ignoring culture has drowned many mergers.

Morale is the result of how the merger was originally communicated and what really happened after the deal was done. Anyone who comes in and says that there won't be any changes is either naïve or a liar. I've been involved in several M&As, and I've never seen one that didn't change many practices, structures, and people. If morale sinks, production suffers, customers are ignored, and people run over one another trying to get out the door. Morale can be managed with honest, timely communication and a recognition of the effects of the merger on the acquirees' culture.

ROI: Key Success Indicators

How do you evaluate a merger or acquisition? A good way to figure that out is to ask, What human capital objectives do you hope to achieve in an M&A?

There are a number of goals common to 90 percent of M&As. Figure 7-7 is a typical list. It includes goals, programs, and measures covering retention, productivity, job satisfaction, motivation, professional-level performance, customer satisfaction, and sales.

Retention of talent is the most common human capital issue discussed in M&As. There are many ways to keep talented people after a merger or acquisition. It starts with an

Figure 7-7. Human capital objectives, programs, and measures in mergers and acquisitions.

Objective	Program	Measure
Retention of key talent	Individual discussion of	Turnover rates
Maintenance of general	opportunities	Productivity levels
productivity	Employee	Job satisfaction
Optimal utilization of	communication	discussions
talent	program	Performance levels
Motivation of key	Intelligent assignment of	Customer satisfaction
personnel	key personnel	Sales levels
Maintenance of	Incentive compensation	
customer service	program	
Increased sales	Assimilation of the two	
	cultures	
	Training and cross-	
	selling programs	

honest, ongoing communication program. This includes general communication to the rank and file as well as individual sessions with key talent. Another way you retain those talented persons is with their insightful assignment to important posts. These are the people who have the most impact and therefore deserve the most attention. That attention should start as soon as possible after you have assessed them and continue until they are firmly committed to staying. Incentives such as stock options and performance bonuses are usually necessary in the managerial and professional ranks. Lajoux makes an emphatic statement that the acquirer's strongest defense against employee defections is a good reputation as an employer, supported by actions consistent with that reputation. Specifically, she states: "The new owner must demonstrate immediately and clearly to all of the new company's employees at all levels that their future is bright individually and collectively."[14] The operative term here is *demonstrate.* Talk is cheap. Everyone on both sides is wondering how the merger will play out. Skepticism and fear abound. Only actions are believed.

Maintenance of productivity and customer satisfaction is critical. Acquiring a company that is losing market share due to inefficiency or poor customer service is not a good deal. Sustained performance depends on a continual, effective general communication program. People need to feel that they are valued. This is especially important to the acquirees. Often the buyer comes in like a conquering army. In 1996, Wells Fargo executives set a cruelty standard surpassed only by "Chainsaw" Al Dunlap when they bought First Interstate Bank (FIB). Wells Fargo announced that it planned to remove 85 percent of FIB's 6,000 employees. Can you guess what happened to customer service over the next year? Wells Fargo's performance in the second half of the decade did not compare favorably with that of previous years. During AOL's acquisition of Netscape in 1999, the attitude of the acquiring managers was, "They should be grateful that we saved them." The problem was that the acquirees didn't feel a need to be saved. They thought that they were doing well enough, thank you. As a result, within less than ninety days, there was a major loss of talent. To this day, the acquirers can't understand why good people left.

Motivation, and therefore productivity, depends largely on how comfortable a person feels in an environment. In a new deal, you have two main cultures and usually a number of subcultures. Assimilating people into the culture of the dominant player is a sensitive issue. It takes time, respect, communication, and often special forms of recognition. This last step is an effective way to show that the acquirer values the acquired employees. A pat on the back is often worth as much as or more than a salary increase. Everyone wants to be valued. Socialization is a higher-order need than security. Once it is clear that a person still has a job, the next step is to assure him or her that the acquirer cares. It is fundamental to self-esteem. People who feel unloved often develop negative attitudes and sometimes countereffective behaviors.

Selling is a function of knowledge, skills, and motivation. Salespeople are inherently motivated to sell, but they expect short-term rewards. To help them sell, they need training in the new product line. This often includes some ongoing coaching and support until they grasp how to present the unfamiliar products. In many cases, salespeople have to learn to sell a different level of product to a different group of customers. Building their confidence through training and coaching is the most effective approach.

In conclusion, a merger is successful if it retains key talent, maintains acceptable levels of productivity and customer service, keeps morale upbeat, obtains top performance out of its managers, and achieves sales targets. All of these are relatively easy to measure quantitatively and/or qualitatively.

Benchmarking: A Value-Adding Approach

In preparing this section, I looked back at my book *Benchmarking Staff Performance*, published in 1993.[15] At the time, I remarked that benchmarking was still a rather new idea. Today, as we march into the new century, benchmarking is an old but still vibrant activity. It would be difficult to find a professional who has not been touched by benchmarking from one side or the other. My approach to benchmarking—and I've done it with companies in at least a dozen countries—is to start with the goals of the enterprise and a description of the intended value of the project. Which of the following values do you have in mind?

- Human—helping people be more productive, less stressed, more satisfied with their jobs
- Production—improving service, quality, or productivity
- Financial—increasing ROI, assets, or equity

Purpose and Expectation

Benchmarking is a tool with a specific purpose. It will help you find out how someone else conducts a process and perhaps allow you to transfer that discovery to your operation. It is a common practice preceding most of the programs mentioned in this chapter. But benchmarking does not provide answers, suggest priorities, or prescribe action. An effective benchmarking project develops a mass of potentially relevant and useful information about functions, processes, or practices. It might help you uncover root causes of problems and paths to more effective applications.

Anyone who is considering being involved in a benchmarking project should realize that it will not provide simple solutions to complex problems. Looking for the Holy Grail of management through benchmarking is a futile exercise. The more difficult or broad-based your problem, the more complicated the solution is likely to be. Only in rare cases will you be able to adopt the discovery directly in your operation. It is much more likely that you will have to interpret the finding and modify the practice to fit your situation.

> Looking for the Holy Grail of management through benchmarking is a futile exercise.

Effective benchmarking starts by finding adaptable practices and understanding the antecedents. In what situation was this practice effective? What was the objective? Is it proving to be effective over time? How does the practice fit your situation and goals?

Common Mistakes

There are several mistakes that people make in preparing to benchmark. The following list tells you what to avoid:

- Too broad a scope: Don't take on world hunger.
- Too many questions: Keep your list short, or you will be buried in data.
- Lack of team preparation: It takes certain skills and commitment.
- Haste: Don't sacrifice speed for quality; do it right the first time.
- Metrics versus practices: Don't ignore one for the other; get both.
- Similar partners: The further afield you look, the more likely you are to find value.
- Famous companies: Just because they are well-known doesn't mean they are good at everything.

Value Benchmarking Model

Our approach focuses on two objectives. First, we want to find value as expressed in human or production terms. If we accomplish that, we will certainly be rewarded with financial value. Second, we want to apply learning in a way that gives us a competitive advantage in the market. This means that the practice we adopt as a result of our learning will help us improve service, quality, or productivity.

Figure 7-8 shows the value benchmarking process. It starts with an expectation of finding and adding value, not just learning something. After you know what you need to learn to add value, then you can formulate questions and gather data. The fun step is evaluating what you have, learning from it, and determining what you can do to add value. Finally, you can act, monitor progress, and start over. Quite often, by the time you have fully implemented the new process, it is time to take a quantum leap and consider benchmarking world-class performance. If you're tempted to stop after improving performance one level, you have to remember that your competition is continuing to move to a higher level.

In practice, the benchmarking process oscillates back and forth across the four steps. Invariably, you learn and modify or expand the process as you go. The recycling keeps you on the value path. This bouncing back and forth makes sure that you will end up with more than just a lot of activity and no real applicable learning.

The ROI of Benchmarking

As in all cases in this book, we want to know how to find a return on our investment in a management process. Benchmarking is potentially a very powerful tool. It has helped some companies pull back from the brink of bankruptcy and regain market share.

Figure 7-9 is a sample of some of the values that companies have obtained by benchmarking various functions. You can see that benchmarking can be applied to any process. I started with human resources activities and then moved on to

Figure 7-8. Value benchmarking process.

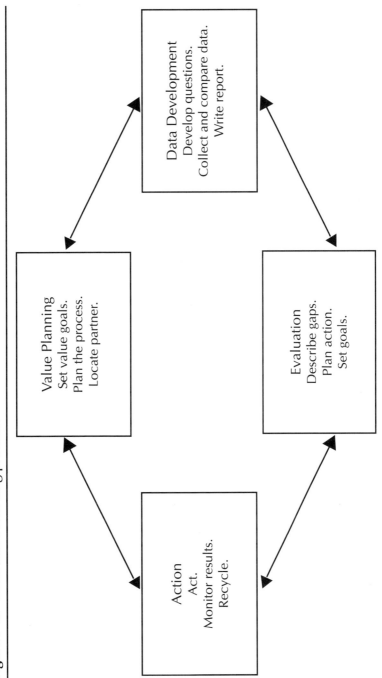

Figure 7-9. Value added through benchmarking.

Process Improvement	Change	Impact	Value Added
Streamline requisition approvals	Hiring process shortened	Quality hires sooner	Productivity sustained
Automate applicant tracking	Number of recruiters reduced	Staffing costs cut	Operating expense reduced
Centralize transaction system	Managers/employees empowered	Less administrative time	Output increased
processing	Less supervisory time	More focus on value added	Production/service improved
Outsource payroll processing	Just in time, relevant training	Lower cost, better outcome	Efficiency/effectiveness gained
Decentralize training delivery	More satisfied customers	Customer retention increased	Marketing cost cut
Streamline customer call center	Cleaner, safer facilities	Fewer accidents	Lower workers compensation claims
Upgrade building maintenance	Timely receipt of good data	Information more useful	Sales increased
Deliver on-time, accurate reports	Employee stress reduced	Less absence/turnover	Lower employee expense
Redistribute workloads			

examples from other functions. The examples run the gamut from specific process or system improvements to general enhancements, such as redistributing workload, which applies anywhere. I did not specify the potential dollar values in the value-added column because they differ across businesses. Using your experience and imagination, you can think of how dollar values could be calculated from similar examples in your company. The thought process is always the same. The questions are:

- What is the current state of the process we want to improve?
- How is that state causing us problems?
- If we "fixed" it, what would the outcome look like?
- How is that different from the original state?
- What is the economic value of that difference?
- Is it worth the effort, or should we focus resources elsewhere?

Benchmarking is a tool that can help you find and generate value in almost any administrative or production function.

Summary

American business is working hard at improving its competitiveness in world markets. This is bringing about great changes within companies. Every day we read about and experience the effects of this effort. Companies are employing a variety of processes in search of more efficient and effective operations. Restructuring, outsourcing, employing contingent workers, merging and acquiring, and benchmarking best practices are the popular tactics. Each offers a different path from the present to the future. But at the end of the day, the most important question is, Did it work? The answer can come only through an analysis of ROI.

Restructuring is, by definition, a disrupting activity. Fundamental organizational dynamics such as power, control, timing, collaboration, and risk come to the surface. As in all cases, success is most often achieved by those who have a well-developed plan. Communication is the lifeblood of a restructuring project. Since many people will be upset and some will be terminated, it is critical that honest, continual communication flow up and down the organization.

During the course of a restructuring, outsourcing is always considered and often adopted. The key question is, What are the comparable costs of processing inside versus outside? Cost is measurable in both dollars and people's reactions. Although outsourcing has been around for more than thirty years, its widespread use is a phenomenon of the 1990s. Human resources and other staff functions are increasing their use of outsourcing. Beyond the traditional applications to payroll and benefits, outsourcing is claiming more of the staffing and training functions. Many employee support programs, such as employee assistance programs, are being outsourced. Outsourcing works most cost-effectively if we look at both the human and the financial aspects of it. Cutting costs while destroying morale is not a cost-effective move. We have learned from the top performing companies that a balance of human and financial value is optimum.

The contingent workforce movement grew dramatically during the 1990s. Starting as a flexibility and cost management tool, it accounted for about 20 percent of the workforce by the end of the decade. Then came the backlash. People started to ask why we used contingents in critical jobs when we claimed that people were our most important asset. The debate about contingent versus regular staff will continue in the new century. I believe that it will be settled when management decides whether people are really valuable or just an expense. To know the cost-effectiveness of contingents, we have to look beyond the hourly rate comparison. We need to study issues of pay, benefits, training, supervisory time, and productivity.

Mergers and acquisitions have generated ungodly amounts of money for investment bankers and some executives while simultaneously putting hundreds of thousands out of work. In the long run, the new organization often provides a good return on investors' money. But in the short run, more

M&As fail than succeed. From a human capital standpoint, the measurable indices of success include maintaining productivity and customer service and meeting revenue and profit targets. These depend on the retention of key talent, because tangible assets generate no value without skilled people to apply them. The most effective tools in a merger are communication and culture management. Understanding the diversity in the merging cultures and maintaining a two-way communication system will greatly enhance the odds for a successful merger.

Benchmarking is a tool that emerged in 1990 after the publication of Camp's book about Xerox's use of benchmarking to recapture market share.[16] Although people have always tried to learn from others, this technique formalized a methodology. After an overwhelming flood of benchmarking in the early years of the decade, benchmarking took a rest. Then, as the century came to a close, there was renewed interest. Benchmarking doesn't answer questions. It uncovers process methodology and, when properly conducted, reveals the rationale and conditions behind the method. The most important things to remember are to keep the project focused, plan, look at both metrics and practices, and don't benchmark a company just because it is famous.

References

1. Francis Engoron, "Human Resources Benchmarks and Best Practices: A Global Survey," *International HR Journal,* spring 1999, pp. 47–49.
2. Chris Ashton, ed., *Transforming HR to Support Corporate Change* (London: Business Intelligence, 1999).
3. *Restructuring the Human Resources Department: A Report by Saratoga Institute* (New York: AMACOM, 1997).
4. Thomas Stewart, "Taking on the Last Bureaucracy," *Fortune,* January 15, 1996, p. 105.
5. Tom Lester, "Spare Me the Details," *HR World,* July/August 1999, pp. 32–36.

6. Mary F. Cook, *Outsourcing Human Resources Functions* (New York: AMACOM, 1999), p. 119.

7. Courtesy of Outsourcing Institute: Survey of Current and Potential Outsourcing End-Users, 1998.

8. Jeffrey Pfeffer, *Competitive Advantage Through People* (Boston: Harvard Business School Press, 1994), p. 21.

9. Stanley Nollen and Helen Axel, *Managing Contingent Workers* (New York: AMACOM, 1996).

10. Courtesy of Mercer Management Consulting, 1997.

11. Mark Clemente and David Greenspan, *Empowering Human Resources in the Merger and Acquisition Process* (Glen Rock, NJ: Clemente, Greenspan & Co., 1999), p. 109.

12. Ibid., pp. 11–18.

13. Robert Stowe England, "When Pensions Change Hands" *CFO*, August 1999, pp. 69–74.

14. Alexandra Reed Lajoux, *The Art of M&A Integration* (New York: McGraw-Hill, 1998), p. 85.

15. Jac Fitz-enz, *Benchmarking Staff Performance* (San Francisco: Jossey-Bass, 1993).

16. Robert Camp, *Benchmarking: The Search for Industry Best Practices That Lead to Superior Performance* (Milwaukee: American Society for Quality Control Press, 1989).

8

How to Leverage Your Human Capital ROI

"People are the one true competitive measure."

—Hal Rosenbluth

Almost everyone agrees that people are the prime resource today. So, it follows that we have the best chance of leveraging our investments if we build on that resource. Hamel and Prahalad claim that all successful strategies have resource leverage at their heart. They offer five ways to leverage resources:[1]

1. Concentrate resources on strategic goals.
2. Accumulate resources efficiently.
3. Complement resources from different areas for higher-order values.
4. Conserve resources wherever possible.
5. Recover the investment in resources rapidly.

In simple terms, this reads as focus, be efficient, combine, save, and manage for ROI. At this point, I trust that you are sold on the premise that people do add value and that this value can be measured in financial terms. So, the most important question for you is, What can you do to get a better return on your investment in your human capital?

There is no shortage of theories and models of management and leadership. In Figure 1-3, I listed over forty management theories that have hit the market in the last fifty years, and they are just the ones that attracted some attention. Each year, several hundred books are published on management and leadership. The total number of titles published on the broad topic of organizational management in the last thirty years of the twentieth century reached nearly 10,000.

The irony of this flood is that we don't know much more about leadership and management of people today than we did 2,800 years ago with Homer's *Odyssey* and Sun Tzu's *The Art of War*. The Golden Rule and common sense seem to be as good as many recent theories, and better than most of them. Most research is characterized either by minute studies with little generalizability or by broad, unsupported hypotheses that are impossible to put into practical terms. Academicians who could not organize a two-car parade regurgitate earlier theories without adding any fresh insights. Consultants and writers offer old material under new titles. In the end, our knowledge has not been advanced.

> We don't know much more about leadership and management of people today than we did 2,800 years ago.

The only research that impresses me is that which is drawn from the daily struggle of human beings trying to make the most of their situations. The less esoteric it is, the more I like it. In this vein, two massive longitudinal studies of the views and experiences of thousands of employees stand out. The Gallup organization conducted one study, and the other emerged from the ongoing work of the Saratoga Institute. As we often find in life, different people working on the same issue from different angles, unknown to one another, sometimes reach similar conclusions at about the same time. Gallup has been studying employee needs and managerial behavior for two decades. Using a standardized questionnaire, it has interviewed over 80,000 managers. The Saratoga Institute has used a consistent script in interviewing 70,000 employees who left their organizations voluntarily over the past four years. Both studies covered a wide range of organizations, from the Fortune 500 to midsize companies across several industries. When the results are viewed together, we find a great degree of similarity regarding employee needs and managerial behaviors. Taken together, the data suggest that there are factors that predict higher-than-average performance and employee satisfaction and lower-than-average voluntary turnover across a broad range of settings. This is the stuff of human capital leverage.

The Managerial Perspective

Buckingham and Coffman detailed the Gallup study in their book *First, Break All the Rules.*[2] Their focus is on what good managers do when working with employees. Underlying those behaviors are data drawn from over a million employee interviews conducted by Gallup over a twenty-five-year period. The authors ploughed into this mass of data in search of the core elements of a good workplace. The determination of *goodness* was based on a balance of human, production, and service criteria against which the interview data were matched. (Remember, my own study of exceptional companies, detailed in Chapter 2, found that the top performers balanced human and financial values.[3]) Applying standard statistical techniques, they looked for patterns and discriminating questions. If they could cull the key items, they would be able to identify the things that made a difference.

The result of their labor pushed twelve questions to the surface (see Figure 8-1). This dozen doesn't cover everything that you might want to know about your workplace, but according to the authors, it does cover the most important information. You will notice that issues of pay and benefits are not included. This does not mean that they are not important. But, as Herzberg found in the 1950s, fair pay and benefits are a given.[4] If your compensation program is not competitive, you won't attract and retain talent. Even if it is better than average, it will not overcome other more important deficiencies.

In Figure 8-1, I italicized what I believe to be the key issue in each question. Some care must be taken in this interpreta-

Figure 8-1. Questions for measuring the strength of a workplace.

---

1. Do I know what is *expected* of me at work?
2. Do I have the *materials and equipment* I need to do my work right?
3. At work, do I have the opportunity to do what I *do best* every day?
4. In the last seven days, have I received *recognition* or praise for good work?
5. Does my supervisor, or someone at work, seem to *care* about me as a person?
6. Is there someone at work who *encourages* my development?
7. At work, do my *opinions* count?
8. Does the mission/purpose of my company make me feel like my work is *important?*
9. Are my *coworkers* committed to doing quality work?
10. Do I have a *best friend* at work?
11. In the last six months, have I talked with someone about my *progress?*
12. At work, have I had opportunities to *learn and grow?*

---

tion. You see that the word *opportunity* comes up twice in the questions. The terms *coworkers* and *best friend* are different, in that the coworker question is focused on the quality of their work, not on the relationship. When you pull out the italicized words, you get a behind-the-words view. This is what people are saying:

1. Tell me what is expected.
2. Give me the resources necessary to do the job.
3. Fit me into a job that is right for me.
4. Recognize my contribution.
5. Care about me as a person.
6. Mentor my development.
7. Show me that my opinions count.
8. Let me see importance in my work.
9. Put me with committed coworkers.
10. Let me find a close friend.
11. Give me opportunity for advancement.
12. Give me opportunity for personal growth.

Further digging sorts the twelve items into two categories:

Personal	*Work*
Recognition	Expectations
Caring	Job fit
Mentoring	Importance of contribution
Opinions heard	Coworker effort
Friendship	Resources
Advancement	
Growth	

You could argue that communication of expectations, a job that fits one's ability, a feeling that one's work is important, and making a contribution are personal issues. In a sense, they are, but they are directly connected to the job assigned. What strikes me the most is how communication or human interaction is so pervasive throughout the list. With the exception of resources, everything else is based on communication between the individual and his or her coworkers and supervisor. This tells me that work is more a human interaction issue than a task issue. I grant that people have to start with some inherent talent and aptitude, and they have to have their skills developed through experience and training. But most important, they need and want social interaction on the job. Work is not a place where people should be isolated and totally focused on a task. Keep this in mind, because we are going to see it come up again in other research.

Connecting to Results

If this were as far as Gallup's research went it would be worthwhile. Fortunately, it did not stop there. The researchers wanted to know whether there was a connection between employee statements about work and their actual results in one or more of four dimensions: productivity, profitability, retention, and customer satisfaction. To build correlations that would stand up across companies, they applied meta-analysis, a complicated statistical process. This gave them a thirteenth item—overall satisfaction—against which they could correlate the four dimensions.

The twelve-question set was administered to 105,000 employees in 2,500 business units within twenty-four companies. The findings revealed that employees who responded most positively worked in the higher-performing organizations. This was interpreted as validating the connection between employee opinion and operating results. Conversely, it could be argued that people were simply responding to their successful units. It is the old chicken or egg quandary. So, care should be taken in accepting the opinion-results correlation premise. Keep in mind that a great deal of effort was put into validating the questionnaire items. Gallup's results do not imply that any set of opinions given by employees correlates with job performance, and certainly not with operating results.

The second general finding was that opinions differed by work unit rather than by company. This implies that the local environment is more important than the corporate culture, structure, or policies. The point hidden in here is that the supervisor is the key. Management behavior is more important than anything. This is exactly what the Saratoga Institute found in its research into voluntary turnover, which is described later. Figure 8-2 shows where the original twelve items and the overall satisfaction factor correlate with the four dimensions.

To make connections between employee opinions and the four factors, we have to eliminate profitability. Whereas productivity and customer service are direct results of employee actions, profitability is a function of executive management. It is true that employees can do a lot of little things to save money, but the impact of executive action far outstrips employee behaviors when it comes to profitability. Voluntary turnover, or quitting, is a choice made by employees. Dis-

Figure 8-2. Correlations generalizable across companies.

Item	Customer Satisfaction	Profitability	Productivity	Turnover
Overall satisfaction		x	x	x
Known expectations	x	x	x	x
Resources and praise			x	x
Job fit	x	x		x
Recognition	x	x	x	
Caring	x	x	x	x
Mentoring of development		x	x	
Opinions count		x	x	
Importance/contribution			x	
Coworker commitment		x	x	
Best friend	x		x	
Opportunity for advancement	x		x	
Opportunity to grow		x		

counting personal reasons for leaving, such as a change in some aspect of one's life outside the workplace, quitting is a result of a series of frustrations. When we get to the Saratoga research, I'll say more about that. So, this leaves us with customer satisfaction and productivity.

Clearly, productivity is the most frequent correlation with employee feelings or opinions. A happy employee is a productive employee. And who has the most to do with an employee's positive feelings? The immediate supervisor, of course. Employee behavior is largely a function of the relationship with the supervisor. Customer satisfaction is a function of customer service, which is the way the employee interacts with the customer. And employee behavior is driven by supervisor behavior. Are you beginning to see a pattern?

Voluntary turnover is driven by only four items in the general list: knowing what is expected, availability of resources to do the job, a good fit between the job and one's talents and interests, and a feeling of being cared for as a human being. Who is it that assigns work and sets objectives, provides the tools necessary to do the job, and shows respect and caring for the employee? Employees who have a good relationship with their supervisors are much more apt to put up with poor

corporate policies, put in extra effort, and endure hardships—
even temporary wage cuts during tough times. Conversely, supervisors who do not take care of
their people always suffer high
turnover. Employees quit their supervisors, not the company. If you
ever quit a good job and company,
it was probably because you
couldn't stand to work for your
boss. Personally, I left a company I
really liked early in my career be-

> Supervisors who do not take care of their employees always suffer high turnover. Employees quit their supervisors, not the company.

cause I could not get a transfer away from my boss, who was
a two-timing SOB.

In conclusion, there are five items with the most power:
knowing what is expected, job fit, recognition, praise, and a
supervisor who shows that he or she cares. If we want to get
top performance and retain talented people, these are the
points to focus on. This will give us a better ROI from our
human capital.

The Employee Perspective

In 1996, the Saratoga Institute offered a retention management service for the first time. This was based on an intensive
exit interview program. Client companies sent lists of employees who had left voluntarily, and the institute contacted the
people and carried out the interviews by phone and written
questionnaire. Over three years, approximately 70,000 interviews for fifty companies were carried out. As the number of
responses mounted, patterns began to surface. Initially, we
found that the drivers of turnover were somewhat different
between low-level employees and professionals and managers. However, as the number of responses topped the 40,000
level, these drivers began to converge, and several generalizable factors emerged.

We discovered that people enter companies with a set of
expectations that are rather common, even across levels and
functions. They expect to:

- Receive job-related training.
- Receive career development support.
- Have advancement opportunity.
- Be treated as contributing adults.
- Have their knowledge and experience put to use.
- Be kept informed about company matters and changes.
- Be compensated fairly and equitably.

When any of these expectations are not fulfilled, dissatisfaction sets in. If enough disappointments or frustrations pile up, they quit.

Development and Training

Employees expect a match between their skills and the jobs they are assigned. Over time, they expect to receive training to build their skill base. On the job, they are looking for training that will make the job easier and the results better. They want their career objectives to be addressed by their supervisors and by the organization. Opportunities to make adjustments that will increase their contributions to the company are important. Most employees consider skill development and career advancement as means to greater earnings first, improved job satisfaction second, and company contribution third.

Communication

Most people are seeking two-way communication. They want their opinions to be considered as much as they want their supervisors and the company to communicate important matters to them. They like to know in advance what is coming so that they can help shape the change, if it is within their power. Complaints from employees point out that when things start going bad, communication dries up and the rumor mill becomes their main channel of information. Lack of communication is translated by employees as a feeling that they don't count for much, which implies a lack of respect. Employees who have direct contact with customers want to pass information up the chain. (By the way, isn't this what we mean when we talk about building a learning organization?) When their firsthand experience with customers is ignored, their disillusionment and dissatisfaction grow.

Compensation

Satisfied employees report an expectation that starting pay and pay adjustments will keep them in a competitive position. Pay becomes an issue only if the company fails to adjust to changes in the market or fails to equitably adhere to its own pay policy. Pay increases were more important than starting pay. When there is no perceived connection between exceptional performance and a clear payoff, people often leave in anger. Benefits are background issues for most people, so long as they are competitive. Women with children are most vulnerable to changes in benefits and are more likely to leave if the policy changes.

Management

Employees expect their managers to be well-trained and experienced. They want their professional opinions to be heard, and they hope that their supervisors are open to influence. When their accumulated special knowledge or experience is ignored, people tend to give up and quit. Employees do not expect managers to be clairvoyant, but they do expect them to be good communicators and responsive to the needs and problems of their employees. Supervisors who are not available or who disappear at the first sign of a problem are resented. The most important behavior trait is consistency.

■ ■ ■ ■ ■ ■

So, there you have the other side of the coin. Gallup talked with people who stayed and were successful or at least relatively satisfied with their lot. Saratoga talked with people who gave up and quit. In both groups, the principal driver of human performance and retention was the immediate supervisor or manager.

A Commonsense Example

Having examined what two large-scale, sophisticated studies found, it might be useful to see if that is the only way to learn to manage our human capital more effectively. Consider the experience and management philosophy of Hal Rosenbluth, CEO of Rosenbluth Travel. He described building his company from a regional to a global travel service in a book with the provocative title of *The Customer Comes Second.*[5] This claim flies in the face of every management theory I have ever heard. Everyone knows that customers always come first. Customers are always right. The customer is the only one who judges quality. In a service business, what could possibly come before the customer? Rosenbluth's answer is, the employees.

One example of a failing office speaks to the insights in Rosenbluth's book. He described how, under pressure from a large client, he rushed into opening a new office without going through his normal procedures. The first sign that everything wasn't going well was the error rate. According to Rosenbluth, this is always a sign of employee unhappiness. The second indication was a number of calls from unhappy employees from that office. Finally, the third signal came from a customer who called to say that corporate travelers were complaining about the service from the new office. The key point is that the customer was the last to see the problem. The employees' performance and morale slipped before the customer felt the effects. The employees clearly come first. If Rosenbluth had responded more quickly, he might have been able to cut out the problems before any of the customers felt them.

Rosenbluth built his business, which was listed among the Fortune 100 best companies to work for, by focusing on the employees. His basic rules of employee happiness drive excellent customer service, leading to improved profits. Those rules are:

1. Remember that happiness in the workplace is the key to providing superior service.
2. Look at areas with rising costs to see if there is a morale problem also.
3. Measure happiness in many ways—formally and informally.
4. Maintain frequent contact between the leaders and the people, and listen to the people, who often have money-saving, service-improving ideas.
5. Be constantly aware of the effect the company has on the personal as well as the professional lives of its people.
6. Involve the people, give them a sense of ownership, and make it fun to be at work.
7. Check the ratio of financial to human metrics of the business. "We have found the two coexist in perfect harmony. The humanistic approach to business yields the financial results companies seek, because people work better where they *want* to work."

Look at the list of employee opinions and expectations that Gallup and Saratoga uncovered. Not only is the tone identical to Rosenbluth's management model; the items map directly onto his basic rules. I am totally dedicated to gathering data before building hypotheses, but it is refreshing to find a case in the field that matches the data in the lab.

Leverage Opportunities

In an effort to contribute something of practical value, Dess and Picken carried out a three-year study of approximately one hundred leading-edge firms selected from *Fortune*'s "Most Admired" lists of 1994–1997.[6] To this list they added another hundred of what they considered to be "up-and-comers" based on their performance and innovative strategies. From this collection of materials and interview data, they built a model that incorporated human and structural capital.

This led them eventually to a compilation of what they termed "opportunities for leverage." They list five central functions, which they believe are basic to the effective management and leveraging of human capital. You will see some points of connection with what I described in Chapters 3 and 4.

The first step is to recruit, develop, and retain human capital. Next comes leveraging human skills through technology. These steps rest on efficient and effective organizational structures. To this system are overlaid the last two functions: incentives and controls, and leadership and a learning culture. This is an integrated approach that combines the value-adding power of each function. If one of them is missing or suboptimized, the total is diminished severely. Collectively, they are a formidable force for productivity and customer service.

To operationalize this system, Dess and Picken cross-matched the leveraging activities. That is, every activity has specific applications within each of the five central functions. The activities include:

- Recruiting and retaining top-notch human capital
- Training, developing, and shaping attitudes and encouraging individual learning
- Concentrating resources on top-priority activities
- Designing core processes to use the capabilities of human capital
- Accumulating and sharing organizational knowledge
- Encouraging and facilitating the sharing of individual knowledge
- Enhancing, extending, and multiplying individual capabilities
- Facilitating organizational learning

There is no best practice here. There is no one way to do these things. If business were that easy, everyone would be functionally effective. Each organization has to figure out for itself what it should do. This is a template from which management can choose the activity most appropriate for its company.

Summary

You recall from Chapter 4 that the principal elements in managing human capital are planning, acquiring, maintaining, developing, and retaining. Let's apply them to what we have learned so far.

Plan

It is clear that having a map of where you are and where you want to go is much more efficient than just setting out on a random drive. Taking the time to gather data is not a luxury; it is essential. The saying "Those who cannot remember the past are condemned to repeat it" applies, no matter how harried we feel. We must take time to plan our strategy and do it right the first time. In the case of human capital management, it requires that we know two things. First, we need to learn the enterprise goals and the rationale behind them, which includes knowledge of outside forces. Second, we need to talk with the functional unit leaders to learn how they are translating the enterprise goals into their business unit objectives. Then we can decide what we have to do, how fast we have to do it, how much money can be spent doing it, and how well it must be done.

Acquire

The first operating step in managing human capital to service the requirements of the enterprise is to develop a strategy and a set of tactics for acquiring talent. Again, we should know the cost, time, quantity, and quality requirements. Knowing the goals and objectives of our management customers will guide us in forming the strategy and tactics that are most cost-effective.

Maintain

People are assets that must be cared for, just like capital equipment. Pay and benefits programs help keep people productive. Money is like a lubricant. If a machine is not well lubricated, it slows down and eventually burns up. If people are not compensated properly, they slow down and eventually retire on the job or leave. Beyond pay, people need to have jobs that fit their talents and interests. They need, expect, and demand communication from their supervisors. And they want to know what is expected in the way of performance.

Develop

Employees want training and work experience that helps them grow. In a rapidly changing, technologically rich environment, people need their skills continually refreshed. Customers are more demanding than ever; therefore, a poorly trained employee cannot be tolerated. Formal training, informal coaching, and mentoring support employees' needs both psychologically and careerwise.

Retain

Employees need to know that their supervisors care about them as people. They want their supervisors to be available when needed. People need to be recognized and praised when they excel. If we pay attention to the items described in the earlier examples, we should have no problem keeping the people we want.

No matter what level we look at, it is clear that the relationship with one's boss is hypercritical. If an organization trains its managers to support their people in these ways, it can expect to retain talent and improve its ROI in its human capital.

References

1. Gary Hamel and C. K. Prahalad, *Competing for the Future* (Boston: Harvard Business School Press, 1994), p. 175.
2. Marcus Buckingham and Curt Coffman, *First, Break All the Rules* (New York: Simon and Schuster, 1999).

3. Jac Fitz-enz, *The 8 Practices of Exceptional Companies* (New York: AMACOM, 1997).
4. Frederick Herzberg, B. Mausner, and B. Snyderman, *The Motivation to Work* (New York: Wiley, 1959).
5. Hal Rosenbluth, *The Customer Comes Second* (New York: William Morrow and Company, 1992).
6. Gregory C. Dess and Joseph C. Picken, *Beyond Productivity* (New York: AMACOM, 1999), p. 228.

9

Quantum Leap

A Strategy for Inventing Your Future

"Life is either a daring adventure or nothing."

—*Helen Keller*

The market belongs to those who get there first. Being number one yields better margins and stronger customer loyalty. This is undeniably true, simply because numbers two and beyond have to compete on price, and as soon as number one drops its price, the rest lose all the customers who came only for the sale price. Becoming number one is not easy. Desire does not equal achievement. Warren Buffet is the most successful investor in history. Starting with $105,000 of friends' and relatives' money, in thirty years he built it into $45 billion. Warren once said, "Risk comes from not knowing what you are doing." One of the more effective paths to market prominence is to make a planned quantum leap into the future.

Planning the future requires a strategic viewpoint. So many forces are at work in the marketplace that we must take them into consideration before we launch a major offensive, or we court disaster. If we engage a consultant to help us develop a strategic plan, the consultant will work from a model. It may be one as well known as the McKinsey Seven S's or one that the consultant has developed. Either way, we will be asked to start by articulating and examining the drivers of our business.

In the same way, if we want to take a quantum leap past our competition, we have to examine the drivers of our business, one of which is our human capital. The difference is that in the quantum-leap process, a strategic plan is not the deliverable. In fact, in this approach, we won't develop a strategic plan at all, even though we go through much of the same research and analysis. The purpose in looking at drivers is twofold. First, we need to stop operations for a minute and think profoundly about all aspects of our enterprise and its position within the marketplace. Second, we need that background data in order to plan the quantum leap, which is itself the deliverable.

Performance Drivers

Every organization is driven by a combination of internal and external factors and forces. They are the causal forces within an organization that make it unique. They are fundamental to every business enterprise. Collectively, they describe why and how an organization's processes work as they do. Any negative drivers are constraints on our ability to act freely. If we ignore or misinterpret the drivers of our enterprise, we will certainly not be a market leader and might not even survive as a significant player within the industry. Figure 9-1 shows the interaction of the drivers with an organization's performance.

> If we ignore or misinterpret the drivers of our enterprise, we will certainly not be a market leader and might not even survive as a significant player.

Internal

An organization is driven first by its vision, articulated or not by the CEO. When there is no clear vision, there is no basis for decision making. Hewlett Packard's "The H-P Way," IBM's "Think," and Motorola's "6 Sigma" gave their people

Figure 9-1. Performance drivers.

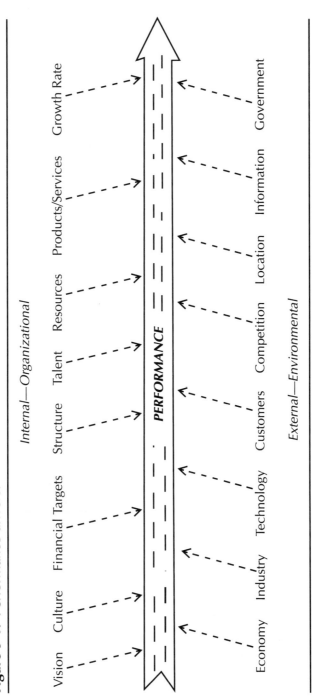

Internal—Organizational

Vision   Culture   Financial Targets   Structure   Talent   Resources   Products/Services   Growth Rate

PERFORMANCE

Economy   Industry   Technology   Customers   Competition   Location   Information   Government

External—Environmental

something to live by. The vision sets up the culture, which drives the design of structure and process and creates communication patterns and protocols. The products and services, financial targets, employee skills, and growth rate of the company all influence the *what* and the *how*. These are the principal drivers that push an organization in one direction or another. They are key questions that have to be answered when any strategic action is being formulated.

External

Since an organization does not live in a vacuum, environmental factors also influence decisions and actions. The state of the economy affects all businesses—some more than others—depending on the types of products or services being offered. Obviously, it is more difficult to sell Porsche automobiles and Piaget watches during a recession. Technology has become an extremely potent force in the last two decades of the twentieth century. In a free market, customer demands and competitors' actions often dictate actions that a company might not want to take, but must, in order to survive or maintain market position. Geographic location can be a positive or negative force. It affects labor availability. Of course, for infrastructure industries such as utilities, transportation, health care and telecommunications, the influence of government regulation is a powerful force.

At the end of the day, a list of performance drivers and their trends is essential to any strategic activity. This is even truer when we contemplate making a quantum leap into the unknown. The longer the leap, the bigger the risk and the more important it is to have a sound launching pad. Keep in mind that labor availability and the skill levels of employees are key issues in any quantum-leap planning. As always, plans and capital investments are essential, but without talented and motivated people to execute them, we will achieve nothing. Once we have a clear idea of the state of our drivers, we can proceed along the pathway toward planning a quantum leap.

Human Capital Signs of the Future

The accounting function does a fine job of telling the state of our past and present financial health. But it says nothing about the future. Additionally, it does not speak to human capital issues. To see the future, we need leading indicators. In Figure 5-6, I offered a set of leading human capital indicators. This is another place where they come into play.

These indicators tell us the state of our human capital as we prepare for the future. Beyond employee skills, leading indicators give us some sense of the degree of stability we can expect as we launch into the future. Factors such as voluntary separation rate, job satisfaction, and commitment let us know how reliable our workforce will be. As we examine our drivers, we can look at the human capital leading indicators. They show us our chances of making a successful quantum leap. If we are going to have a problem with the workforce, it would be good to know it now.

The Lead Questions

The future belongs to the customer. No matter what we do inside our companies, the customer will ultimately decide how well we do in the marketplace. That being so, it seems reasonable to begin an investigation of the market by asking our customers what they want from us. Market surveys are common, ongoing events. Such surveys can be enriched if they go beyond the standard questions such as, What do you like and not like about our products and services? These questions focus on us, not on our customers. Even if we respond to the deficiencies, we are talking about improving on past performance. Like most people, our customers are buried in their daily routine of battling the alligators. Seldom can they articulate strategic solutions to their problems. What they can tell us in detail are their daily frustrations. It is up to us to figure out how to help them overcome those frustrations. If we do that, we win customer loyalty that low prices can sel-

dom erase. I have been with one insurance company for almost forty-five years because of its understanding of my needs
and its customer service. When other insurers approach me, I
tell them not to waste their time talking about lower rates.
Personal concern and service have won my loyalty for life.

An effective tack to take if we want to jump the curve and
get ahead of the competition is to focus on the frustrations the
customer is experiencing within the scope of our product or
service range. Two ways of asking this type of question are:

1. What are you doing that you wish you could do better?
2. What bugs you?

I grant that these are not the most articulate questions, and I
doubt that any marketing research firm would pose them in
those words. But sometimes if we
cut through the brain and get to the
gut, we learn the truth. The following section illustrates this theory
with an example that anyone over
forty can relate to.

> Sometimes if we cut
> through the brain and get
> to the gut, we learn the
> truth.

Evolution of a Solution

When I started in business, everyone used typewriters—
manual typewriters. The two performance issues with typing
are speed and errors. Speed is measured in words per minute,
and errors per page are counted. If a marketing research firm
of the 1960s asked what the customer liked about the typewriter company, it would have gotten answers about product
reliability and service. From that, the company could have
made incremental improvements, but seldom any break-
throughs. But someone was smart enough to look at the two
basics of typing and come up with solutions that typists never
thought of.

Speed

The smart company realized that it took a good deal of pressure to depress some keys. If you ever tried to lift the carriage mechanism by depressing the Shift key with your pinky, you understand the problem: It took a lot of pressure. So the first change was to make the bank of type bars movable. The bank was much lighter than the carriage and required less pressure to move. The next change was to introduce a power assist. Electrical power was introduced to trigger the key strikes. This greatly relieved fatigue and increased speed.

Errors

When a typist made a mistake, he or she had to stop and erase it with a hard eraser and then brush the residue away. This made a mess in the typewriter and required periodic service calls to clean the machine. It also severely slowed down the process. The first advancement was correction fluid. This was better than erasing, and the end result didn't look too bad if you applied the fluid very lightly. But it did take several seconds to dry. Then came correcting swatches. These little pieces of paper had dry white material on one side. You put it over the error, typed the same key to blot out the error, then backspaced and typed the correct letter over the correction—voila, less mess and a better look. Finally, someone put a roll of correcting tape on the typewriter just below the ribbon. By simply backspacing and rekeying, you could cover the error and type in the right letter. This was high-tech.

In the end, typists were less fatigued, could type faster on an electric keyboard, and spent less time correcting their errors. All these improvements came from asking about the biggest problems typists faced rather than how well the company was doing.

■ ■ ■ ■ ■ ■

That was improvement in functionality. The next insight was to expand functionality. From the electric typewriter, we went to the electronic word processor and the computer with memory and the first word-processing programs. I still remember the excitement the first time we saw automatic word wrap—no more carriage return lever. After word processing came spreadsheets, desktop publishing, presentation graphics, and portability. You know the rest.

This little trip down memory lane had a purpose beyond reminiscence. It was about opening up to new ways of thinking and learning how to institutionalize it. Thinking about the opportunities of the future rather than the problems of the present will help us invent our future. To do that, we need data. To obtain the data, we need to make quantum leaps; we have to learn the right questions to ask. I believe that one of the best data-gathering systems is people—namely, our employees. We need to arm them with forward-thinking questions.

The Number-One Information Center

Every employee is an information repository. Knowingly or not, people pick up data in the course of doing their jobs. In many cases, they are not told to do that. What is worse, when they offer data to managers, they are rebuffed with the attitude, You're not paid to think! I believe that the companies that learn how to turn on the information- and intelligence-gathering capability that lies dormant in most employees will dominate the future. And the ROI of human capital in those firms will be astronomical. They will be able to produce much more per person. They will be opening new product lines faster, creating new markets while competitors are reworking old ones, and continually improving life for customers and employees. When that is achieved, management will truly be leveraging the potential of its human capital.

> Companies that learn how to turn on the information- and intelligence-gathering capability that lies dormant in most employees will dominate the future. Their ROI of human capital will be astronomical.

There are four requisites to making this a reality:

1. Turning employees into intelligence-gathering machines
2. Developing systems to collect and classify the intelligence gathered
3. Assigning someone to analyze the data for market opportunities
4. Establishing a culture that drives and rewards intelligence generation

Employees

Every employee sees things every day that have potential value for beating the competition. Even staff departments such as accounting, information technology, and human resources that are focused on supporting the corporate infrastructure can be taught to keep their eyes open to possible new ventures. Telling our people that we see them as sources

> Challenge people to keep their senses tuned to wild and crazy ideas that just might work.

of competitive intelligence rather than as administrative drones will inspire them. Challenge them to keep their senses tuned to wild and crazy ideas that just might work. Let them know that probably eight out of ten will not work, but every once in a while, someone will come up with a blockbuster that can change the world. Most of the great ideas do not come out of the R&D labs. Post-it Notes didn't. Xerography didn't. They were products of one frustrated person.

Systems

Make data collection and submission an easy task. Create an internal, secure Web site or a knowledge exchange that only employees can access. This is the tool that people need to make intelligence gathering an exciting and rewarding challenge. Without it, the plan will die quickly.

Analysis

Assign someone to review the inputs. Make this his or her primary job. If it isn't enough for a full-time job in the beginning, set that person onto some research. Work out the ideas that have at least a 10 percent chance of adding value (don't wait for the fully finished grand idea). Set up a "wild and crazy idea" task group. When an idea is developed, pass it on to management and report back to the employee what happened. At the very least, you will have turned on employees, because someone is honestly communicating with them and asking them to think.

Culture

Instill in the culture the value of knowledge sharing. Recognize people who come up with good ideas. When you get a blockbuster idea, reward the person *lavishly*. Make a spectacle of it to show Everyman and Everywoman that ordinary people like themselves are winners.

An idea that seems really silly at first glance just might have a kernel of profound truth buried in it. Look at the craziness of it with an open mind. Be childlike for a few minutes. Make believe that you really want to make that quantum leap. It is going to be a lot easier to leap the gap if you have a stout pole to use in vaulting over it.

This concept is not the same as a suggestion award program or building a learning organization, although it shares many of the same elements. Both focus on gathering and sharing information from internal operations for the purpose of improving productivity. The intelligent company gathers data from everywhere, by everyone, from outside and inside, for the purpose of making a quantum leap in the market. This is how it applies to managing human capital. Beyond doing their jobs better, people become intelligence agents. The many ideas that you receive can be levers to pry open executive minds for the next step in preparing for a quantum leap.

Building Scenarios

Now, we know our company. We are getting wild and crazy ideas every day. Energy is flowing. It takes a lot of energy to make a quantum leap. NASA didn't get a man on the moon by launching him with a firecracker. The next step in preparing for the leap is to build a short list of possible future scenarios using the data from the review of internal and external drivers. I propose a quantum leap of five years, later in this chapter. To prepare for that, I suggest a set of three scenarios, each of which looks three years ahead. This will prepare us for looking into the future without straining our imagination too much.

The scenarios can be built around a number of driving forces. I recommend we look at the following:

- Demographic trends to tell us about population, education, and labor trends
- Technology developments to give us an idea of what might be possible
- Customer lifestyles to suggest what might be most salable three years from now
- Economic trends to alert us to major shifts in demand
- Government tendencies to give us a clue as to forthcoming regulations

Of course, other drivers can be added to the scenarios. I left out the competition purposely. If we are enlightened enough about what we are doing, the competition will be playing for second place. Of course, it is your choice to include or exclude any driver, depending on how important it is for your future.

The Possible, Probable, and Unthinkable

Three scenarios should be constructed around each of the five forces. One should be the worst-case scenario, one should be the best-case, and the last should be the most probable. I suggest doing them in this order so that we experience some reality before we go euphoric. Then, we can end with what is most likely to happen. Figure 9-2 is a matrix layout that keeps everything in view at one time. By forcing ourselves into a cramped matrix cell, we have to think and write sharply. Cutting down on the adjectives helps us stick to the essence of the points.

The objective of the scenarios is not to come up with a plan to execute over the next three years. It is to continue to open our minds, expand our thinking, and practice looking ahead. By starting with the key driving forces and then looking out a few years, we are breaking away from the daily grind. This is vital if we are to make a quantum leap. We have to gather our full speed and strength before we jump. A little limbering up and practice are called for. Metaphorically, when we take that quantum leap, we will jump off the cliff and must land on the other side. We can't jump halfway across the gap and then change our minds. This is not a cartoon. If we misstep and fall in a trench, it will really hurt.

How to Make a Quantum Leap

Everyone knows that the world changed drastically in the last twenty years of the twentieth century. Clearly, the major driver of that change was the rapid advancement in information technology that transformed communication from the individual to the global level. When I think back to the 1960s, there were no copy machines, faxes, personal computers, pagers, consumer mobile telephones, personal digital assistants, or the worldwide net. To wish that we could operate tomorrow as we did in 1960, or even 1990, is foolish.

Imparato and Harari offer four organizing principles that are useful for positioning ourselves for the exigencies of the new market.[1]

1. *Look a customer ahead.* Today's products and services will not meet the needs of tomorrow's customer (think of the

Figure 9-2. Scenario matrix.

	Demographics: Population, Education, Labor Availability	Economy: From Recession to Boom	Technology: Trends in Sciences	Customer: Emerging Needs and Desires	Government: Likely Responses to Events
Unthinkable					
Hopeful					
Probable					

computer versus the typewriter). Beyond products, this suggests that we might have to create new markets rather than push harder into existing markets.

2. *Build the company around the software and the software around the customer.* The key corporate assets today and in the future are people and information. The intangible asset of employee brainpower is the lever of profitability. This intelligence is the software of the company. Design to support the employee in supporting the customer.

3. *Ensure that those who live the values of the organization are the most rewarded and most satisfied.* To make a quantum leap, the organization needs to harness the diverse skills and values of the workforce. This must be done in such a way that everyone sees a consistent commitment and fair dealing for those who support the change effort.

4. *Treat the customer as the final arbiter of quality by offering an unconditional guarantee of complete satisfaction.* The traditional arrangement with the customer was legalistic—doing what the contract called for. That is no longer sufficient. The organization must build into its systems and attitudes the notion that nothing short of total customer satisfaction is acceptable.

These principles, though not radical, are certainly not traditional. They represent the type of thinking that is necessary to serve the emerging marketplace. What was good, right, and true yesterday has not only changed but will continue to change. We are in an era of transformation that calls for expanded perspectives. Making a large-scale change in an organization is an entirely different challenge than reengineering a process. The difference is not only one of scope but also one of nature. The vast majority of changes that take place in organizations are incremental amendments, alterations, or modifications in an existing structure or process. These can be small scale, such as a process adjustment, or large scale, such as a corporate downsizing. In either case, it is a change in the way something is organized or conducted. American business has been going through change in a big way since the 1980s, with the introduction of quality programs. We have a number of tested methods for managing change. We know how to reduce costs, make quality improvements, reengineer processes, and restructure business units. All these hold the potential for adding value. Unfortunately, around two out of three change programs in the last twenty years have failed to achieve their initial value objectives. This is an amazing statistic, considering that most businesspeople are not stupid bunglers. They know their processes and their people well enough to make positive changes. So, why is there such a high failure rate?

Reversing the Failure Rate

Change projects can fail for many reasons. However, assuming that the people driving the projects are not total idiots, there are about four reasons for failure:

1. Quick-fixes
2. Obsolete solutions
3. Incorrect analysis
4. Organizational resistance

Quick Fixes

These don't achieve lasting change because they can't. By their nature, they deal with symptoms, not causes. They don't allow for the time necessary to find the root of the problem. They deliver aspirin tablets to people with broken legs. The pain and inflammation might be reversed, but the person still can't run the 100 meters in less than ten minutes.

Obsolete Solutions

To state that change is constant and often invisible is to reiterate the obvious. Yet some people attack today's problems with yesterday's attitudes and methods. This is most obvious in employee relations. Some older managers apply their values when attempting to motivate young people. The old-timer forgets that today is different from yesterday, no matter how much he wishes it weren't. If you are a child of the depression, you never forget the anxiety your parents went through regarding job security. If you are a baby boomer, you might still be living with Woodstock rather than rap. The images that frighten or inspire you are a function of your generation, not later ones. You can't use them to move other people.

Incorrect Analysis

If we don't understand the problem, it is difficult to fix it. There are many sources of problems: lack of motivation, inferior materials or equipment, missing data, capricious last-minute changes, awkward processes, coworker friction, no cooperation from other units, incompetent supervisors, inadequate pay, and so on. If we misinterpret the source of the problem, we will apply the wrong methodology to solve it. Giving motivational speeches or offering incentives to people who don't have the skill to do the job only adds to their frustration. Reengineering an awkward process but not improving the equipment or materials will not result in lower rework rates. Taking the time to correctly identify the problem greatly improves the odds of a successful solution.

Organizational Resistance

Sometimes being right isn't enough. You also have to have the power to push the right solution through the organization. People resist for many reasons, most of them very personal. Threatened loss of face or power stops many change programs. Ignorance, fear, and resistance to learning new ways are also powerful stoppers. So many books have been written about resistance to change that I don't need to restate the reasons. The solution, of course, is to change the power balance in your favor. This often means convincing people to stop resisting because the change is not going to hurt them, or invoking a greater power from above the resistance point to support and drive the change.

The bottom line on change failure is simply that these

projects deal with *doing* something differently. The only way to make bedrock, large-scale change in an organization is to teach it how to *be* different. *Doing* focuses on processes. *Being* focuses on context. This is a seminal difference. It is a difference not of magnitude but of essence. Rather than trying harder to change more processes, the idea is to change what *is* to what *must be*.

> The only way to make bedrock, large-scale change in an organization is to teach it how to *be* different, not how to *do* something differently.

Dogs Don't Fly

One of my favorite expressions is, Dogs don't fly. It means that if you want a pet that flies, don't spend your time and energy trying to teach your dog to fly. Get a bird. The point is that everything has limitations, and no matter how much you wish for it or how hard you work on it, things cannot change their nature. I tell women that if they want someone who is attentive, listens, is supportive, and cares deeply about human relationships, don't marry a man. Get a girlfriend. We men are like dogs; we can't change our nature, and we don't fly.

So it is in business. If you want major, lasting revitalization of the organization, don't waste your time on incremental change improvements. Instead, decide how you want the organization to *be* as a place to work and as the provider of choice. Customers don't care how an organization's processes work, but they care deeply about what kind of organization it is. To win that special place in the hearts and wallets of your customers, you have to be an extraordinary organization. That translates into superior service, quality, and productivity. Process changes can give you more efficiency, but they cannot give you the sustaining energy in the workforce to make your customer service the best there is. The reason is that service is not a process issue. Granted, there are processes by which you deliver service, but at the end of the day, customer satisfaction is based not on the efficiency of the process so much as on the desire of the employee to deliver world-class service. You don't get that desire from process change. You get it by making your company a special place to work. That comes from *being* the best organization.

Reexamining Our Nature

Quantum leaps require a reexamination of the nature of the organization. Rather than focusing initially on behaviors that are driven by processes, which are the result of management's vision, we have to reverse the process. It is a redefinition of the context of the organization.

Context is an all-inclusive term that covers everything from technological investment to culture management. It defines the nature of an organization. Nature is a constant, and behavior is a variable. If we can clearly define, communicate, and support a new nature, we will obtain the behaviors we want. Fundamentally, it is a question of *who we are* versus *what we do*. In the mid-1990s, the U.S. Army ran a series of recruiting ads that focused on the activities of soldiers. I remember one very energetic ad showing soldiers sliding down ropes from helicopters, climbing cliffs, and setting up command posts, all at high speeds. The punch line was, "We do more by 6 A.M. than most people do all day!" It was a very effective campaign. Concurrently, the Marine Corps was running an ad showing a single marine in a dress uniform with his ceremonial saber, standing rigidly at attention. I only remember the punch line, which was, "The few, the proud, the Marines." It still makes my hair stand on end. While the army was talking about *doing* exciting things—an idea that would appeal to energetic young men and women—the marines were talking about *being* something. At a time when many young people were seeking something to believe in, this ad provided it. That is context. If you are a marine, or ever talked to a marine about his or her service, you can feel the difference. There's nothing wrong with the army. It is just different.

Context tells everyone inside and out, all stakeholders, what the organization believes is possible. It drives all decisions, supports all actions, and predicts subsequent results.

BEing = Vision × Culture × Strategy × Commitment

An organization that seeks to change its nature and be something different focuses on four requisites: vision, culture, strategy, and commitment. These four issues are interactive rather than additive. If one is missing, the multiplicative power is severely diminished.

The first requirement is a clear vision of what the organization must become. The vision must be basic, honest, positive, and inspiring. It can't be hyperbole. It must be backed with evidence of why it is imperative. The reasoning must be not only commercial but also humanistic. You win the hands and minds with commercial reasoning. You win the hearts with humanistic reasoning.

The second requirement is culture. Great companies are built on great cultures. Culture is the powerful, driving life force of an organization. It is the corporate blood that carries the nutrients throughout the system to nourish, support, and revivify. Legally describing an organization as a corporation (Inc.), or in some countries as a society (S.A.), recognizes the intrinsic parallel to a body, a corpus. I can't think of any organization that sustained greatness over decades that did not have a powerful, positive, inspiring culture.

The next requirement is strategy. There has to be a grand plan to carry out the vision. The strategy focuses on the internal tactics that will be deployed to deal with the external market factors. Externally, the state of technology; competition; global, national, and regional economies; government policy and regulations; and community support influence a corporate strategy. Strategies that ignore external forces ultimately drive a company to inappropriate and belated actions. When the strategy or the culture gets out of sync with the marketplace, the company suffers. One of the best examples of the 1990s was IBM. For thirty years a most admired and successful company, IBM gradually lost touch with the changes in the marketplace and the shifting needs of its customers. Tied to a mainframe mind-set backed by three decades of commercial success, IBM executives refused to see that new forces were at work. Someone once said that success is the first step on the road to failure. What that means is that success often breeds arrogance, the "you can't argue with success" cliché. Arrogance is a slippery slide that quickly propels anyone on it to the bottom.

The final and critical requirement is commitment. Without commitment, everything else is just words. So it is in many organizations—inspiring words on plaques, promises of a new culture, grand strategies in impressive folders. Then the first bump in the road overturns the shiny new vehicle. Everyone at the top of the organization must demonstrate every day that there is commitment behind the words. A story about an aborted commitment will make the point.

The CEO of a large, famous corporation hired a well-known human resources director. The chief executive recruited the director on the premise that the culture needed to be changed even though the firm was financially very successful. One day shortly after arriving, the new director witnessed a high-ranking executive treating an employee extremely rudely in front of her peers. The director took the executive aside and suggested that this was inappropriate. When the issue rose to the owner's level, his response was, "Yes, that is not good, but he is a big producer." Nothing was done. Commitment died at the first bump. The HR director, to his credit, promptly quit.

A side note: I had been asked by the company to consult on performance measurement a few months before the new director was hired. I found that there were plaques all over the building stating the new vision of the company. After this incident, the message was clear to everyone: Forget the words, it's the same old BS. If we're not going to totally support the new order, it is better that we never start in that direction.

How to Create a New Context

Motorola under the leadership of Bob Galvin offers an example of a company that reinvented its context several times over a fifteen-year period. Galvin saw in the early 1970s that the world was changing in many ways. The culture of the founder, his father Paul, had been paternalistic and had worked well for four decades. But Bob saw that a paternalistic system could not move fast enough to compete as the marketplace was increasing its speed. So, he decreed that the company was going to shift its culture to be more participative. The stated vision was to become the "highest-quality manufacturer." The famous 6 Sigma program drove this. Bob supported it with major investments in training and his personal, very visible enthusiasm for it. Over about eight years, he got his culture change. At that point, he pushed for a new, even better context. The vision was now to become the "premier world company," with all that that implied. Finally, five years later, he went for the next context, which was to be the "best company to work for in the world." By continually driving new, exciting contextual changes, Galvin kept Motorola in the forefront of American business. Unfortunately, when he retired in the early 1990s, the next generation of leadership was not as strong, wise, or committed to providing the sustaining energy, and the company fell behind in several of its main product lines.

The fundamental concept of quantum leaps is to manage tomorrow from the future. That is not a typo. It is the key difference between quantum leaping and other management strategies. We need to stand mentally in the future marketplace. As we envision it, the question is, How do we want to *be* when it arrives? Keep the *be* word in front. This is not about reengineering or downsizing. Those are not context. Those are tools or tactics that might be necessary to help make the move, but they are not the thing we are talking about. Quantum leaping demands that we manage tomorrow by *being* there *today*.

Taking the Leap

To be in the future today, we have to imagine it. There are four steps in making a quantum leap. In order to navigate them successfully, we have to apply several key questions to each of the steps:

1. What will be important five years from now?
2. What will be the most difficult things for competitors to copy?
3. Where do we find data to answer these questions?
4. What can we do about it today?

The first question is the foundation. It presumes a total view of all aspects of the future marketplace. If we get this right, all subsequent decisions and actions have a much better chance of being appropriate and effective. In addition, it will give us the answer to the second question, and that is where we find our competitive advantage. The third question is a matter of research, and there is no dearth of economic, social, or technological data in this country. We will see the answer to the fourth question when we reach the fourth step in the process.

Step 1. Description

Describe the organization as we want it to be five years from now. Concentrate on the enduring qualities behind the visible parts of the company. The components of a business enterprise over which management has some influence are people, facilities, technology, material, products and services, suppliers, shareholders, and customers. Think about them in the most basic sense. We are laying bedrock here. This is the foundation for everything to come. Ask these questions:

- What kind of place do we want it to be for people to work in?
- What types of people do we want to work with? Profile the personality traits we would like to see in our co-workers. Technology will surely evolve, but people don't change as easily.
- What should the physical facility look like? Let's avoid the temptation to adopt the latest fad. What kind of workspace would we like to work in in the future? More important, what type of space will attract people and

make them comfortable so that they can perform at top level?

- Where in the price–performance continuum do we want our products or services to be? Do we want to be the low-price or the high-quality company?
- What types of customers do we want? This is a question that people often ignore. But it is important because it must mesh with the product question. We won't sell many Ferraris to retired people or cheap clothing to the nouveaux riches.
- How do we want to work with our suppliers? Will the low-cost guy win, or are we willing to sacrifice a few pennies in favor of establishing a long-term, mutually beneficial relationship?
- What type of investors do we want to attract? Do we want the day-traders or the institutional funds? Each will be attracted by a different business strategy and performance profile.

Answers to these and other related questions should spark a lively debate. If everyone in the decision-making group is in violent agreement, we probably ought to rethink our answers. Maybe we need an outsider to come in and probe our answers for validity.

Step 2. Context

Analyze the descriptive terms we used. What are the adjectives that keep appearing? Do we see words like these?

flexible	competitive	open
fast-paced	low-cost	focused
accessible	automated	leading-edge
humanistic	fair	collaborative
driven	team-based	committed
balanced	never satisfied	high risk/
responsive	opportunistic	high reward

Pull them out and make a list. How does that feel? Is that what we imagined for our organization five years from now?

Step 3. Barriers

What is going to get in the way of our being that way? Life seldom goes as we planned. Even less frequently do grand strategies play out as desired or anticipated. In this case, what (or maybe who) will resist our plan? What prevents us from leaving the past and moving on to confront the realities of the future? It's time for another list. This is the barrier list—the forces that might resist our contextual change.

Lacking strong, committed leadership
Preferring slow, evolutionary change
Waiting to be told what to do
Avoiding confrontations with difficult people or issues
Not punishing those who resist the change
Promoting people who are poor role models of the change
Having no sense of urgency to change at all
Lacking financial resources
Having tired technology
Not understanding the new marketplace

It is highly predictable that we will encounter some if not all of these barriers. Of course, there may be other resisting forces not on the list. The question becomes, How do we deal with the resistance? The answers are unique to each company.

Step 4. Enablers

A potential stumbling block is to get so involved in dealing with resistance that we have no energy left for making the change happen. After we have a strategy for dealing with any antici-pated resistance and we are certain that we have the courage and com-

How do we manage tomorrow from today?

mitment to see the change through, it is time to answer the strange question, which is, How do we manage tomorrow from today? We have stood in the future and designed a set of blueprints for our new company. Naturally, one wonders how we are going to pull it off. The solution is found principally with corporate system design.

If you follow my logic that says that processes are a function of vision, strategy, and culture, then it is a less formidable task. We have a vision, strategy, and culture plan. Systems, processes, and policies are the operational forces that drive behavior. We have listed the characteristics we want to see in our new company, but they must be designed into our systems. Let me repeat it: *designed into* our systems.

It is very difficult for someone to resist a concentration of culture and systems. Systems enable us to do our jobs, and culture tells us why we do it this way. Therefore, if we redesign our systems now to meet the specifications described in step two, we will begin to live in the future. This means that we need to look at:

> Strategies and processes for selecting people and housing them
> R&D philosophy, investment, and methodology
> Production methods
> Sales and marketing strategies and processes
> Distribution channels
> Customer service systems
> Finance and accounting systems
> Information technology investment and management
> Facilities management

Every major strategy, process, and policy needs to be reviewed and updated to match the descriptors in step two. We can do this. The trick is making it work. Notwithstanding all the reasons why it can't work, if we are truly committed to contextual change, we will succeed. Contextual change will give us the leverage to make the quantum leap into tomorrow, today. And people will make it happen.

Summary

Change programs have not been especially effective more than half the time. The reason is that they focus on improving a process rather than changing the underlying drivers. In other words, we don't have time to drain the swamp because we are too busy fighting the alligators. Attempts at quick fixes, using obsolete methods for poorly analyzed problems, and not being able to overcome resistance to change kills many good ideas. If we really want change, we have to shift the focus from *doing* something to *being* something. The context has to change in order for real progress to occur swiftly. Context gives us a picture of what is possible and preferred. It is the sum total of everything from technology investment to corporate culture.

To establish a new context, we have to have a clear vision, positive culture, forward-looking strategy, and commitment to persevere. Once we have those things, there is a four-step process that will take us through to a new organization suited for the future. The four steps are (1) describe the organization as we want to see it five years out, (2) make a list of the descriptive terms we use to ensure that this is what we want, (3) recognize the resistance we might encounter, and (4) design the systems that embody the descriptors in step two.

The lesson of this chapter is that we have to take on two challenges. One is to gather data that will help us see ahead of the curve. This enables us to redesign the organization in a way that makes quantum leaping a natural event. The other is to find a way to make a leap across that curve to position us in front of the competition. This requires a process for doing it not once but every three to four years. It takes a year to change systems, policies, and processes. It takes another year to get the new ways to work. This means that within a year you'll be ready to start planning another quantum leap.

From a human capital standpoint, we need leading indicators to give us an idea of how well prepared we are for the future. Without the right people, we have no chance of succeeding. Measures of competence, readiness, employee commitment, satisfaction, climate, and voluntary turnover produce a view of our position. Finally, a competitiveness index combining all those indicators plus any unique company factors yields a single, overall indicator of support for a quantum leap.

Reference

1. Nicholas Imparato and Oren Harari, *Jumping the Curve* (San Francisco: Jossey-Bass, 1994).

10

Guiding Principles

"You may be flexible on strategy, but must remain consistent on principle!"

—Anonymous

Throughout the writing of this book, I made notes about the principles that underlie my thinking and experience. Originally, my thought was to place them in the book where their point would fit in the text. However, I now believe that it makes more sense to put them all in one place. As you review these principles, please pause for a moment on each one and ask yourself what the point is behind it. Why did I decide that it would be useful to reinforce these issues?

The Foundation Stones of the Human Capital Measurement Pathway

Principle 1: People Plus Information Drives the Knowledge Economy

You've heard it before and you'll hear it again: This is the Information Age, and people are the most important resource. It is true—profoundly true—with implications that are still difficult to fully grasp. Imagine going into the twenty-first century without current telecommunications technology. It would be impossible to sustain the growth of the world market without the rapid movement of information. And, as we increasingly automate our organizations, we change our cultures. Since communication is so central to a culture, new channels and media force a culture change. Bringing people and organizations along as fast as technology is the primary challenge.

Principle 2: Management Demands Data; with Relevant Data We Start Managing

To say that we have no data is not accurate. We collect data constantly through our senses in interaction with our colleagues and our environment. However, we need relevant information with which to make good decisions. Many decisions are made without adequate data. Sometimes it can't be helped. An apparent emergency springs up, and we must respond. Nevertheless, this does not provide an excuse for the lack of a human capital information database and reporting system. People who have the best information are the winners.

Principle 3: Human Capital Data Shows the How, the Why, and the Where

Since people are the only self-determining assets, it follows that they are the cause of everything that happens. If something goes well, it is due to the behaviors of the people involved. If it blows up, literally or figuratively, that is also the result of human behavior. It must follow, then, that in order to know how to improve something, we must know how people are dealing with it. Cost, time, quantity, and quality data on human capital provide the base for effective action.

Principle 4: Validity Demands Consistency; Being Consistent Promotes Validity

The principal criticism of human capital measurement is that it is neither as consistent nor as accurate as financial information. This is because people have started measurement programs by adopting unproven external metrics or by making up their own. When the system is not standardized, everyone who comes along is free to change it to suit their personal needs. Then there is no way to compare their view with that of others, since the definitions are idiosyncratic. They build a modern Tower of Babel. However, when a standard set of metrics is established and used consistently over a long period, they are as accurate as a financial system.

Principle 5: The Value Path Is Often Covered, and Analysis Uncovers the Pathway

One of the major barriers to measuring qualitative, intangible human capital factors is the belief that we cannot demonstrate cause and effect. Many unknown and unknowable forces constantly in action make it impossible to prove anything in business. Nevertheless, being clear about our destination, knowing the positive and negative forces along the way, and understanding the process necessary for the journey increase the odds that we will travel by the most expeditious route and arrive ahead of the hunch players.

Principle 6: Coincidence May Look Like Correlation but Is Often Just Coincidence

It is a great temptation to claim that factors moving in parallel are correlated. Unfortunately, often what we observe is only a random variation. This error can be avoided if we start our observation from valid principles. Believing that two things that are basically unconnected to each other are related is the basis for most misperceptions. To produce a true correlation, we must first demonstrate the probability that A and B have something to do with each other. Starting from this base avoids false conclusions.

Principle 7: Human Capital Leverages Other Capital to Create Value

People make things happen. Equipment, processes, and intellectual property are leveraged not by their inherent capability but by the actions of human beings. Employee skill, knowledge, and motivation generate the incremental values that lie within the potential of organizational assets. Management provides the structural capital at the best cost possible. Employees give life to that capital and create value through interaction with coworkers and outside stakeholders.

Principle 8: Success Requires Commitment, and Commitment Breeds Success

The history of sustained excellence in business shows that commitments were made to a long-term core strategy. That strategy described the organization's dedication to dealing with employees, customers, suppliers, competitors, and other stakeholders, including community and government. Frequent oscillations between divergent philosophies and behaviors are a recipe for failure. Despite accounts of sensational results in isolated and short-term situations, the rule is inviolable. Building an institution of value is the only management practice that guarantees long-term excellence.

Principle 9: Volatility Demands Leading Indicators, and Leading Indicators Reduce Volatility

Walking into the future with our eyes glued to the results of the past is a very dangerous act. The wide-open, volatile, global marketplace of the twenty-first century allows everyone to compete. Cyclonic changes in technology make yesterday's processes obsolete overnight. The instantaneous access to information and the annual doubling of knowledge demand a constant view of the horizon. We absolutely must have intelligence systems that provide clues to what is coming. That includes intelligence on human, structural, and relational capital. It is as vital to a successful future as a healthy lifestyle is to extended longevity.

Principle 10: The Key Is to Supervise, and the Supervisor Is the Key

All evidence points to personal relationships as the cornerstone of employee performance. The talented employee depends on the supervisor for guidance, support, and development. Throughout one's career, the supervisor is the principal route for two-way communications. This person interprets what is happening and what is coming. This person describes how change will affect the employee. This person defends the employee and is the primary channel through which employee ambitions are fulfilled.

Principle 11: The Future Is Harder to Prepare for Than the Past

I leave you with this business koan. Think about it. Let me know what it says to you (my personal e-mail: source@ netgate.net).

11

Summing Up and Looking Ahead

"A core skill to understanding the future is the willingness to see it."

—*Jennifer James*

If you have made it this far, I admire your perseverance. I've bombarded you with numerous graphics and dozens of formulas covering the whole of the enterprise from the strategic corporate level down to the human resources function. I realize how complex this exposition is, but we are dealing with a complex topic. This is the end product of over twenty years of measuring human behavior in organizations. In essence, they are my argument for the valuation of human capital. Still, like any complex issue, it doesn't include everything that could be said.

Each company is unique. It is a combination of management philosophy, financial strength, culture, employee relations, market reputation, competitors, and customers in a singular mix. Many people don't like to look deeply into a complex topic. They find it disconcerting to admit that something may require a reconfiguration of their frame of reference. They spend precious energy defending the status quo. So, when people respond to your suggestion that they apply these metrics and practices with the ancient avoidance, "But we're different," agree with them. Then point out that this is a framework within which they can construct a system that suits their needs.

Bringing It All Together in One Place

I would like to sum it up for you. Given the three levels and the connections I outlined in Chapters 2 through 5, I now en-capsulate them in one display of all the common possible mea-sures. Figure 11-1 restates those metrics and their formulas. I suggest that you look at the figure and decide which elements you need to understand and apply at each level of your organi-zation. Yes, every company is different; nevertheless, we all use one system of financial accounting. We can use one system of human capital evaluation as well. The good news is that you can choose from the list in Figure 11-1 to make a set that will work for you. No one from the FASB or the SEC is going to come knocking on your door to tell you it is wrong.

Remember to set up your system so that you can see the connections between the levels. When you make an improve-ment in one of the four human capital management areas— acquiring, maintaining, developing, and retaining—where does it touch the operating units? If that improvement sup-ports a cost reduction, a shortening of cycle time, a gain in output over input, a reduction in errors or defects, or an im-provement in someone's attitude or satisfaction, how does it add value in the operating unit? It should be traceable to cost reduction, time to market, customer retention, reputation for quality, or other value-adding outcomes. And if that improves, which of the strategic corporate goals does it support? After you have traced that pathway, you will be able to show tangi-bly that better human capital management leads to better cor-porate performance.

Looking Ahead

In September 1999, *Business Week* published a special supple-ment focused on the explosive e-commerce phenomenon.[1] The

Figure 11-1. Composite human capital scorecard.

CORPORATE

Human Capital Revenue
Revenue divided by FTEs

Human Capital Cost
Average cost of pay, benefits, absence, turnover, and contingents

Human Capital ROI
Revenue − (expense − total labor cost), divided by total labor cost

Human Capital Value Added
Revenue − (expense − total labor cost), divided by FTEs

Human Economic Value Added
Net operating profit after tax − cost of capital, divided by FTEs

Human Market Value Added
Ratio of market value to book value, divided by FTEs

FUNCTIONS

Exempt Percentage
Number of exempt FTEs as a percentage of total FTEs

Contingent Percentage
Number of contingent FTEs as a percentage of total FTEs

Accession Rates
Replacement hires and hires for new positions as a percentage of the workforce

Total Labor Cost Revenue Percentage
All labor costs as a percentage of total revenue

Readiness Level
Percentage of key positions with at least one fully qualified person ready

Commitment Level
Percentage of employees committed to the corporate vision and expecting to stay at least three years

Depletion Rate
Percentage of exempt separations among top-level performers

Performance Level
Average performance score compared to revenue per FTE

Satisfaction Percentage
Percentage of employees scoring in top quintile of satisfaction survey

Corporate Climate
Percentage of employees scoring in top quintile of culture and climate survey

Outsource Ratio
Ratio of employee pay and benefits to outsourced and contingent worker cost

Training ROI
Return on training investment

(continues)

Figure 11-1. (Continued).

HUMAN RESOURCES

Acquisition	Maintenance	Development	Retention
Cost per hire	Total labor cost as percentage of operating expense	Training cost as percentage of payroll	Total separation percentage
Time to fill jobs	Average pay per employee	Total training hours provided	Voluntary separations: exempt/nonexempt
Number of add hires	Benefits cost as percentage of payroll	Average number of hours of training per employee	Exempt separations by length of service
Number of replacements	Health care cost per employee	Training hours by function, job group	Cost of turnover
Quality of new hires			

opening statement reinforced my principal argument about the importance of people.

It's clear that while technology laid the foundations for the Web's first wave, it is sharp thinking by individuals that is powering the second wave—the e-business revolution. . . . the innovators and influencers who are doing the most to spark a transformation that is every bit as profound as the Industrial Revolution.

Later in the introduction, Scott McNealey, CEO of Sun Microsystems, is quoted:

The beauty of the Web is that it's open to everybody. Everybody gets to stand on the shoulders of everybody else's work. That's why everything is accelerating.

Clearly, 2000 is bringing in the millennium of people—the human capital—at a speed and with an intensity never before encountered. I pointed out in my 1990 book *Human Value Management* (San Francisco: Jossey-Bass) that we are witnessing "evolutionary change at revolutionary speed," and you are seeing it. Anyone with an idea and a few hundred dollars can open a Web site and be in the world market overnight. Even more

> The pace of business and life will be incomprehensible to us twentieth-century folk. It will be a whirlwind of people and information.

than that, they can quickly inflict serious injury on established enterprises (see Amazon.com and Barnes and Noble). Never before has this been true. It is because now human rather than financial capital is the driver. The most dazzling aspect is that e-commerce is only five years old! Imagine how in a few years people will be accessing the Web with pocket-size, voice-driven gadgets from anywhere, any time. That pace of business will be incomprehensible to us twentieth-century folk. It will be an integrating whirlwind of people and information.

The new millennium question is: What does this imply for organizational management?

Zuboff brought this issue of people and automation to our attention in the 1980s with her studies of the effects of electronic technology on organizational life.[2] She called it "automating and informating." By this, she meant that as we introduce electronic technology, we simultaneously automate the process and "informate" the culture. Informating is an outgrowth of automating. Informating transforms the culture with new conceptions of work and power. Zuboff points out that:

> History reveals the power of certain technological innovations to transform the mental life of an era— the feelings, sensibilities, perceptions, expectations, assumptions, and, above all, possibilities that define a community . . . the medieval castle, the printed book, the automobile—each example drives home a similar message.

No one born after 1930 remembers the effect that the automobile had on the relationship between parents and teenagers. With a car, a teen was suddenly out from under the visible control of a parent. The horseless carriage profoundly changed the dynamics of the family, just as much as the availability of the printed book undermined the dominance of the church in the 1500s. Putting mobility and information in the hands of the populace upset the existing patterns of society.

New technology always makes the world a new place. Today, the availability of information changes the relationship between worker and supervisor. It shifts power to the keepers of knowledge, no matter where they sit on the organizational chart. This demands a new form of leadership. Leaders have to create conditions in which new visions, concepts, and languages for workplace relations can emerge.

> Power is shifting to the keepers of knowledge, no matter where they sit on the organizational chart. This demands a new form of leadership.

Strassmann has been writing on the human and economic effects of information technology since the 1980s. In his book *Information Payoff,* he gave us a historic perspective when he stated:

> The organizing principle of a hunting society is tribal.
> Its primary resource is nature.
> The organizing principle of an agrarian society is feudal.
> Its primary resource is land.
> The organizing principle of an industrial society is nationalism.
> Its primary resource is capital.
> The organizing principle of a service society is global cooperation.
> Its primary resource is knowledge.[3]

Strassmann argues that when a society's production reaches its natural saturation point—that is, where capacity outstrips the ability to consume—it has two choices. One is to develop elaborate and expensive institutions to redistribute income to solve problems of the past. In my view, this is what happened in many northern European countries and, to some extent, in North America in the 1970s. Social programs in Europe have become so costly that they are now being modified or dismantled; industrial production can no longer support them, and individual tax rates have become too burdensome. The better choice is to invest in growth opportunities of the future. In our case, this means information technology and management of the knowledge potential that it generates. Fortunately, America realized this before most other nations and is shifting capital investment rapidly from hardware through software to knowledge management.

But all is not rosy just yet. In his most recent work, Strassmann claims that the returns on investment in information technology are seldom as great as the promises.[4] He points out that in a ten-year tracking of over 1,000 firms, there was no correlation between investments in information management per employee and return on shareholder equity. However, in his studies, one important point stands out: The companies with positive financial returns spent an average of $36,405, versus $50,168 for those reporting negative returns. In short, one group was able to produce higher financial returns with lower per-employee investments. This differential may be a proxy for the effective application of knowledge.

It is work such as Zuboff's and Strassmann's that shows us that we need to support studies aimed at improving the ROI of knowledge management, as well as the effects of information technology on people's work experience. Already, some firms are reforming their supervisory and management practices to deal with the emerging values and dynamics of the new marketplace. We need to know more, and we need to know it today.

References

1. "The e.biz 25," *Business Week*, September 27, 1999, e.biz supplement.
2. Shoshanna Zuboff, *In the Age of the Smart Machine* (New York: Basic Books 1988).
3. Paul Strassmann, *Information Payoff* (New York: Free Press, 1985), pp. 203–6.
4. Paul Strassmann, *Information Productivity* (New Canaan, CT: Information Economics Press, 1999).

Index

ability, innate, *x*
absenteeism, 34, 167
accession rate, 41–42
accounting
  human capital, 114–117
  traditional, 4–5
acquisition, 242
  and becoming an employer of choice, 141
  on human capital management scorecard, 112
  as human resources activity, 154
  and increasing customer satisfaction, 139
  as management activity, 94–97
  and reducing time to market, 138
Adams, Scott, on quality initiatives, 79
ADP, 201
Alexander the Great, 7
Allstate, 65
AMA, *see* American Management Association
Amazon.com, 281
American Management Association (AMA), 190, 198

American Productivity Center (APC), 186–187
American Society for Training and Development, 44
analysis, incorrect, 260
Andersen Consulting, 20
AOL, 219
APC, *see* American Productivity Center
appraisals, performance, 166
Armstrong, Lance, 160
The Art of War (Sun Tzu), 230
assets, 1
  intangible, 156, 158
  processes as, 62, 64
AT&T, 63, 117
authority figures, 161
Axel, Helen, on contingent workforce, 95

The Balanced Scorecard (Kaplan and Norton), 45–46
balanced values, 49–50
balance sheet, 5
Bank of America, 95
Barnard, Chester Irving, *ix*
Barnes & Noble, 281
being, doing vs., 261

benchmarking, 119–120, 187,
    220–225
  common mistakes with, 221
  of competitors/customers, 30
  limitations of, 220–221
  purpose of, 220
  and restructuring, 194
  and ROI, 222, 224–225
  value, 222, 223
*Benchmarking Staff Perform-
    ance* (Jac Fitz-enz), 220
benefits, employee, 34, 104,
    112, 123–124
  and contingent workforce,
    210
  outsourcing of, 201
  Saratoga Institute bench-
    marks for, 175
best practices, 120–121
Bigos, Gus, on what is arguably
    right, 163
Birchard, Bill, 65
Bodek, Norm, 186
Bontis, Nick
  on human capital, 3
  on voluntary terminations,
    151
bonuses
  awarding unearned, 165
  sign-on, 97
bookkeeping, double-entry, 4–5
Brache, Alan P.
  on enterprise processes, 62
  on measurement, 4
Buckingham, Marcus, 231
Buffet, Warren, on risk, 245
Bureau of Labor Statistics, 95,
    154
Business Intelligence, 190
business ratios, 5
business units, 20–21
Business Week, 278, 281

Canada, 182
capital, invested, 5–6
Capital One, 215–216
career-planning services, 141
cash assets, 5
causality, correlation vs., 163–
    164, 274
Ceridian, 201
change
  incremental, 261–262
  measurement of, 79–80, 108,
    110
  resistance to, 161, 260–261
change projects, *see* improve-
    ment initiative(s)
Clemente, Mark, 214
clichés, 161
climate, corporate, 148
coaching, 155
Coffman, Curt, 231
collaboration, 53–54, 131
commitment, 275
  as foundation trait metric, 50
  level of, 148
  to restructuring, 194
communication(s), 7, 54–55
  as employee need, 237–238
  and mergers and acquisi-
    tions, 215, 216
  and restructuring, 194
compensation, 123
  as employee need, 238
  Saratoga Institute bench-
    marks for, 174–175
competence, 148–149
competitive advantage, 80–81,
    139
competitiveness, 152–154
competitive passion, 55–56
competitor benchmarks, 30
Conoco, 202
consequences, 71

consistency, and validity, 273–274

consortia, management, 119–120

consultants, 13–14

context, 262, 267–268

contingent percentage, 40–41

contingent workforce, 31, 95, 112, 206–212

  advantages/disadvantages of using, 209–210

  efficient use of, 208–209

  growth of, 207–208

  measuring cost-effectiveness of using, 210–212

Cook, Mary, 202

corporate culture, *see* culture

correlations, 47

correlation(s), 163–164, 274

Cortada, James W., on performance measures, 76

Cosby, Phillip, 187

cost management, 42–43

cost(s)

  employee, 3

  hiring, 41–42, 103, 117–118

  in human capital performance matrix, 103–105

  replacement, 105

  termination, 104–105

  training, 43–44

  vacancy, 105

criterion-referenced competencies, 149

culture, 11–12

  for encouragement of ideas, 254

  as foundation trait metric, 50–52

  and mergers and acquisitions, 214, 217

  and quantum leaps, 262

customer benchmarks, 30

The Customer Comes Second (Hal Rosenbluth), 239

customer needs/desires, 249–250

customer satisfaction, 258

customer service, 132, 136, 139–140

dashboards, 143–145

data

  collection of, *xii*, 253

  on effective enterprise practices, 48–49

  human capital, 273

  on human capital, 3

  linking of, to people, 6–7

  production of, 19–20

  relevance of, 273

  sharing, 7

  sources of, 181–183

data sensors, 167–171

data-to-value cycle, 8–10, 114

deadlines, missed, 86–87

Deal, Terrence E., on corporate culture, 12

Death of a Salesman (Arthur Miller), 48

defect rate, 75

delight, customer, 64

Deming, W. Edwards, 107, 187

  on barriers to performance, 43

  on reducing variance, 167

demographics, workforce, *xi–xii*, 39–41

depletion rate/cost, 148, 151–152

Derby, Elias, 2–3

Dess, Gregory C., on leveraging, 241

development, 124, 243
  and becoming an employer
    of choice, 141–142
  as employee need, 237
  on human capital manage-
    ment scorecard, 113
  as human resources activity,
    155
  and increasing customer sat-
    isfaction, 139–140
  as management activity,
    98–99
  Saratoga Institute bench-
    marks for, 177
  see also training
Dilbert, 79
DiMaggio, Joe, 162–163
directionality, 163
disabilities, persons with, 96
doing, being vs., 261
double-entry bookkeeping, 4–5
downsizing, 43, 208–209, 214
Drucker, Peter, *ix*
  on attaining one's objectives,
    25
  on data collection by enter-
    prises, *xii*
  on greatest challenge for or-
    ganizations today, 3
Dunlap, Al, 132, 219
Dunningan, James, on great
  generals, 7

early-warning signals, 167–171
e-commerce, 278, 281–282
economic value added (EVA),
  32, 181
effective practices, enterprisewide, 47–49
*The 8 Practices of Exceptional
  Companies* (Jac Fitz-enz),
  48, 51

electronic technology, *xiii*
employee assistance programs,
  104
employee benefits, *see* benefits,
  employee
employee costs, 3
employee development, 124
employee development investment, 43–44
employee mind-sets, 150–151
employee need(s), 230–231,
  236–240
  communication as, 237–238
  compensation as, 238
  development/training as, 237
  management as, 238
employee-relations (ER) function, 202–203
employee(s)
  as information repositories,
    252, 253
  loss of, 151–152
  with personal problems,
    100–101
  sales per, 31
employer of choice, becoming
  an, 137, 140–142
enterprise goals, 8, 25–59
  and effective practices,
    47–49
  and financial-based human
    capital metrics, 31–38
  and foundation traits, 49–52
  and human-based human
    capital metrics, 39–45
  and human-financial inter-
    face, 27–30
  and need for data/measures,
    30
  pathways to, *see* pathway(s)
  and processes, 62–63
  and structural traits, 52–56

enterprise level, 20
enterprise-level futures,
146–147
Epstein, Marc J., 65
ER function, *see* employee-
relations function
error rate, 75
error(s)
in human capital perform-
ance matrix, 107
increases in, 167
EVA, *see* economic value added
evaluating (as management activity), 93
exceptional performance, 25
exempt percent, 39–40
experience, on-the-job, 155
"experts," 161
external performance drivers,
248
Exult, Inc., 204

FASB, *see* Financial Accounting Standards Board
Fayol, Henri, *ix*
Federal Express, 11
federal government information sources, 181–182
FEDSTATS, 182
feedback, 71
Feynman, Richard, on turning
around human capability,
67–68
FIB (First Interstate Bank),
219
Fidelity Investments, 40
Financial Accounting Standards Board (FASB), 5,
116, 156, 158
financial-based human capital
metric(s), 31–38
human capital cost factor as,
33–35

human capital market value
as, 38
human capital return on investment as, 36–37
human capital revenue factor as, 31–32
human capital value added
as, 35–36
human economic value
added as, 32–33
financial ratios, 5
financial statements, 5
First, Break All the Rules
(Buckingham and Coff-
man), 231
First Interstate Bank (FIB),
219
First Union, 215–216
fixed assets, 1
Flamholtz, Eric, 114
forecasting, *see* trends
foreign countries, outsourcing
to, *xii*
Fortune magazine, 12, 50, 61–
62, 192, 240
foundation activities, 154
foundation trait metric(s),
49–52
balanced values as, 49–50
commitment as, 50
culture as, 50–52
FTE, *see* full-time equivalent
fulfilling work, *xi*
full-time equivalent (FTE), 31–
32, 34–36, 38–40, 173,
178, 179
functional futures, 147–148
future(s)
enterprise-level, 146–147
functional, 147–148
preparing for the, 276

Gallup Organization, 230–231,
    233, 234, 238, 240
Galvin, Bob, 52, 263–264
Galvin, Paul, 264
General Electric, 52
Genghis Khan, 7
geographic location, 248
globalization, 2
goals, enterprise, *see* enterprise
    goals
Golden Rule, 230
Goldman Sachs, 2, 38
Gompers, Samuel, *ix*
Gould, Stephen Jay, on data
    analysis, 162–163
Grayson, Jack, 186
Greenspan, David, 214
gross national product, 1
gross sales metric, 28
guarantees, unconditional, 258
guiding principle(s), 272–276
    coincidence vs. correlation
        as, 274
    commitment as, 275
    human capital data as, 273
    leading indicators as, 275
    leveraging as, 274–275
    people plus information as,
        272–273
    preparing for the future as,
        276
    relevant data as, 273
    supervising as, 275–276
    validity and consistency as,
        273–274
    value path as, 274

Hamel, Gary, on failure of
    change programs, 30
Handy, Charles, *ix*, 91
Harari, Oren, on positioning
    for new markets, 256

Hay Group, 50–51
HCCF (human capital cost fac-
    tor), 33–35
HCCI (human capital cost
    index), 178
HCMV, *see* human capital mar-
    ket value
HCPI (human capital profit
    index), 178
HCRF (human capital revenue
    factor), 31–32
HCRI (human capital revenue
    index), 173, 178
HCROI (human capital return
    on investment), 36–37
HCVA (human capital value
    added), 35–36
Hermanson, Roger, 114
HEVA, *see* human economic
    value added
Hewlett-Packard, 139, 246
hiring
    costs of, 41–42, 103, 117–118
    process of, 96
Homer, 230
Honda Civic, 117
*How to Measure Human Re-
    source Management* (Jac
    Fitz-enz), 104
HRA (human resources ac-
    counting), 114
HRM (human resources man-
    agement), 204
HR World, 198
human-based human capital
    metric(s), 39–45
    accession rate as, 41–42
    contingent percentage as,
        40–41
    employee development in-
        vestment as, 43–44
    exempt percent as, 39–40
    separation rate as, 42

total labor cost revenue percentage as, 42–43
human capital, 10, 11, 91
acquiring, 94–97
components of, *x*
developing, 98–99
economic value of, 4
leverage of, 20
maintaining, 97–98
need for measures of, 3–4,
17–18
origin of, as term, *ix–x*
planning for, 93–94
retaining, 100–101
spiritual value of, 4
human capital accounting,
114–117
human capital cost factor
(HCCF), 33–35
human capital cost index
(HCCI), 178
human capital management
scorecard, 45–47, 110–
114, 278–280
acquisition on, 112
development on, 113
maintenance on, 112
retention on, 113–114
human capital market value
(HCMV), 38, 146, 156
human capital metrics
financial-based, 31–38
human-based, 39–45
human capital performance
matrix, 72–76, 101–109
cost in, 103–105
error in, 107
quantity in, 106–107
reaction in, 107–108
time in, 106
human capital profit-and-loss
(P&L) statement, 117–119

human capital profit index
(HCPI), 178
human capital return on investment (HCROI), 36–37
human capital revenue factor
(HCRF), 31–32
human capital revenue index
(HCRI), 173, 178
human capital value added
(HCVA), 35–36
human capital value circle,
28–29
human economic value added
(HEVA), 32–33, 146, 156
human-financial interface,
27–30
human reaction, 107–108
*Human Resource Effectiveness
Report*, 27
*Human Resource Financial Re-
port*, 25–27, 42, 97, 105,
118, 173
human resources accounting
(HRA), 114
human resources function, 154
and mergers and acquisi-
tions, 213–215
outsourcing of, 198, 201–204
and restructuring, 188–197
Saratoga Institute bench-
marks for, 174
see also management activ-
ity(-ies)
human resources management
(HRM), 204
Human Value Management (Jac
Fitz-enz), 281

IBM, 139, 246, 262–263
"If Japan Can, Why Can't We?"
(W. Edwards Deming), 187
immigration, *xii*, 96

Imparato, Nicholas, on positioning for new markets, 256
improvement initiative(s), 28, 186–227
  benchmarking as, 220–225
  contingent workforce management as, 206–212
  failure of, 30, 259–261
  first human capital, 187–188
  and focus on cost reduction, 132
  in Information Age, 187
  mergers/acquisitions as, 212–220
  in 1970s, 186–187
  outsourcing as, 197–206
  restructuring as, 188–197
incentive programs, 139
incorrect analysis, 260
incremental change, 261–262
industrial age, *xiii*
inflation rate, 179
information
  and cultural transformations, 282
  exchange of, 2
  and people, 6–7, 272–273
  relational, 12–13
  value of managing, 7–8
Information Age, 187
information culture, 20
Information Payoff (Paul Strassmann), 283
information sector, 1
information technology, 3, 282–284
initial public offering (IPO), 2
innate ability, *x*
innovation, 54, 117, 282
intangible assets, 156, 158
intellectual capacity, 10

intellectual capacity pathway, 14, 16
intellectual capital, 10–11, 91
intellectual property, 10, 11
interferers, 69, 71
Interim Services, 123
internal performance drivers, 246, 248
internal Web sites, 253
International HR Journal, 189
intervention, 78–79
invested capital, 5–6
investment management, 43–44
IPO (initial public offering), 2

James, Jennifer, on willingness to see future, 277
Japan, 187
Juran, Joseph M., 107

Kaplan, Robert S., 45
Keen, Peter G. W., on enterprise processes, 62, 64
Keller, Helen, on life as adventure, 245
Kennedy, Allan A., on corporate culture, 12
knowledge
  application of, 8
  exchange of, 20
  and fulfillment, *xi*
  right of individual to trade on his/her, 13
knowledge economy, 3, 155, 272–273

labor trends, 154
labor unions, *xii*
late filings/deliveries, 86–87
leading indicators, 147–148, 249, 275

learn, ability to, *x*
learning organizations, 13
Lev, Baruch, 116
leverage/leveraging, 1–2, 20, 26, 229, 240–241, 274–275
Levi Strauss, 40

Mager, Robert F., 69
maintenance, 242–243
  and becoming an employer of choice, 141
  on human capital management scorecard, 112
  as human resources activity, 154–155
  and increasing customer satisfaction, 139
  as management activity, 97–98
  and reducing time to market, 138
management, as employee need, 238
management activity(-ies), 91–101, 154–156, 229–243
  acquiring as, 94–97
  developing as, 98–99
  and employee needs, 230–231, 236–240
  evaluating as, 93
  leveraging as, 229, 240–241
  maintaining as, 97–98
  and perspective of managers, 231–233
  planning as, 93–94
  and results, 233–236
  retaining as, 100–101
  see also human resources function
management consortia, 119–120
management panaceas, 14, 15

managers, outmoded beliefs of, *xii–xiii*
Manhattan Project, 67
Marx, Karl, *ix*
M&As, *see* mergers and acquisitions
Masterson, Daniel, on great generals, 7
McClellan, David, on competency, 148–149
McDonalds, 96
McKenna, Regis, on building relationships, 12–13
McKinsey Seven S's, 245
McNamara, Robert, on what cannot be easily measured, 61
McNealy, Scott, on World Wide Web, 281
meaning, looking for, 163–164
measurement(s)
  of improvement initiatives, *see* improvement initiative(s)
  meaningfulness of, 160–161
mentoring, 155
Mercer Management Consulting (MMC), 213
mergers and acquisitions (M& As), 212–220
  evaluating success of, 217–220
  key issues in, 216–217
  risk factors with, 215–216
  success factors with, 214–215
metrics, 28–30
Miller, Arthur, 48
mind-sets, employee, 150–151
MMC (Mercer Management Consulting), 213
monetary incentives, 139

morale, and mergers and ac-
    quisitions, 217
motivation
    and mergers and acquisi-
        tions, 219
    to share data, 7
Motorola, 44, 52, 74–75, 187,
    246, 263–264

NASA, 255
needs
    customer, 249–250
    employee, 230–231, 236–240
Netscape, 219
Nike, 40
Nollen, Stanley, on contingent
    workforce, 95
Norton, David P., on balanced
    scorecard, 45–46
null hypothesis, 164

obsolete solutions, 259–260
Odyssey (Homer), 230
older workers, 96
on-the-job experience, 155
operational excellence, 139
organizational capital, 10
organizational culture, *see* cul-
    ture
organizational effectiveness,
    Saratoga Institute bench-
    marks for, 174
organizational resistance,
    260–261
outsourcing, 96, 197–206
    argument for, 198–199
    at Exult, Inc., 204
    to foreign countries, *xii*
    and ROI, 204–206
    success factors with,
        203–204
    trends in functional, 199,
        201–203

panic management, 97
participative culture, 51
partnering, 52–53
passive resources, 1
pathway(s), 129–142
    basic, 130
    to becoming employer of
        choice, 137, 140–142
    cost reduction as, 132
    to improved time to market,
        134–135, 138–142
    and people, 132–133
    to world-class customer ser-
        vice, 136, 139–140
patterns, 160–162
Paychex, 201
pay programs, 123
payroll, outsourcing of,
    201–202
performance, 43
    drivers of, 246–248
    evaluation of, 101–109, 166
    standards for, 166–167
permanent jobs, 95–96
personal problems, employees
    with, 100–101
Peters, Tom, *ix*
Pfau, Bruce, on best predictor
    of company excellence,
    50–51
Pfeffer, Jeffrey, on importance
    of strong workforce,
    206–207
Phillips, Jack, 99
Picken, Joseph C., on lever-
    aging, 241
Pipe, Peter, 69
planning, 242
    as management activity,
        93–94
    for restructurings, 193–194
    workforce, 121

P&L statement, human capital, 117–119
post-industrial age, *xiii*
Prahalad, C. K., on failure of change programs, 30
prediction, 160
preparedness, 148–150
PricewaterhouseCoopers, 189
principle(s), guiding, *see* guiding principle(s)
processes, 61–89
  as asset, 62, 64
  case example of, 81, 83–84
  components of, 69–71
  effects of human intervention in, 76–81
  and goals, 62–63
  human capital in, 65, 67–68
  improving efficiency of, 61–62
  measuring, 84–88
  multiple gains from improvement of, 64–65
  performance matrix for evaluation of, 72–76
  and productivity, 61, 75
  and quality, 74–75
  and service, 74
  and situation analysis, 77–78
  and value creation, 64–66, 80–83
process management, 11
process value analysis, 76
productivity, 1
  as answer to talent shortfall, *xiii*
  of contingent workforce, 211–212
  and employee feelings/opinions, 235
  and invested capital, 5–6
  manufacturing vs. employee, 61

measuring white-collar, 21
and mergers and acquisitions, 219
of new employees, 105
in performance matrix, 75
Productivity Inc., 186, 187
profit-and-loss (P&L) statement, human capital, 117–119
punishment, 71
Purcell, Ed, 162
purpose, enterprise, *see* enterprise goals

qualitative measures, 3
quality
  measurements of, 107
  in performance matrix, 74–75
quality movement, 74
quantitative measures, 3
quantity, in human capital performance matrix, 106–107
quantum leap(s), 245–271
  barriers to, 259–261
  and customer needs/desires, 249–250
  examples of, 250–252, 264–265
  fundamental concept of, 265
  and human capital leading indicators, 249
  incremental changes vs., 261–262
  at Motorola, 264–265
  and nature of the organization, 262
  and performance drivers, 245–248
  positioning for, 256, 258–259
  requisites for, 252–254, 263–264

quantum leap(s) (*continued*)
    scenarios for, 255–257
    steps in making, 265–269
quick fixes, 259

R. G. Barry Corporation, 114
ratios, business, 5
reaction, in human capital per-
    formance matrix, 107–108
readiness, 149–150
recruitment, 13, 96–97
reengineering, 28, 62
relational capital, 10, 11
relational information, 12–13
relationships, 160–162
relevant data, 273
renting, 112
repetitive tasks, 160–161
replacement costs, 105
replacement hires, 41–42
reporting, 142–145
research organizations,
    182–183
resources
    leveraging, 229
    passive, 1
restructuring, 188–197
    critical issues with, 192–193
    evaluation of, 195–197
    order of, 189
    prime question in, 190–191
    and role of human resources
        function, 191–192, 195
    studies on, 189–190
    success factors in, 193–194
Restructuring the Human Re-
    sources Department, 190
retention, 124–125, 243
    and becoming an employer
        of choice, 142
    on human capital manage-
        ment scorecard, 113–114

as human resources activity,
    155–156
and increasing customer sat-
    isfaction, 140
as management activity,
    100–101
and reducing time to market,
    138
retirees, 96
return on investment (ROI)
    of benchmarking, 222,
        224–225
    outsourcing of, 204–206
    restructuring of, 195–197
rewards, 71, 254
Rifkin, Jeremy, on government
    job-creation statistics, 95
risk, 54, 245
risk management, 215–216
ROI, *see* return on investment
Rosenbluth, Hal
    on employee happiness,
        239–240
    on people as competitive
        measure, 229
Rummler, Geary A.
    on enterprise processes, 62
    on measurement, 4

salespeople, and mergers and
    acquisitions, 219–220
sales per employee, 31
Saratoga Institute, 25–27, 32,
    42, 43, 48, 97, 101, 105,
    116–118, 121, 173–177,
    190, 202, 209, 230, 234,
    236, 240
satisfaction, employee, 148
scenarios, building, 255–257
Schultz, Theodore, on human
    capital, *ix–x*
Schwarzkopf, Norman, 7

scorecard, human capital, 45–47
Sears, 11
Securities and Exchange Commission, 116
Senge, Peter
  on information exchange, 2
  on learning organizations, 13
separation(s), 151
  rate of, 42, 153
  Saratoga Institute benchmarks for, 175
service, in performance matrix, 74
service, quality, or productivity (SQP), 77–78
Signet Bank, 215–216
sign-on bonuses, 97
situation analysis, 77–78
6 Sigma program, 76, 187, 246
Smith, Fred, 11
software, 258
solutions, 78–79, 259–260
SQP, *see* service, quality, or productivity
staffing, 122–123, 175–177
Statistics Canada, 182
Stewart, Stern, on economic value added, 32
Stewart, Thomas, 192
stochastic rewards, 115
stock market, valuation of human knowledge by, 1
Strassmann, Paul, on organizing principles, 283–284
strategic-level metrics, 30
strategies, 262–263
structural trait metric(s), 52–56
  collaboration as, 53–54
  communication as, 54–55
  competitive passion as, 55–56

innovation/risk as, 54
partnering as, 52–53
Sun Tzu, 7–8, 230
supervision, 211, 275–276
supervisory coaching, 155
surveys, 47, 51–52, 140, 141, 249

Taco Bell, 105
tactical-level metrics, 29–30
talent, shortage of, *xi–xiii*, 93–94
targets, enterprise, *see* enterprise goals
teamwork, and restructuring, 194
technology
  electronic, *xiii*
  as passive asset, 18–19
telecommuting, 96
temporary work, 95–96, *see also* contingent workforce
termination(s)
  costs of, 104–105
  voluntary, 151, 209, 234–236
Theory X, 99
time, in human capital performance matrix, 106
time to market, improving, 134–135, 138–142
time to start, reducing, 118
Tobin's Q, 38
total labor cost revenue percentage, 42–43
training, 19, 98–99, 113, 155
  of contingent workforce, 211
  cost of, 43–44
  as employee need, 237
  and mergers and acquisitions, 215
  Saratoga Institute benchmarks for, 177
  see also development

Training magazine, 98, 99
transfers, requests for, 167
Transforming HR to Support Corporate Change, 190
trends, 160–184
  business applications of, 165–167
  and datasources, 181–183
  developing human capital financial index to identify, 171–181
  fallacies in identification of, 162–164
  and identification of relationships/patterns, 160–162
  using data sensors to identify, 167–171
  value of identifying, 172
turnover, 34, 118–119, 151
typewriters, 250–251

unconditional guarantees, 258
United States Information Agency, 148
U.S. Army, 262
U.S. Congress, *xii*
U.S. Marine Corps, 262

vacancy costs, 105
validity, and consistency, 273–274
value added, 8, 28, 30
value benchmarking, 222, 223
value(s)
  balanced, 49–50
  creation of, 80–81
  in data-to-value cycle, 8–10
  generation of, *x*
  organizational, 258
  process, 62–63
  processes and creation of, 64–66

variance, 163, 167
The Vest-Pocket Guide to Business Ratios, 5
vision, 262
vocational training, 96
Volkswagen Beetle, 117
voluntary activities, reduced participation in, 167
voluntary terminations, 151, 209, 234–236

Wal-Mart, 11, 52, 139
Walton, Sam, 52
Web sites, internal, 253
Welch, Jack, 52
Wells Fargo Bank, 188, 219
Wheatley, Margaret, on understanding organizations, 129
Willy Loman syndrome, 48
Woods, John A., on performance measures, 76
word processing, 251–252
workforce demographics, *xi–xii*, 39–41
workforce management/readiness, 94
workforce movement, metrics of, 41–42
workforce planning, 121
workplace, "good," 231
world-class customer service, 136, 139–140
World Competitiveness Report, 183
World War II, 186
World Wide Web, 281
W-2 form, 33

Zuboff, Shoshanna, on technological innovations, 282